COLDHEARTED RIVER

COLDHEARTED RIVER

A Canoe Odyssey down the Cumberland

Kim Trevathan

Photographs by Randy Russell

OUTDOOR TENNESSEE SERIES
JIM CASADA, SERIES EDITOR

The University of Tennessee Press / Knoxville

To my mother, for her wisdom, support, and optimism

 The Outdoor Tennessee Series covers a wide range of topics of interest
to the general reader, including titles on the flora and fauna, the varied
recreational activities, and the rich history of outdoor Tennessee. With
a keen appreciation of the importance of protecting our state's natural
resources and beauty, the University of Tennessee Press intends the series
to emphasize environmental awareness and conservation.

Some passages from the book were published in the summer 2004 issue of
Experience Outdoors magazine.

This book is printed on acid-free paper.

Library of Congress Cataloging-in-Publication Data

Trevathan, Kim, 1958-
Coldhearted river : a canoe odyssey down the Cumberland / Kim Trevathan ;
photographs by Randy Russell.— 1st ed.
    p. cm. — (Outdoor Tennessee series)
ISBN 1-57233-468-1 (hardcover) — ISBN 1-57233-530-0 (pbk.)
 1. Cumberland River (Ky. and Tenn.)—Description and travel.
 2. Cumberland River Valley (Ky. and Tenn.)—Description and travel.
 3. Trevathan, Kim, 1958-—Travel—Cumberland River (Ky. and Tenn.)
 4. Canoes and canoeing—Cumberland River (Ky. and Tenn.)
 5. Cumberland River Valley (Ky. and Tenn.)—Social life and customs.
 I. Title.
 II. Series.

F442.2.T74 2006
917.68'5—dc22   2005025938

CONTENTS

FIGURES

Rhonda Frattarelli's Bass
Fort Donelson Overlook
Barkley Lake Campsite
The Beach at Eureka Campground
Barkley Dam Lock
The Reception Party in Smithland
My Dog, Jasper

MAPS

EDITOR'S FOREWORD

The Cumberland Plateau and Cumberland River have, for reasons I cannot really explain, always held me in thrall. Part of it goes all the way back to adolescence, when as a senior in high school I read Harriet Arnow's wonderful book, *Seedtime on the Cumberland*. Those familiar with the work will no doubt find that a strange choice for a teenager, but for a youngster with a voracious reading appetite, a keen interest in anything that dealt with living close to the land, and the limitations imposed by a small-town public library, it was a logical one.

The better part of a decade later, while pursuing doctoral studies at Vanderbilt University in Nashville, I had a better opportunity to come to know a portion of the Cumberland first-hand. I fished some of the impoundments along its course, along with feeders of the river, marveled at a portion of its drainage in the lovely Cumberland Plateau, and gained some sense of the rich, varied history connected with this ribbon of water that wanders across the Tennessee landscape.

It was not until I read Kim Trevathan's delightful work, however, that true appreciation of the Cumberland's lure and lore really came home to me. As he did in a previous volume in the Outdoor Tennessee Series, *Paddling the Tennessee River*, Trevathan brings to the reader a meaningful feel for the solitude one finds in a canoe. His odyssey begins in the headwaters of the Cumberland in 2003, five years after his travels down the Tennessee.

This time the author's trip is a bit longer, and he paddles without the erstwhile canine companion of his first book, Jasper. Instead, he is accompanied by a photographer, Randy Russell. Readers will find the pages that follow an intriguing tapestry of human history, natural history, environmentalism, and philosophy, with a spicy bit of quirkiness and a buoyant sense of good humor thrown into the mix.

Personally, I find the early portion of the travelogue, which focuses on the geography of the headwaters, the most appealing. There are whitewater stretches in the scenic splendor of the Daniel Boone National Forest, with deep, dark gorges that let fertile imaginations dream of the days when this was the land of Boone, the Wetzel brothers, and the type of fictional figures one encounters in Zane Grey's *Spirit of the Border*. Or maybe the mind delves even deeper into the past and ponders the splendid hunting Native Americans once knew along the Cumberland. As an avid hunter, I constantly found myself thinking what wonderful opportunities a canoe voyage of this sort offers.

Yet all too soon the remoteness of place and links with the past give way to something quite different. One of my favorite outdoor writers and a man who was probably the most productive sporting and environmental scribe of the twentieth century, Archibald Rutledge, was almost always a gentle, genteel man. When it came to impoundments on major waterways, however, be they his beloved Santee River in Low Country South Carolina, or Tennessee Valley Authority or Corps of Engineers dams anywhere, he unequivocally said: "Damn the dams."

Doubtless Trevathan came to understand, and perhaps share, some of Rutledge's frustration in seeing a lovely, free-flowing stream undergo an unattractive, depressing change. That transition takes many forms—stilled waters with the detritus of careless humans filling the back of coves; armadas of fishing boats, pontoons, and jet skis with roaring engines and, often, uncaring operators; unsightly barges at work in the lower reaches; ranks of plush homes lining shorelines as the affluent proclaim the lure of water; docks jutting into reservoirs; and most of all, a loss of the sense of wildness and solitude to be found in free-flowing streams.

Those of an insightful or introspective bent, and Trevathan certainly belongs to their ranks, might also pause while paddling and ponder the world that has been lost to the stair-stepping reservoirs that line the Cumberland: rural communities now submerged, bottomland farms, bank fishing for smallmouth bass in deep pools or, in hot weather, swimming in those same pools, and a vanished time of simpler days and ways. When thoughts turn to such matters, the word "coldhearted" from the book's title seems singularly applicable.

Title and the foregoing thoughts notwithstanding, it would be wrong to suggest that this is a chronicle of doom and gloom. Far from it. There's magic in the rugged terrain of Land Between the Lakes, a vast recreational area that opened to the public after residents underwent reluctant relocation four decades ago. I've hunted turkeys in this strip of land situated between the Cumberland and Tennessee Rivers, and to walk its steep ridges and deep hollows, with evidence of long-ago settlers greeting you at every turn, is to tread paths of wonder.

There's likewise mystique and the occasional bit of mesmerism on the water, especially for those conversant with the Cumberland's history. Trevathan has immersed himself deeply in the stream's past. I once lived in Donelson (a suburb of Nashville), but even though I'm a trained historian it shames me to admit that I only know bits and pieces of the life of the man who gave the location its name. In this book I learn more about him, the Chickamaugan leader Dragging Canoe, the military exploits of Ulysses S. Grant, and more. Much of this history connected with the Cumberland is dark, as is in many senses the character of the stream; hence the book's title. When the author employs phrases such as "empty and desolate" or "haunted, distant, [and] aloof" to describe the stream, you understand that.

Again though, there is warmth and comfort in these pages, as the author unravels its mysteries with the same sense of delight one experiences when traveling gravel roads in lovely country, far from the hurly-burly and sterility of interstates and urban settings. One pleasant surprise after another, along with occasional disappointments and Trevathan's ongoing process of self-discovery, greets the reader. The author gives his age as forty-five, and some might suggest that he undertook this long trip down a sometimes foreboding river as a novel solution to what it is fashionable for psychologists to describe as a "mid-life crisis."

Personally, I prefer the assessment he offers at the conclusion of the introduction: "There might be other extended river trips, but . . . the Cumberland would be my last chance to slip into some other realm in search of those moments of nirvana, those feelings that stop time and take you out of yourself and your worries." The delight of this book, and perhaps its strongest point, is Trevathan's ability to share that personal nirvana. Join him for a splendid session of armchair adventure with an underlying theme of concern for and devotion to the good earth, and its life's blood, water, that makes this a welcome addition to the Outdoor Tennessee Series.

JIM CASADA
Series Editor

ACKNOWLEDGMENTS

KIM

I am grateful to my family, especially my wife Julie, for putting up with another long canoe trip. Thanks in particular to my mother and Julie for bringing supplies and moral support along the way. Thanks to river brothers Vic Scoggin and Mack Prichard, whose knowledge and emotional connection to the Cumberland served as valuable inspiration. Thanks to Lara Edington, Curt Roberts, Bryan Capps, and Tammy Ailshie for help around the falls and the fine dinner they made for us slacking voyageurs. To Paul Threadgill for guiding me to the Cumberland's source. To Murray Browne and Ian Joyce for transporting us to the headwaters. To Murray and Scot Danforth for reading early manuscripts and making insightful and helpful suggestions. To Maryville College for its support. To David Noyes for publishing an excerpt from the book in *Experience Outdoors* magazine. Finally, thanks to Jasper, my dog, for understanding that it was best he didn't go along this time.

RANDY

I would like to thank my mom and dad and friends for their love and support, and especially my girlfriend, Lara, for being my inspiration.

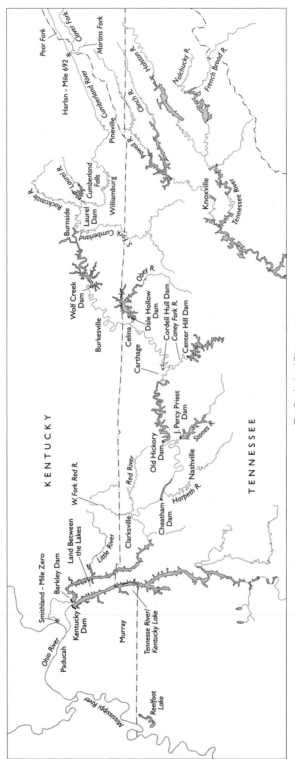

The Cumberland River.

INTRODUCTION

"The rivers are our brothers," said Chief Seattle. "They quench our
thirst. The rivers carry our canoes and feed our children. . . . You
must give to the rivers the kindness you would give your brothers."

EDWARD ABBEY
Down the River

When I started out on a canoe trip down the length of the Tennessee River
in late August 1998, I was propelled by a desire to break free from the corporate cubicle land where I had worked for three long years. Confined, exploited, and resentful, I sought therapy in simple hardship. I was obsessed
with being alone, outdoors, far from the bewildering mazes of technology
and the political maneuvering required to succeed. Long-suppressed anger
fueled 652 miles of monotonous paddling under a sun that glared hard at the
wide-eyed absurdity of such an undertaking.

Five years after the Tennessee River trip, I set out to paddle another mostly
dammed-up river, the Cumberland, 696 miles to the Tennessee's 652. By the
time of the Cumberland trip, having been ejected from the high-flying dot-
com economy without a golden parachute, I was teaching at Maryville College,
a small liberal arts school near Knoxville, at a job where I had autonomy,
flexibility, and a clear sense of purpose. I felt no pressing need to escape to
another river away from my life of work on land. This I *intended* as a trip
where I would focus more on the river, less on internal demons. In short, after
getting to know one major river from beginning to end, another called to me.

Jasper, my canine companion on the Tennessee River trip, would be unable to accompany me down the Cumberland. Although he still sat in the
bow on day trips, he would not, at his age, eleven, be able to withstand the
rigors of a five-week voyage. I would miss him. In his place, I invited photographer Randy Russell, thirty-three, with whom I'd worked in my corporate days. He agreed without hesitation. This relieved me because I couldn't
face this trip alone, but it also brought up an entirely new set of worries. I
wouldn't have to take care of Randy, who was an experienced outdoorsman,
but if anything did happen to him, it would be my wacky trip, my conception, that caused it. Though I loved Jasper and would have deeply mourned

any suffering on his part, replacing him with a human in the bow raised the stakes and would complicate and enrich the trip in ways I could not have anticipated.

Randy and I weren't close friends, but we had worked together three years at iPIX, an Internet photography corporation. We'd collaborated as writer/ photographer on a few projects, such as an online photographic tour of landmarks in St. Paul, Minnesota, and "live" Internet coverage of the international hot-air balloon fiesta in Albuquerque. On the job, Randy was meticulous at his craft, some said to the point of eccentricity. From working with him, I knew that although he retained a high level of professionalism, he was not afraid to take risks.

Randy also had a quirky sense of humor. From iPIX projects, he always brought home the odd shot of a coworker caught dozing at a terminal or an unflattering candid portrait of a self-important, overpaid executive. At the balloon fiesta, where four of us toiled long hours inside a cramped trailer, Randy, taking a short break, was creating tooth decay with PhotoShop on an executive's Web site portrait when that particular executive, with nothing better to do, wandered into our work space. We think he only caught a glimpse of his distorted image, and he was too startled to say anything.

After iPIX laid us off (not for satiric photos), Randy and I shared a disdain for corporate America and a desire to make a living free from the constraints of an office and layers of meddling, overpaid management. I knew that Randy, a competitive cyclist, was in good enough shape to paddle 700 miles, and I hoped, though I didn't know for certain, that he had the mental doggedness to complete such a trip. Spending long days together in a small, tippy boat and evenings in isolated, weedy camps would test our levels of tolerance and senses of humor.

Its geography suggesting a warped sense of humor, the Cumberland, like the Tennessee, cracks a crooked smile across what used to be the hunting grounds of the Cherokee, Shawnee, Chickasaw, and Chickamauga tribes. It starts in southeastern Kentucky, dips down through Middle Tennessee and turns north back into western Kentucky before it empties into the Ohio River. A small stream at its headwaters in the eastern Kentucky coalfield region, it meanders down the long narrow valley between Cumberland and Pine mountains, and then descends in a generally southwestern direction through Barbourville and Williamsburg, where it sneaks under busy I-75, the link between Knoxville and Lexington. It veers northwest, toward the Daniel Boone National Forest, where it widens and flashes whitewater through dark gorges lined with thick forests and rounded gray outcroppings of sandstone and conglomerate rock.

At this point, having passed through over 130 miles of sparsely populated pastureland and forest, it plunges down sixty-eight-foot-high Cumberland Falls, where people, lots of them, suddenly appear, leaning against railings gawking at the power and beauty of the roaring spectacle. After the falls, the river continues to roar, but only for about 5 miles. Near the mouth of the Laurel River, under the influence of Wolf Creek Dam, 100 miles downriver, it begins to pool, its waters flooding the coves, once the mouths of major tributaries such as the Laurel and Rockcastle rivers, and smaller ones, such as Buck Creek, Fishing Creek, Wolf Creek, and Bee Lick Creek. On the surface of Lake Cumberland, fishing boats, houseboats, and cabin cruisers jet along the rocky shorelines, a buzzing cotillion of activity. Below, decaying in the murky silence, lie towns such as Point Isabel and Rowena, rich bottomland, broken steamboats, and the bones of keelboatmen, many of them put there by treacherous Smith Shoals, also buried under water.

At Point Isabel, now called Burnside, tall bluffs overlook the slackwater confluence of the Cumberland and the Big South Fork (of the Cumberland), flowing due north up from Tennessee. It is here, writes William Lynwood Montell in *Don't Go Up Kettle Creek*, that the Cumberland becomes a major river. Below Wolf Creek Dam, south of Somerset and Jamestown, Kentucky, the river once again narrows and picks up the pace, its waters flowing frigid from the dam's power generation toward Burkesville on a stretch that is famous now for the trout supplied by the hatchery below the dam. The river, freed from the dam's constraints, is back to twisting through high gorges as it works its way "in great loops," as Montell says, into Tennessee at Celina, where the Obey River joins the flow.

The river becomes Cordell Hull Lake here, its current gradually stolen by yet another dam, this one named for the Tennessean who was secretary of state under Franklin D. Roosevelt. The dam blocks the river a few miles upstream of Carthage, Tennessee, north of Interstate 40. Next is Old Hickory Reservoir, backed up by Old Hickory Dam, completed in 1956. Here, as the pooled river spreads itself out among increasingly affluent neighborhoods and resorts, the barges and big boats become more numerous. Below Old Hickory, the Cumberland, its current quickened between narrow banks, takes in the waters of the Stones River and flows right through downtown Nashville, past the Tennessee Titans' stadium.

From here it changes its mind about heading southwest and turns northwest, under the influence of the same ancient geologic lift that tilts the Tennessee River up from Alabama and back into Tennessee, where it started. It takes in the waters of the Harpeth River and sluices through a small dam in West Tennessee—Cheatham. It noses closer and closer to its sister, the

Tennessee, as it passes through Clarksville, where the Red River flows in, and through Dover, Tennessee, on its return to Kentucky. Once in Kentucky, it spreads out to form Barkley Lake, which at over 100 miles long, is the biggest reservoir that the Corps of Engineers created on the Cumberland. On the west bank of the reservoir is the Land Between the Lakes, a strip of land separating the Cumberland from the Tennessee, once inhabited by farmers, moonshiners, iron ore miners, and renegade Confederate sympathizers such as Jack Hinson, who, sniping from the bluffs, methodically killed thirty-six Union soldiers during the Civil War.

Now, after the Tennessee Valley Authority relocated its residents in the early 1960s, the Land Between the Lakes is devoted entirely to outdoor recreation and wildlife conservation. The bays of the east bank of the river shelter clusters of marinas and resorts, such as Barkley Lodge, and large homes overlooking the lake. Below Barkley Dam, the Cumberland hooks northwest into a sparsely populated rich bottomland region in the proximity of three other great rivers: the Tennessee, the Ohio, and the Mississippi. It gives itself up to the Ohio River at Smithland, just a few miles north of the Tennessee's mouth at Paducah, 50-odd miles north of the Ohio's confluence with the Mississippi.

The Cumberland spends around 300 miles of its length in Tennessee, but it dallies most in Kentucky, where much of it is free flowing, finding its own natural way through the landscape. Looking at the Tennessee and Cumberland rivers on the same map, one would conclude that the former is far longer, as it covers a vast watershed, including not only Tennessee and Kentucky, but also a significant portion of northern Alabama. Because of its tortuous route, the Cumberland is the longer river.

Much of the Cumberland is a working river, managed by the Corps of Engineers for multiple purposes: generating electricity, controlling flood waters, and providing a maritime highway for commercial barge traffic. Where the river has been turned into a reservoir, not only has the landscape changed but also the culture around it. From the free-flowing river in eastern Kentucky, where cattle graze on the banks, the flooded coves of the reservoirs attract tourist dollars and subdivisions, the dredged channels marking safe passage for craft big enough for the high seas.

As on the Tennessee, I pursued in my imagination the old river as it existed before the dams, trying to relive in my canoe the lives of the river's first inhabitants and to meditate on the great historical events that took place along its banks. Many historical heavyweights wet their feet in both rivers: Ulysses Grant, who won battles at forts Donelson (the Cumberland) and Henry (the Tennessee); Colonel John Donelson, who led a flotilla of rafts down the length of the Tennessee, then *up* the Cumberland to modern-day Nashville in the historically frigid winter of 1778–79; and Dragging Canoe, the fierce, smallpox-scarred leader of the Chickamauga tribe that terrorized Donelson and other white settlers in the region of both rivers. Where I had grown up, in western Kentucky, the lower part of each river lay only a short drive away, and I knew Barkley Lake (the Cumberland) almost as intimately as I knew Kentucky Lake (the Tennessee). This, like the other journey, would be a long, slow trip home on mostly flat water in the type of self-propelled boat—a canoe—that sensible folks use for shorter, more leisurely voyages on clear northern lakes or picturesque streams.

Despite the similarities between the two trips, the essential personalities of the rivers clashed. For one thing, even though canoeing the length of the Cumberland is generally unheard of, sections of it attract recreational paddlers. The Cumberland, unlike the Tennessee, still flows freely for long stretches, flashing whitewater near its headwaters and in a short, turbulent section below Cumberland Falls. In fact, from the headwaters in Harlan, Kentucky, to a few miles below the falls—about 130 miles—the Cumberland flows unimpeded by dams (with one small, unforeseen exception). Everything resembling a free-flowing river has been submerged on the Tennessee, few if any vestiges of its former wildness surviving nine high dams. The Cumberland has five of those riverine road blocks.

While Chief Seattle considers rivers masculine siblings, I think of the Tennessee and Cumberland as sisters. Unlike the Tennessee, the Cumberland was cold, in both a literal and figurative sense. Long stretches ran empty and desolate. It seemed haunted, distant, aloof, while the Tennessee was warm, embracing, pliant, the friendly sister, outgoing, perhaps older, its sibling younger, with a reputation for trouble. Like a renegade, the Cumberland was complex and difficult as it twisted and turned through the landscape, roaring between high bluffs and narrow gorges. It fogged up. It flooded. It resisted control. The Tennessee had been sedated and trussed up, an old gal whispering stories in gentle dreams, while the Cumberland wailed through the night like a vengeful ghost, telling lies of mischief and desire.

I prepared for the Cumberland the same way I had for the Tennessee. I read histories and guidebooks, consulted the Corps of Engineers Navigational Charts, made a few scouting trips, and asked people who lived near the river about navigation and camping. Randy and I put in at Carthage a few months before we started the voyage and paddled several miles up the Caney Fork River, a major tributary in Middle Tennessee. Jasper and I canoed a bit on Lake Cumberland, several miles below the falls, and I drove to Harlan and Bell counties a couple of times, trying to scout tricky rapids and likely campsites from the road. Cumberland Falls became one of my favorite places to visit, a spiritual shrine, and Randy and I rode the rapids below the falls in an inflatable kayak.

Consulting a variety of maps, I wrote out an itinerary based upon an average of a twenty-mile day, planning stops, when possible, at official campsites and what I thought were likely places for primitive sites, such as an island, a town, or the confluence of a major tributary. With the bits of knowledge I collected in my scouting and reading, I found that segments of the river, particularly in the upper region, still held quite a bit of mystery and uncertainty, even for those who lived nearby. One man, Vic Scoggin, who had swum the length of the river in 1996, gave me the most reliable and cautionary information, but even he didn't have all the answers, even he acknowledged that things happen on a river that resist explanation and light-of-day description. I didn't want all the answers. I wanted to leave much of the river a mystery so I could experience its surprises firsthand.

There was never any question about the craft—a canoe—never any consideration that it would lack a motor. Such a mode of transportation creates access to experiences mostly denied to travelers in cars and planes and motorboats. To write *Blue Highways*, William Least Heat-Moon explored America's back roads in a van, and he captured the nature of the kind of quest I had in mind:

> On the old highway maps of America, the main routes were red and the back roads blue. Now even the colors are changing. But in those brevities just before dawn and a little after dusk—times neither day nor night—the old roads return to the sky some of its color. Then, in truth, they carry a mysterious cast of blue, and it's that time when the pull of the blue highway is strongest, when the open road is a beckoning, a strangeness, a place where a man can lose himself. (1)

Working rivers like the Cumberland and the Tennessee are the last back roads, the few places left in America where mysteries remain deep in the night, in the early mornings, sometimes surprising you in the midday glare. They wind far away from strip malls and four-lanes into lives that have retained distinction, originality, and character. Canoeing, you set your own pace and rest assured that no matter how much concrete is poured, no matter how many trees are cut, no matter how much riprap smothers the banks, humanity will never succeed in obliterating a river. Rivers will endure forever, and in canoeing them, you become a part of their immortality.

At forty-five, my life probably half over, it wasn't really immortality I sought but a chance to test myself once again, to drain myself of physical and mental toxins and to embark on a quest for transcendence above ordinary experience. For me that threshold to the world of spirit and transcendence can only be entered in a narrow boat on moving water. I guess the river is like my church. There might be other extended river trips, but probably not for a long time, so the Cumberland would be my last chance to slip into some other realm in search of those moments of nirvana, those feelings that stop time and take you out of yourself and your worries about success, dignity, passion, confidence, purpose, and the transience of life. If only I could get Randy to stop singing Garth Brooks at the top of his lungs.

CHAPTER 1

HEADWATERS

HEADWATERS

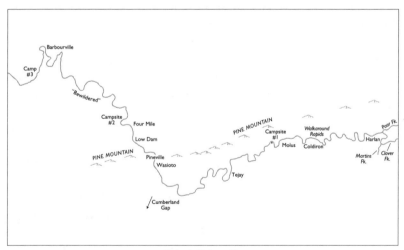

Harlan to Barbourville.

"And this also," said Marlowe suddenly, "has been one of the dark places of the earth."

JOSEPH CONRAD
Heart of Darkness

Night One: Randy and I lay on a narrow, sloping strip of flat rocks under a low canopy he'd rigged with his black tarp and ropes. The river flowed fast just a couple of yards below our feet. Rain seeped from the sky as night fell and the air grew chilly. Behind us, the muddy, brush-covered bank rose steeply twenty feet to the CSX Railroad, formerly the Louisville and Nashville, the famous L & N, as in the song that says "it don't run here anymore" (though it does, as we would find out). If the river rose, we'd have to break camp, get back into the boat, and paddle through the darkness. From the looks of the clothing, toys, lawn furniture, and lumber suspended thirty feet high in the trees, we knew the river could stick out its chest and swell to great heights. Up until the last month or so, I had worried that we might not have enough water to float from Harlan to Williamsburg, three or four days downriver. Bob Sehlinger, author of *A Canoeing and Kayaking Guide to the Streams of Kentucky*, reports that the gauge at Williamsburg should read at least 1,300 cubic feet per second (cfs) in order for the uppermost Cumberland to be runnable. On the day before we left, the gauge read 3,255 cfs.

The river had already overflowed its banks at least a couple of times that year. In February, it crested at twenty-one feet, five over flood level, requiring some families to evacuate their homes. It rose above flood stage again in April, and rainfall had been consistently heavy all spring, though nothing like 2002, when in March, five inches of rain fell over a twenty-four-hour period, swelling the Cumberland to twenty-seven feet.

As we lay there in silence, the rain slackened to a fine drizzle, and whirring insect chatter filled up the night. In the distance, four-wheelers grumbled down the railroad tracks from one hamlet to the next, towns with names like Coldiron, Loyall, Molus, Ponza, Tejay. The river sloshed powerfully over fallen trees and boulders, but it hadn't risen, as far as I could tell. As Randy snored, big splashes jolted me out of shallow drowses throughout the night. It sounded as if some joker were standing on a bridge dropping bowling balls into the river.

The day that preceded that first miserable night—May 25, a Sunday—had been, in retrospect, idyllic, though at the time, to my hyperactive imagination, it seemed full of bad omens and veiled cosmic threats. Murray Browne and Ian Joyce had accompanied us on the four-hour drive from Knoxville to Harlan in my old blue Buick Century, a four-door hand-me-down that my mother had sold me for cheap. At over sixty miles an hour, the Buick trembled like a spaceship on reentry to Earth's atmosphere.

"We're breaking up!" Randy would say whenever I surpassed my car's threshold for stability.

The Buick's thin roof buckled under the weight of my eighty-pound canoe, secured to the plastic bumpers with the same frayed cotton ropes I'd used for five years. When a gust of wind buffeted the bow, the canoe shifted abruptly a half-foot, the cheap blue pads attached to the gunnels skidding against the metal roof. From a family of accomplished worriers, I put on a brave face for my companions, who I thought perceived me as a seasoned expedition leader, confident and focused on the tasks at hand, ready for anything that might happen, including, say, my canoe breaking free and tumbling end over end until it got tangled beneath the wheels of a tractor trailer, the catalyst for a jackknife and a chain-reaction crash that would turn the highway behind us into a spectacle of carnage and mayhem.

Murray and Randy, in the back seat, were conducting a sort of mock interview. Randy seemed hopped up on coffee, his mood excessively upbeat at the prospect of the long journey. He joked about replacing Jasper, the German shepherd mix who had accompanied me down the length of the Tennessee River. "I'm trying to learn to bark like a dog," he said, his voice high-pitched, the volume, I thought, a little loud for inside the car.

I'd suggested he read my first book before deciding to go with me on this trip. Instead, he'd asked to borrow a copy that morning, in my driveway. He told Murray, "I didn't *want* to know what to expect."

Drizzle fell as we approached the gaping mouth of the tunnel at Cumberland Gap. Listening to National Public Radio, we made light of the orange Homeland Security alert that had been raised just before this Memorial Day weekend. Then we entered the tunnel, tons of earth and rock suspended above us, and the familiar voices on the radio stopped, the signal blocked. Chatter ceased. I fought the old demons—claustrophobia-borne anxiety attacks— and fended off hyperventilation, barely resisting an impulse to speed through the mile-long tunnel at one hundred miles an hour. For me, so sensitive to the myriad possibilities of doom, worrying had become an obsession in these times of disasters and warnings of disasters. A headline in the Blount County, Tennessee, newspaper (where I live) was particularly soothing and helpful: "Have a nice weekend," it said, "but watch out for terrorists."

As if that weren't enough, Murray and Ian cracked *Deliverance* jokes. Randy and I had already agreed that the words "Deliverance" and "Blair Witch Project" would be taboo on our canoe trip, but we put up with the ribbing of our companions, who by driving the Buick back to Blount County were doing us a big favor. Unlike the unfortunate paddlers in James Dickey's novel, who had to hire locals to drive their cars to meet them at river's end, we were being sent off by friends and picked up at our destination—696 miles and thirty-eight days hence, in Smithland, Kentucky—by my loyal wife, Julie; Randy's steadfast girlfriend, Lara; my beloved Jasper; and an entourage of friends and relatives.

Early that morning at my house, I had packed Dickey's novel into the bottom of a sealed dry bag, snapped the catch, then dragged out all the bag's contents to replace it with *The Narrow Road to the Interior*, a travel dairy of haiku and prose by seventeenth-century Japanese poet and Buddhist monk Matsuo Basho. Recommended by my friend, poet Jeff Hardin, I thought the monk's musings might distract me from night worries. I did not want to think about *Deliverance*, the book or the movie, with which I had a complicated relationship. On the one hand, I identified with the main character, played by Jon Voight, a man dissatisfied with work and city life, searching for deeper meaning and a clean and simple feeling of accomplishment on a wild river. On the other hand, the violence of the movie, particularly the rape of one character, Bobby, seemed exaggerated and lurid, and the portrayal of the locals, though shockingly authentic in one sense, also made mountain people out to be perverse, violent, and damaged.

Among friends, in a car on good roads high above the river, it was easy to laugh about what might happen if the depraved characters of Dickey's fiction came to life. And it wasn't just a Yankee ("Midwesterner," he protests) like Illinois native Murray who razzed us about the hostile natives of eastern Kentucky. Dr. Paul Threadgill, a colleague of mine at Maryville College and a native of Middlesboro in Bell County, next to Harlan County, had delighted in fanning the flames of my paranoia. The January before the trip he accompanied me on a hike to Bad Branch Falls on Pine Mountain above the Poor Fork of the Cumberland. At the top of the ridge, he lay on his belly and drank from what we agreed was the source of the great river, a spring that trickled through limestone and dead leaves. I waited a couple of seconds to see if he would keel over; then I drank a little myself. It was cold and sweet, tasting faintly of leaves.

A member of his high school marching band, Paul remembered that after away football games against Bell County, the Middlesboro busses would be ambushed by home fans who hid behind trees and jumped out to throw stones at the bus windows. One player from Corbin, Kentucky, had his eye put out by a rock that crashed through the glass. During that spring before our trip, Paul sent me eastern Kentucky newspaper articles on Oxycontin, the addictive painkiller known as Hillbilly Heroin. He suggested I take along Bibles, Oxycontin, and Kentucky whiskey (not Jack Daniels!) to give away like wampum. A couple of days before I left, during graduation ceremonies at Maryville, he advised me that there had been a run on ammunition at the Middlesboro Wal-Mart.

In short, I was worried, sure, but these were worrisome times, and my friends, the ones who had the good sense not to set out on five-week canoe trips, seemed to delight in multiplying the possibilities of doom. In a way I appreciated the ribbing, the ridicule of the possibilities our imaginations create before we do something out of the ordinary. It reminded me of whistling in a graveyard, though these guys, Murray and Ian, would soon return home to their kitchens and soft beds and electricity, to the familiar routine of stoplights and offices, and wonder what the hell was happening to the pair of lunatics canoeing through eastern Kentucky without a clue. There's a price for transcendence, whether it's self-created anxiety or the cold, hard reality of risk.

Driving to Harlan, my eyes often strayed from the road. Something watched us. A toddler, his head as big as a hot-air balloon, gazed down at us from billboards in Bell and Harlan counties. It was a face full of derision and knowing beyond its years, lacking the endearing innocence of childhood, disturbing in its dimensions and the implications of its omniscient squint-eyed gaze across the landscape. The kid, of indeterminate sex, wore a polka dot bow on its hairless head and laughed open-mouthed, showing a full row of upper teeth. We laughed at the ads for hardwood floors, but the laughter covered up our deepest fear: confronting ways of thinking that, as outsiders, we could not fathom. I hoped that the billboards would not be within visual range of the river. I could imagine them glowing in the dark, the pupils pulsating red, like coyote eyes.

Murray said the kid reminded him of the banjo boy in *Deliverance*, the one who sits on the rickety bridge over the river and stares down at the doomed canoeists on the day they launch, a symbol of indifferent otherness.

The Buick barely fit through the narrow threshold at Harlan's concrete floodwall, which was thirty feet high. Beyond and above it, downtown Harlan clung to the side of a mountain, tight little streets full of vibrant businesses: law offices, convenience stores, diners, pawn shops, dress shops, a square with an old gray courthouse and a statue of a World War I soldier, holding a rifle that mysteriously drooped, as if gravity were dragging it down the slope on which the town perched.

Randy and I put in on Martins Fork, one of three streams—along with the Poor Fork and Clover Fork—that meet to form the Cumberland. Beside a flat gravel bar where we dropped our boat, Martins Fork murmured thoughtfully, a small creek, almost ditchlike, though the floodwall suggested its mood could change. Across the creek were four tennis courts and a football field where Harlan High School athletes performed, the hillside where the school itself perched too crowded for such spacious sporting venues. Up the creek from us, on the four-lane that ran outside the floodwall, sprawled the usual outlets of American angst and desire: Wal-Mart, Burger this, Taco that, those symbols of prosperity and bad taste that had obliterated the personality of place the world over. In spite of the corporate sameness that threatened the brooding town, Harlan was still Harlan, unlike any place I'd ever been.

Even though I am a native Kentuckian, I felt like a tourist and rank stranger, even voyeuristic, for I knew that on this part of the river, more than any other section, we would be traveling through backyards, taking in the private objects of people's lives, and that some of those people would be poorer than anyone I'd ever met. They might not take kindly to a couple of strangers in floppy, wide-brimmed hats and sunglasses, one with a camera, gawking at them from a plastic green canoe. I was glad that Richard Haynes, the burly Harlan County children's librarian, accompanied us in his canoe for the first day. Though Richard's presence was reassuring, I couldn't help but be troubled by the fact that he had never canoed this river or saw a reason to. He told his wife we'd be in Pineville—the next major town—by late that afternoon. His timing was off by a long shot.

At the time of the launch, it was probably best that I didn't know about certain historical events. Had I known, for example, that in 1967 Canadian filmmaker Hugh O'Connor was shot and killed by an angry landlord named Hobart Ison in nearby Letcher County, I might have asked Randy to leave his cameras at home. Ison's reason for shooting O'Connor? He was offended that the filmmaker and his crew were documenting the life of one of his tenants, Mason Eldridge, a coal miner who sat on his front porch with his daughter in his arms, who had graciously given O'Connor permission to roll the cameras. Ison saw the filmmaker as a trespasser who was trying to humiliate him, to make the people of the area look bad, and as those interviewed in Elizabeth Barret's film *Stranger with a Camera* testified, Hobart was not a man with whom to trifle. I had an idea about the Hobart Isons of eastern Kentucky (and elsewhere), but nothing concrete like what Barret's documentary explored in all its tragic detail.

Martins Fork flowed through green-grass islands, passages just wide and deep enough for a canoe loaded with camping gear for two (tents, cookware, stove, two propane canisters, sleeping bags, tarps), five weeks of provisions (including some cans but mostly noodles and rice and soup mixes), two full five-gallon water jugs, a suitcase-sized hard plastic case full of Randy's camera gear, extra clothes, and other objects of comfort and survival for a trip that would often but not always stray far from plumbing, electricity, convenience stores, and hard-roofed dwellings. Richard, who kneeled in the stern of his canoe, put some of our gear in his bow as a counterweight for him and a load lightener to help us over the shallow places.

We pushed off and followed Richard through the tight passages, the current sweeping us around islands and bridge piers without much rudder action from me, in the stern. A few dogs barked lazily from the banks, the water too cold for pursuit. The sun broke free of the clouds, and we floated without paddling, chatting with Richard and gazing up at sycamores, maples, and river birches, where fabric of all colors flapped in the breeze. Randy said it reminded him of the prayer flags in Tibet. Driving along Highway 119 (part of Thunder Road, the old moonshine run from Harlan to Knoxville), you'd think that the river was lined with houses. But we floated in bends far away and below roads and houses, the noise of cars and lawn mowers faint next to the frenzied cries of wood ducks, the powerful slosh of the current, and the low white noise of approaching shoals.

Trees leaned out over us to form a canopy of shade that leaked shafts of sunlight. Before we left Harlan proper, we glanced behind us at three tunnels drilled in 1989 through Ivy Hill to divert the Clover Fork of the Cumberland, a flood control project. Richard said that the wealthy residents on top of the mountain had to endure many tremors as workers blasted their way through, but that no one had to move. Richard had kayaked some of the Poor Fork, near where he lived, in the town of Cumberland, but he had not had his canoe in the water for some time, and he was excited about this run and about persuading his wife into joining him on day trips such as this one. She, the two babies, and her niece had gone to Norris Lake that day, in the direction that we had come from, to enjoy a peaceful day beside those calm, clear waters backed up by Norris Dam, TVA's first on the Tennessee system. Richard, who was working on a summer reading program that would incorporate the Lewis and Clark expedition, then being commemorated on its two hundredth anniversary, had opted to confront the unknown with us, our little paddle trip giving him a personal connection with the great adventurers. When we reached the confluence of the Poor Fork and the Clover Fork, where a Dairy Queen presided, we were on the Cumberland proper.

The first Harlan Countian we saw on the bank stood in his backyard and waved big, the anti-Hobart. He asked two of three questions we would hear repeatedly: "Where you from?" and "How far you going?" The third, "Catching any?" I asked him before he could ask us. In the time that it took us to float past, he told us he liked to catch carp from the river and keep them as pets. There was no time to ask further questions about this somewhat novel hobby. As we followed Richard through gentle riffles and forgiving shoals, I began to think that all of my misgivings about this part of the trip were totally unfounded, that this was an undiscovered part of the river that should be attracting paddlers from all over. Nobody that I talked to had canoed from Harlan to Williamsburg, and only Bob Sehlinger's guide book referred to the run: "Although only steep, wooded hillsides meet your searching eyes, you are never out of earshot of the rumbling coal trucks or the raspy barking of a dog defending an unseen cabin in some lonely hollow. . . . The section from Harlan to Williamsburg is best suited to *one-day runs . . . rather than canoe camping* [my italics]" (150).

We hadn't heard any coal trucks, it being Sunday, and not that many dogs had barked at us, but we had seen a couple of houses in the first hour of the trip, and we would see more. Before the trip, I had talked to one of Richard's college classmates, Russell Alred, a Harlan lawyer who raved about how much he enjoyed hunting and fishing along this part of the river. He told me to turn over rocks and use the "grampus" larvae for bait to catch smallmouth bass and walleye. Most of the river is really beautiful, he said, but some parts "will just break your heart."

As we rounded a bend, one of those parts struck us silent. An avalanche of trash flowed down the thirty-foot-high bank to the surface of the water. I wanted to catalogue some of the contents of the riverbank dump, but it was so vast in its hideous entirety that I could not seem to settle my eye on details. And there were dwellings to consider as we floated past, awestruck, our paddles held above the water. Two trailers and a blue panel truck sat just above the trash avalanche. From the truck a white plastic pipe ran down the bank to the water, what is known as a straight-line pipe, a direct conduit for raw sewage. A junked car sat next to a charred area, still smoldering, where it looked as if a dwelling had burned to the ground. Farther downstream, we heard voices. A man stood in the open doorway of a trailer, another older man sat in a chair outside, and a boy stood between them. They waved, and the old man said something we could not understand. The boy, shirtless and without shoes, spoke up in a high voice: "Don't you fall in that river. You'll drown." Randy, in the bow, had a camera poised, hesitated, and put it back into his dry bag.

"Are the skeeters bad?" asked the boy. We said they weren't and floated on. Randy later said that when he saw the trash and the truck, he had his camera ready to shoot, but when he heard voices, he put it away. As much as I wanted to remember what the place looked like, I had just as strong an impulse to avert my eyes, as some do when they pass a disabled beggar on a city street. None of us spoke about these people during the day. Richard, the native, later said that he wanted to be quiet and minimize contact as we passed the trash bank. If people didn't care about the land any more than that, he said, they probably didn't give a damn about anything, meaning, in particular, that obeying laws of any kind was not a priority.

Russell Alred got it right when he called such scenes heartbreaking. The sheer volume of the trash was enough to make you feel powerless, and the fact that people had thrown it there and lived above it made us sad and embarrassed for them. Some might want to scold them. Others to punish them. Still others might want to help them understand what was wrong about the way they lived. We chose to glance furtively, to exchange small talk, and let the river carry us onward. There would be more to see, and some of it would sadden us, though nothing to this extent.

Harry Caudill, a native of Letcher County, up the Poor Fork, wrote most eloquently about this region in several books, but *Night Comes to the Cumberlands*, published in 1962, was probably his best and most comprehensive work. A lawyer by trade, Caudill was one of the first to describe the ills of the region and to expose the causes of those ills, much of which he blames on destructive and exploitative coal mining practices. Even before the mines, the timber industry had decimated the forests, the greatest giants bringing as little as a dollar a tree: "The Goliaths were the superb, pencil-straight poplars, some of them towering one hundred and seventy-five feet and achieving a width of seven or eight feet" (62). Strip mines added to the destruction of the hills and forests, the pollution of streams and rivers. Locals toiled in dangerous conditions for little pay and were conned into selling the mineral rights to their land for a pittance.

Coal mining also left a legacy of violence during labor wars as late as the 1970s, giving the town the nickname "Bloody Harlan," though Caudill notes that violence was part of the culture before the strikes. In the 1920s, when coal mining put cash in the pockets of Harlan Countians, the homicide rate was the highest in the country. In describing the region's people, Caudill does not shy away from negatives, and some think he dwells too much on inbreeding, a distrust of education and the educated, and a propensity toward moonshine guzzling and brawling. In fairness, Caudill also emphasizes the courage, hospitality, and strongly individualistic character of the early frontier people and mourns how that character had eroded into a dependence upon government aid.

Caudill's book, notes Elizabeth Barret in *Stranger with a Camera*, got the attention of journalists and social activists all over the country, who began to visit the area with cameras and notebooks to document the poverty that was escalating during the 1960s, when many coal mines were shutting down. Hugh O'Connor was one of many outsiders aiming a camera at the unfortunate, his intentions misconstrued and resented by many locals.

Caudill's work is often criticized for its focus on poverty and neglect, making the area seem like a sprawling rural ghetto. His work is best read as a product of its time, urgent in its appeal for action, eloquent in its details and its passion, though like any book it doesn't tell the whole story of Harlan County, which, as I would find out on my trip, was probably the most intriguing and in some ways most beautiful part of the entire river. Still, I had my guard up. The truth about any place almost always lies between extremes.

Vic Scoggin, a Nashvillian who swam the length of the Cumberland in 1996 to draw attention to the woeful state of the river, said he wanted to get out of Harlan and Bell counties as quickly as possible. Someone shot at him from a bridge, and others hid behind trees or bushes on the bank as he approached, unwilling to talk to him. After thinking about Vic and the .45 pistol he carried, I considered taking my Uncle Ed's shotgun (which takes one shell at a time), as I had on my Tennessee River trip. I decided not to. Going armed would only increase our chances of trouble, and if we got into a situation where one of us might use a gun, no good would come of it. In those times of Homeland Security alerts, it was probably best to be unarmed under the watchful eyes of Uncle Sam, especially since we had to lock through four dams. The only weapon we carried was a thirty-ounce wooden baseball bat bearing the signature of Harmon Killebrew, the slugging first baseman who played for the Minnesota Twins in the 1960s. Randy would be the only one to use it. One evening he swatted rocks into the river until I asked him to stop.

By midafternoon on that first day, Richard started wondering how far we were from Pineville. We had passed under several bridges, including a rusty iron railroad trestle and a footbridge with so many planks missing a squirrel would have trouble crossing it. Richard thought the next one would be the Coldiron bridge, which would only be about halfway to Pineville. We back-paddled in the current to ask our whereabouts from three old men sitting in front of a trailer on the bank above us. They confirmed that the Coldiron bridge was nearby.

"There's a couple of bad shoals coming up," said one of them.

"Can we make it across them?" asked Richard.

"Not in that boat," he said, nodding at ours, I thought, though he probably meant both of them. We joked about the old man's warning. If our boats couldn't make it over the shoals, what boats could? How bad could it be? We had already passed over numerous shoals without bumping a rock or a stump, and now this character was telling us to watch out? Natives on the banks of the upper Cumberland seemed to relish giving us dire warnings about dangers on the water, this being the first of many prophets of doom that we would meet. We'd seen a couple of small fishing boats earlier and a few more on the banks, but there didn't seem to be many locals enjoying the river. More likely, people feared its strong currents and cold temperature, saw it as a treacherous force that could take property and lives. The farther we got downriver, the more seriously I took people's warnings about current, weather, animals, or troublemakers, no matter how hysterical they seemed. The first time we dismissed a doomsayer, I reasoned, that doom would come to pass.

We took the old man seriously enough to scout an upcoming shoal that murmured a little louder than the others. Beaching the canoes, we tiptoed over rocks and mud for a good view of the white water flashing over a rock field that extended twenty yards downstream. The only place deep enough for us to pass required three quick changes in direction. The first rock reared up like a jagged molar and created a "hole" in the water behind it at least two feet deep. Richard, with his one-day's worth of gear, might have tried it, but with our weighted-down canoe and lack of expertise, we decided to walk around the disturbance on the far shallow side, holding onto the canoes. Wading Walkaround Rapids, as we called it, might have been safer than plunging through in the boats, but it was considerably more tedious and time consuming. Though we followed Richard's lead, each step in the ice cold water was uncertain. One step took us from knee-deep to mid-chest on the uneven river bed. The current pushed from behind like a schoolyard bully, and we took baby steps to keep our balance. Getting a foot caught between rocks and falling could be fatal. I survived with a stubbed toe, and soon we were back in our boats.

Dusk approached, and we began to consider campsites, finding few, either because of nearby residences, steep banks, heavy vegetation, or otherwise unsuitable terrain. Although Pineville was only a thirty-minute drive from Harlan, the river had its own ideas about getting there, and going in a straight line was not in its nature. Thinking we should have been in Pineville by now, we pulled over at a sandy beach below a bridge and walked with Richard up a four-wheeler path to the road. He determined that we were in Molus, several miles from Pineville. It was about six o'clock. We hauled Richard's gear and canoe up the muddy path and left it next to the road while he called his wife. He assured us he would be fine waiting on the side of the road and that we ought to use the remaining daylight to find a good campsite. Randy and I deliberated. The sandbar where we had landed the canoe was relatively flat but rose only a couple of feet above the water. Four-wheelers motored up and down nearby paths and the railroad tracks. I didn't like the sound of the town—Molus. What was it? Mole-us? It sounded too much like "molest." Reluctantly, we continued on without our guide. We should have stayed. Even though the area was populated with the rumbling four-wheelers, it was superior to the campsite we would settle for a few miles later, near dark.

We considered only campsites on the left bank, following Russell Alred's recommendation that we were less likely to be bothered on railroad land. The few sites we considered were unsuitable either because the bank was too steep and muddy for us to climb or there wasn't enough of a clearing to pitch our tents. As day dimmed, we passed a big sandbar that would have made an excellent campsite, except that two men were pushing a four-wheeler up a steep bank. (Richard called the four-wheeler the "Kentucky state animal.") The boy in the driver's seat looked embarrassed, and after he succeeded in climbing the bank and motoring away, one of the men, breathing hard, explained to us that the boy had "gone where he shouldn't have." The man, who wore a thick gold chain around his neck and slurred his speech, said that he and his friend were setting trotlines on the river before the rain. The friend, who had a black mustache thick as a fireplace brush, silently readied his fishing gear in a flat-bottomed johnboat with a small motor. We were floating slowly toward a shoal during the conversation. It roared as loud as Walkaround Rapids, and aside from the potential trauma of capsizing, getting wet and cold, and then having to gather all our gear in the dark, we didn't want to have a crisis in front of these guys.

We asked the man with the gold chain how bad the shoals were, and he said he hadn't lived in the area since the 1950s. That was all the talk we had time for. We blundered into the fast water, bumping a couple of rocks and turning sideways against one, where the current pinned us. It was then that quick thinking and sophisticated paddling techniques saved us. We scooted in our seats and hacked at the rock in panic with our paddles until the river pushed us on downstream. After that, we stopped at the first wide spot on the bank. I slept little that night, not only worrying about the rising river but also about the trains that roared past only a few feet above our heads, their whistles hooting painfully and the thunder of their passage shaking the hard ground beneath our backs.

I welcomed the lightening of the skies and the twittering of birds like I had no other morning. When we pushed off the loaded canoe, I felt at home, more secure on the moving water than on the narrow shelf below the tracks. I'd hoped to float out of Harlan County on the first day, but the river, the ultimate travel guide, would alter our plans more than just this once.

CHAPTER 2

THUNDER ON THE RIVER
THUNDER ON THE RIVER

At our campsite somewhere between Pineville and Barbourville, the bowling balls fell with greater frequency and volume than the night before. We were hunkered down in a dark forest on a sloping crop of poison ivy twenty feet above the river. Fog lay low on the water like a layer of cotton thick enough to crawl across. The canoe was tied bow and stern to the exposed roots of a sycamore. Fifty yards behind and above us, car tires crunched on gravel all night. I told myself that the bowling ball splashes were monster turtles falling off logs, but that didn't seem right because we hadn't seen any turtles. I slept for a while, and then sat up, awakened by a plunging splash close to the canoe, invisible to us below the sheer bank. Convinced now that some backwoods prankster was throwing rocks at our boat, I opened the zipper of my tent and turned on my headlamp. Randy's tent was gone. Panicked, I crouched and leaned out of the tent to try to see the canoe and realized I had turned in my sleep and was looking out my tent's "back door" opposite Randy's tent.

"Hey, you all right?" asked Randy.

I whispered that I thought someone was throwing rocks at the boat. Seeing me at the opposite door of my tent, Randy had perceived an illusion even more alarming than mine: that someone (not me) was standing over my tent.

After listening for a while longer, we told ourselves that the splashes were turtles and went back to our fitful sleep. Much later in the trip, after many nights of speculation, we would discover that the splashes were beavers, flopping their tails as a warning signal.

That morning it had taken four more hours of paddling to leave Harlan County. In its course between Pine and Cumberland mountains the river had widened, at some places two hundred yards across, high bluffs towering a thousand feet above us. At one of them, Seven Sisters Bluff, a series of craggy, four-story-high profiles jutted out from the greenery. One of the shoals extended downriver about a quarter mile. At every bridge swift, shallow water swirled and bubbled around gardens of rocks, some of them protruding above the surface, others lurking just below—"strainers" that Randy, in the bow, had to spot by reading the water. As we approached these stretches, Randy and I would plan what looked like the best route. Sometimes he would stand up for a better look. Then I would stand and look (never both of us). Then we might argue until the river shut us up. As we entered the fast water, he would call out "Right, left, right, right, left, left, straight ahead, paddle hard," in quick succession, and I would execute a pry or draw—paddle strokes to push the canoe to one side or the other. The general idea was to miss rocks and trees but specifically to avoid getting caught sideways against an obstruction, in which case the current would trap us and quickly fill the boat with water. A strong enough current could do serious damage to the boat, and rocks could dent tailbones, pierce thin skin, and crack thick skulls.

Randy and I had canoed a few times together on the Little River near Townsend, Tennessee, in the shadow of the Smoky Mountains, where his parents live. To give you an idea of our skill level, each time we made a run on the Little River, whose shoals are slightly more difficult than the Upper Cumberland's, we had fallen out of the boat. The last time, we blamed it on my dog, Jasper, who, having gained a few pounds in his retirement, lurched at a wave at the exact wrong moment and capsized us in frigid waist-deep water. In short, even though I had canoed many miles, I was far from an expert on moving water. What paddling skills I possessed were self-taught. What skills I lacked, which were considerable, I tried to make up for with stubbornness. Randy was learning fast—quick with directives, strong with the paddle.

As we approached Pineville and left Harlan County behind, the trash in the trees and on the banks diminished, as did the number of people living near the river. All in all, the float through Harlan County had been a pleasant surprise. Even though the river could have been much cleaner, I got the feeling that the area had improved in the last fifty years or so. Rebecca Caudill, who grew up on the Poor Fork a few miles upriver from the trash compound that we saw, describes in *My Appalachia* (1966) how the coal industry and other forces from outside transformed her beloved home into a wasteland:

> I felt a sinister change had come over that part of Appalachia that was mine. The river seemed the most changed, and all for the worse. I remembered it as clear and clean and deep and sparkling in the sun. . . . Now there were no fish in the river. . . . The Poor Fork was not only low; it was apparently the local refuse dump. Tin cans, pop bottles, and discarded automobile tires lined the banks, while the river itself was full of debris which apparently it was too sluggish to move along. Across the river, on the mountainside, both above and below the road, clung unbelievably unsightly shacks. Dirty-faced, ragged children played on coal piles in dirty dooryards. Open privies drained into the river. (54)

We had seen only one dwelling on the main river that approached this description, and much of what we traveled through showed few *visible* signs of abuse or impact by man. At least the river still flowed, unimpeded by dams, its surface untroubled by powerboats, jet skis, and barges, the likes of which awaited us. Even since 1996, when Vic Scoggin swam the river, some improvements had been made. The video that Vic made documenting abuses on the river was nearly pornographic in its detail, showing at eye level trash that floated on the surface and mounds of detritus along the banks. Enough Kentuckians saw the video to organize a group called PRIDE (Personal Responsibility In a Desirable Environment), which was formed by Congressman Hal Rogers and others in 1997 to "[unite] volunteers with the resources of federal, state and local governments in order to clean the region's waterways, end illegal trash dumps and promote environmental awareness and education, while renewing pride in the region [southern and eastern Kentucky]" (www.kypride.org). Rogers secured more than $66 million in federal funding for cleanup projects. In particular, the Homeowner Septic System Grant Program provides funds for Kentuckians to install proper septic systems or to repair faulty ones that pollute the river. Money has also gone to cities, counties, and utility companies to improve their wastewater treatment infrastructure. So far, we had seen only one straight-line pipe; Vic said that he had swum past many.

Despite our fears, no one had bothered us on the first two days. We did get curious stares, no doubt justified by the uncommon sight of us, strangers floating the river, in a canoe—and *not fishing*. Speaking seriously, Paul

Threadgill had told me that the area's fear and distrust of outsiders came from Scotch-Irish clannishness and from the fact that the culture as a whole had been blatantly exploited by outsiders who made big money on the coal mines at the expense of the environment and people's traditional ways of life. We would meet someone on Day Two who defied these commonly held conceptions about the distrustful and violent highlander.

Just beyond the Highway 119 Bridge, at Pineville, a long shoal bared its teeth and let loose a watery growl. It made us particularly nervous because we imagined people would see us from the bridge if we capsized.

Several miles south of us was the famous Cumberland Gap, where we had driven through the tunnel two days previous. A declivity in Cumberland Mountain, the pass and the river were named by land speculator and medical doctor Thomas Walker, who led an expedition through the passage in 1750 and erected a cabin outpost in Barbourville, the next significant town on our itinerary. Walker named the river and the gap after the Duke of Cumberland, reputedly because the duke shared the river's crooked character. Following Walker were more land speculators, long hunters/surveyors such as Daniel Boone, and settlers, most of them continuing north on the Wilderness Road to the more fertile Bluegrass Region. According to Ted Franklin Belue, who wrote *The Long Hunt: Death of the Buffalo East of the Mississippi*, Walker's discovery "cast a pall" (97) over the world of the Shawnee, who knew Kentucky as "Kanta-ke," "the land of great meadows" (98), and the pass through the gap as the Warrior's Path.

Where we floated under the bridge, the river cut through Pine Mountain at the Narrows or Wasioto, Shawnee for "where deer are plentiful." One thousand feet above us, on Pine Mountain, loomed a rock with a thick chain attached to it. Paul Threadgill told me that the idea of the "chained rock" was to calm the fears of frightened children that the rock would fall on them. ("You know it's a hoax [about the rock's threat]," said Threadgill, never missing a chance to ridicule a neighboring town or county. "Otherwise people from Middlesboro would be up there working on that chain with hacksaws.") A few miles downriver, at the Highway 66 Bridge, was the Cumberland Ford, where early settlers crossed the river to continue on their trek to the Bluegrass. Confederate General Braxton Bragg crossed here with his thirty-two-thousand-man Army of the Mississippi on the way south to Cumberland Gap after the mixed success of the Battle of Perryville, Kentucky, which ended the Kentucky Campaign of 1862, the Confederates' attempt to reassert control over neutral Kentucky after losses at forts Henry and Donelson.

After crossing the shoals below the bridge, Randy and I landed for lunch on the bank opposite the chained rock and the highway. With cell phone towers in sight on the mountain above Pineville, we were able to get a signal for the first time on the trip. Julie and Lara, dedicated worriers, were delighted to hear from us, and glad that we'd made it out of Harlan. For our part, we were thankful to have someone worrying about us. This was one of the better lunch sites of the trip, a wide beach, flat to the water, with big gray outcroppings to sit on and use as tables. I dumped tuna fish from a vacuum-packed foil package into a tortilla, and Randy mixed tuna salad inside his package, adding relish and mayonnaise from condiment packages he'd collected over the past few weeks. I blotted mine with Tabasco sauce. It was a sunny, cool day with no rain predicted for the night, and from Pineville on, the water carried us along on strong current with few rocks to dodge.

In a lighthearted mood, we began an informal hydrological study, formulating technical terms for our observations of the water's character. What looked like an oncoming rock garden but turned out to be a riffle from some change in the gradient below, I termed "wavy gravy." Because the boat rocked merrily over these sections, I declared this my favorite kind of water. Randy preferred what he called chocolate Yoohoo water, fast flowing and boiling without the crazy waves.

We saw only a couple of fishermen on the banks, and this was Memorial Day, making the river seem strangely neglected. One young fisherman, cutting up a turtle for bait, gestured with a long bloody knife at a good fishing spot downriver. Another, wearing a red bandanna, said to watch out for the big drop coming up. "They call it Cumberland Falls," he said.

I had heard about a low dam across the river at an old Kentucky Utilities power plant somewhere between the towns of Four Mile and Artemus. I pictured the kind of mill dams we'd seen on the Little River, with convenient paths that meant a portage of just a few yards. I thought it would take us an hour at most to unload all the gear, carry it across, then go back and get the canoe and reload, tying everything in, as we always did, in case we turned over. When we heard the roaring of the low dam a few yards ahead and saw the pooling of water above it, we landed the canoe at the path that I had anticipated. Steep, muddy, littered with bottles, cans, wrappers, and human feces, including toilet paper, the path led to a blacktop road where a few cars were parked. From there, another narrower path snaked downhill through a wooded area to the dam, where water spilled over a wall six feet high. Without looking closely at the put-in below the dam, Randy and I started to haul gear up to the road, what we thought was the halfway point of the portage.

On the way back to the boat, I met a young fisherman wearing a tan baseball cap, tan bib overalls, and a blue shirt. He lived on a nearby farm. I told him what we were doing and he said that sounded cool, like something he'd try if he had the time. He offered right off to help us portage our gear in his car. I thanked him and refused, thinking that he really wouldn't want all of our soiled gear in his car, plus the heavy canoe on top. He walked on down to fish where our canoe was beached, and I labored up the hill with the first load, the two five-gallon water jugs. After the second load, I explored the wooded path to examine the put-in below the dam. What I saw made my stomach sink. There was no put-in, just a sheer wall with a six-foot drop, no place to load our gear, much less ourselves into an unstable boat.

When I got back to the landing, the fisherman, John Holbrook, glanced at me with some concern; I must have been breathing pretty hard from carrying the gear. Probably my face had bloomed a devilish red. When I caught my breath, I asked him how far it was to a place where we could load the canoe below the dam. He said it was at least a half mile and again offered to help us. Randy and I looked at each other and agreed to accept. We loaded our muddy gear in the trunk and back seat, the canoe on the top of what turned out to be his wife's car.

"What's the baseball bat for?" John asked.

"Snakes," I said, worried that he'd think we were looking for trouble from the locals.

"You guys aren't snake killers, are you?"

John was a snake lover, a high school biology teacher who had recently graduated from the University of Kentucky. After refusing payment for driving us to the landing under a highway overpass and helping us unload, he wished us luck and went back to fishing. He had saved us four to six hours of backbreaking labor.

John, with a closely trimmed black beard, dark eyes, and a quick smile, fit Rebecca Caudill's portrait of an Appalachian more than James Dickey's. After moving away from Poor Fork, she considered the people she left behind: "Money was of no importance in the life of anyone I knew. If a man was sick, womenfolks helped nurse him to health, while the menfolks tended to his planting, his plowing, his harvesting. A man was judged by what he was, never by what he had" (28–29).

And so John Holbrook, taking time out from his day off to help not a neighbor but two fools portage a canoe down a river that no one canoes, demonstrated that generosity still thrived along the Upper Cumberland. John's good deed didn't help that night, though, when under the influence of the darkness, the fog, and Vic Scoggin's stories about dope growers and threatening camp invaders, I heard the flap of beaver tails and thought someone was throwing large rocks at our canoe. An email Vic sent me before the trip made Harlan and Bell counties sound like a place to sleep lightly: "I had all kinds of trouble in the upper Cumberland. Almost every day or night somebody would come into our camp and threaten us. I had to sleep with a .45 every night. There is a whole lot of dope growing going on up there. They just don't like strangers."

The next day (Day Three) we were lost, which is difficult to accomplish on a river carrying you one way. "Lost" may be the wrong word. As Daniel Boone said to the one man who painted his portrait, "No, I can't say as ever I was lost, but I was once bewildered for three days." We weren't lost. We just didn't know where we were. Somehow we missed an entire town—Barbourville—a significant landmark in terms of how far we wanted to get that day. After passing under an iron railroad bridge, we looked up a two-hundred-foot bluff, where a boy stood with two girls.

"Yeeeeeee!" he screamed down at us.

We waited for the rest, but that was all. We waved back uneasily. Another couple of boys near the next bridge hid behind trees as we passed. The river had narrowed to the point where the trees shaded its entire surface, and it twisted tortuously between muddy banks, the current silent and slack. For navigation we were relying upon the *Kentucky Atlas and Gazetteer*, a booklet of maps that showed roads of all sizes, power lines, official campsites, state parks, and boat ramps, but few mile markers or other detailed maritime information found in the Corps of Engineers' charts of the Cumberland that we would use later in the trip. We spent a couple of days on the upper river not really sure where we were or how far we'd been. There was brief talk of wishing we had a Global Positioning Satellite device, but we concluded that such a gadget would take some of the mystery and fun out of the trip. It wasn't so bad, being lost, not knowing exactly where we were, an achievement these days, when the landscape contains more directional signs than trees. Already we had quite a few gadgets, some of which would fall into the river or otherwise break: Randy's video camera and two still cameras, my binoculars, microcassette recorder, transistor radio, weather radio, and our two cell phones.

Night Three we spent on a shelf of flat land twenty feet above the river below a cow pasture. It had a fire ring and a trampled-down grassy area where others had camped, but there were no four-wheeler tracks and no roads or houses in sight. We tied the canoe to a tree's roots and climbed up the bank, gripping the roots with hands and feet like monkeys, our gear on our backs, a task that took about forty-five minutes, then another twenty minutes to put down tarps and set up tents. Since Pineville, the land above the river was mostly pasture or uncultivated farmland. We had seen no houses on Day Three.

Just before nightfall, when supper was almost ready, the rumbles began. For the next hour, as we ate, they got louder. When the storm blew in, at dark, strong winds tossed the tops of the massive limbs high above us and threw down heavy rain for half an hour. "I want my mommy," said Randy, who was videotaping from his tent. Lightning slashed a few yards upriver, followed in an instant by a gut-shriveling whiplash of thunder. But the storm was quickly finished, and we felt secure high above the water, with the canoe tied bow and stern. That, I figured, was the worst storm I'd ever been through while camping, and I didn't expect anything more severe.

Next day, as the river got cleaner, we began to ponder recurring trash items: some kind of fluttering white fabric that hung from the trees, and numerous abandoned cars, half submerged in the water or buried in mud or sand on the bank. Randy speculated that the fabric came from a road construction site we had passed; in the high water it had caught in the branches, whipping in the breeze now like garments discarded by river spirits, some pieces trailing several feet long, as if pranksters had "papered" the river for fools like us to wonder about. One 1970s-era sedan, roofless, stared at us with mud-bleary headlights as bushes grew up through its motor and inside where the seats had been.

What decisions had to be made, what efforts exerted, to dispose of a car in the river, miles from a road? Did the owner assume the car would only run so much longer and drive it across the pasture to the riverbank, abandoning what he might have repaired? Did he tow it from the road to the riverbank? Push it? It all seemed like a lot of trouble; why not just let it sit and metamorphose into a yard ornament, something for the birds to nest in? Why add it to the river's troubles with a car's toxic fluids and decaying metal, plastic, and cloth? Where we saw cars pushed into the water, we were again reminded of war zones, except that the destruction and ruin had been self-inflicted. I must also admit, somewhat guiltily, that these ruins—cars, sunken boats, abandoned houses and buildings—added interest to the river. It led to speculation about a bygone human presence, a history apart from the plants and animals that blended in more naturally. I'd rather the ruins not be there, of course, but since they were, we spent time photographing and conversing about them.

In Redbird, the village at the entrance of Daniel Boone National Forest, billboard-sized signs warned us in thick red letters about the "danger" of an upcoming obstruction. A gate of metal bars, fifty feet high, extending out into the river from the outside bend, had been placed to catch debris from upstream, an attempt to sanitize the tourist experience at Cumberland Falls downstream. This was the trash gate. It seemed to be working, to an extent, but most of what the gate caught was organic: logs and limbs and brush. PRIDE had installed the gate—officially known as the Lake Cumberland Debris Management System—in 1999. As of 2000, according to Carol Cox,

PRIDE's grant compliance specialist, "the trash gate [had] collected over 1,500 cubic yards of material."

The trash gate had been our third landmark on Day Four. The first had been a walking, talking biped on a bridge above us. As we approached, Randy yelled, "Hey . . . where are we?"

"Hey," said the man, caught off-guard by someone yelling from the river, then infusing his voice with the exaggerated tone of a promoter: "You're in downtown Williamsburg."

And just as quickly, we were not. We passed under I-75—landmark number two—found a country music station on AM radio, and floated toward the trash gate. Just downstream of I-75, we noted our first discarded television. It would not be the last.

Camped below Redbird, just within the Daniel Boone National Forest, I began to suspect the river and sky of intentional malice. After one storm of heavy rain that lasted about an hour, I poked my head out the tent door and said, "Well, that one wasn't so bad. At least the winds weren't as strong as last night."

An hour later, another storm: thunder and lightning, sure, no problem, but this rain made the deluge of the night before seem like a sprinkle, a Gene Kelly "Singing in the Rain" kind of storm. Tonight, raindrops hit the roof of my tent like pellets fired from the sky, and this was not hail. That would not have been so bad had the storm not persisted, at the same intensity, for three hours. Puddles began to form under the waterproof floor of my tent, bubbling up like a lumpy waterbed. The trickling creek next to our site turned into a roaring torrent. When the worst was over, at about one in the morning, Randy shouted for me to look out my tent window at the moving water. It looked as if the stars themselves had plummeted onto the Cumberland's surface. The hard rain had struck down a host of hovering fireflies. They floated past helplessly, their glows fading on the dark moving water.

The next morning, the first thing I did was make sure the boat was still there. It was, though it held several gallons of rainwater. Behind my tent, a small indentation next to a tree had become a pond. Soon we had company. A group of cows—ten or twelve—appeared in the pasture above our shelf of land. They looked at us a few minutes, then one by one galloped down the incline toward camp. One of them prodded at Randy's yellow dry bag, unrolling her long pink tongue for a taste. Another touched the pan of boiling water that stood on top of our precarious propane stove. The pan teetered but stayed upright, and the cow jumped sideways away from it. A couple reached up and chomped on leaves from the hickory behind my tent. Randy soothingly talked to our guests while holding the video camera, then I, ever wary, asked, then suggested in a stern tone, that they move on. When I clapped my hands and shooed them, they galloped awkwardly up the hill.

Apart from the storm, this had been a fairy-tale-like campsite, a forest of widely spaced trees with soft green grass that the cows had cropped. It reminded me of the manicured forests that you might see in Europe, with few weeds or shrubs or thorns. Even the most thriving plant of the Cumberland—poison ivy—was scarce here. But we had to move on, to paddle through what would probably be our most turbulent water the next two days. On the second day, a Saturday, we were to meet Randy's friends, including Lara, just above Cumberland Falls. Unlike some who had come before us, we planned to go around the sixty-eight-foot-high falls instead of over them.

Randy kept asking me how far the falls were from our takeout on Saturday. He was worried that we might be swept downriver, unable to stop before a plunge which many had not survived. I had canoed the stretch from Redbird to the Falls, so I knew the takeout was obvious and the danger minimal, but for him, as for most of us, the unknown creates anxiety, and there was little I could do to get him to worry about something more appropriate, like the weather.

CHAPTER 3

ELBOW ROOM

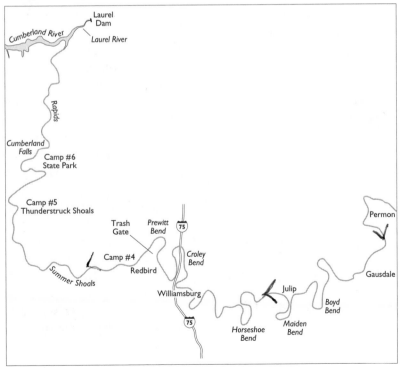

Gausdale to Laurel River.

Day Four dawned a drizzly smear, the river swollen and angry from the night's hard rain. The water was cold enough to take our breath if we fell in, our lives if we floundered in it too long. Many rocks that would have been visible before the rain lurked just beneath the risen water, while others were far enough under the surface that we would pass over with impunity what we would have had to dodge at lower levels. Though we were a bit on edge about confronting the biggest shoals of our trip, experienced paddlers would not be nervous about this part of the Cumberland; hard-core adventurers would be bored.

Every summer weekend, families and beginning paddlers rented canoes or kayaks from Sheltowee Trace Outfitters (STO) to make the seventeen-mile run from Redbird to the falls. On its Web site, STO cites the American Whitewater Association safety code, which classifies water according to difficulty. Our stretch was a mixture of Class I, "moving water with a few ripples and small waves . . . few obstructions"; and Class II, "easy rapids with waves up to three feet and wide, clear channels that are obvious without scouting." This sounds almost scornful. But high water tends to raise the ratings, and we had a canoe fully loaded, including expensive camera gear and five weeks of supplies. Randy had his cameras stowed in waterproof cases, and we had dry bags for clothes and food, but we weren't certain just how well these bags and cases would work if we capsized in strong current. We had so much gear tied in, so much weight, that I worried about it dragging the capsized boat to the bottom. I knew from experience that falling out of a boat, even in shallow water, could be painful and tiring.

The gazetteer listed five shoals between Redbird and the Falls: Summer Shoals, Bee Shoals, Crow Shoals, Thunderstruck Shoals, and Slick Shoals. We planned on paddling at least to the Rock House, about ten miles, and camping thereabouts, leaving a short paddle on the next day, when we were to meet Randy's entourage. Even though we had endured the hard rain at a great campsite the night before, we were intent on finding an even better one where we could relax for a good part of the afternoon and admire the river from the bank. Well within the National Forest, we would be camping legally for the first time.

The personality of the river and its landscape had changed. No more farmland and friendly cows. No more houses on the bank, just a few cabins hidden in the trees. The river was wider here, in some places three hundred yards across, and the shoals roared from a quarter mile downriver, their turbulence louder and crisper on the misty day, the sound insulated by the moisture in the air and the walls of the gorge rising on both sides. On the banks dense stands of trees stretched up toward the tops of cliffs, gray rectangular building blocks that the river had carved its way through over the ages. Big-leaf magnolias grew here, their foliage as broad as a palm tree's, the dry fallen leaves like a crunchy gray carpet on wintertime trails. Mountain laurel sprouted from crevices in the cliffs, and tall bushy hemlocks and hickories appeared for the first time. Instead of the muddy banks we'd been scrambling up to make camp, much of the riverside hospitably extended wide sandy beaches or rocky shelves for us to land on.

We were approaching the edge of the Cumberland Plateau, a dropoff that ran from northeast to southwest across Kentucky (and Tennessee), separating the Eastern Coalfield region from the Bluegrass, north of us, and the Pennyrile Region, which we were entering. Called the Cumberland or Pottsville Escarpment, the ridge was formed where sandstone meets softer rock worn away by erosion, creating waterfalls like the Cumberland and other natural wonders such as Kentucky's Red River Gorge and the grand arch at Natural Bridge State Park.

Above us in the steep-sided forest snaked 269-mile Sheltowee Trace, a hiking trail named after Daniel Boone, who was nicknamed Sheltowee or Big Turtle, by the Shawnee chief, Blackfish. Explorer, surveyor, settler, long hunter, tavern owner, and Indian fighter, Boone is one of those historical figures who was so mythologized by writers, then by television producers and tourism promoters that now it's hard to figure out who he was and what he did that's so important. Pondering Boone, I can't help thinking of Fess Parker, the actor who played Boone in the long-running 1960s television series. In contrast to the tall, statuesque Parker with the pleasant, well-proportioned face (he also played Davy Crockett, leading to much confusion among those who get their history from the tube.), Boone himself was a short, squat man with a wide, full face, thus his amphibious nickname. The Cherokee, more blunt and focused than the Shawnee, called him "wide-mouth."

The catchy theme song for the TV show was belted out by a squadron of strong male voices, their confident delivery underscoring lyrics that created a sort of brawling Goliath of the woods, who was successful at everything he tried: "Daniel Boone was a man, yes a big man."

Boone was tough, sure, and he was brave, but he avoided a fight when he could. After laying claim to a small empire in Kentucky, he died almost landless, hardly the "dream-come-a-truer" of the TV song. He was so bitter that after he moved to Missouri, he vowed never to return to Kentucky, a promise he kept until his body was exhumed in the mid-nineteenth century, decades after his death, and re-interred in Kentucky's capital, Frankfort. TV-show Boone's best friend was a half-white, half-Shawnee named Mingo. An Oxford-educated woodsman with an English accent, Mingo (played by Ed Ames) pretty much went along with whatever TV Boone proposed.

In reality, Boone's relationship with the Shawnee and other indigenous Americans was much more complex. He knew more about the Indians than most whites of the time, but he also fought them and was often able to survive such fights and help others survive because of how well he knew the enemy. In 1778 the Shawnee captured Boone for the second time. He had been hunting and scouting for a group of men who were harvesting and processing salt in the wilderness. Boone convinced the saltmakers to surrender to the war party without a fight. While captive, he ingratiated himself to the tribe and carefully planned his escape. He was adopted as a son by Blackfish and given hunting privileges and supplies, which eventually enabled him to break away and survive the long trek to Boonesborough, where he prepared the settlers for a large-scale attack that the Shawnee and British were planning.

Instead of recognizing that his crafty negotiations intentionally misled the enemy, many white men saw him as a collaborator with the Indians and the Redcoats, and after the siege of Boonesborough, which he was instrumental in repelling, he was brought up on formal charges of treason. The charges were dismissed, but the accusations embittered Boone.

Despite the reputation built around his ability as a fighter and killer of Indians, Boone once told his son Nathan that he could only be sure of having killed a couple of Indians in his lifetime, the first a tomahawk-wielding brave he was compelled to throw off a bridge into a deep gorge (a TV-like image). At the tragic Battle of Blue Licks, he was sure that he killed another with his long rifle. One of Boone's many biographers, Lawrence Elliot, notes the kinship that the Shawnee felt toward Boone, despite their many battles against him:

> And the Shawnee saw in Boone what the white man did not, that he was somehow outside the white man's world. It was true that he stalked the Indians' game and had driven them back on their own land, but he killed neither Indians nor animals for sport, only to defend and feed himself and those dependent on him. He was a true hunter. Like the Indians, he was touched with reverence for the land and the game he pursued. (124)

The most famous inscription attributed to Boone, on a tree in East Tennessee, illustrates how popular myth oversimplifies the complexities of a personality. "D. Boon cilled a bar," it says, the name itself spelled without the "e," something Boone never did. Though he didn't attend much school, Boone was not illiterate. In fact, on one long hunt, notes biographer John Mack Faragher, he carried with him Jonathan Swift's *Gulliver's Travels*, his favorite book, and read aloud from it to his companions. The day after Boone read about Gulliver's encounters with the giant Brobdingnags, Alexander Neeley returned to camp and announced that he'd been to "Lulbregrud," his approx-imation of Swift's Lorbrulgrud. The creek where Neeley killed two buffalo that day has since been known as Lulbregrud, what many assume is an exotic Indian name. In the last year of his life, Boone told tall tales of killing hairy giants that he called Yahoos, after Swift's savage, humanlike characters.

In a tourist brochure or a one-hour television series, it's difficult to cap-ture these kinds of complexities—a white man struggling with his cultural and racial identity, having to fight those whom he emulated, becoming impa-tient with whites who did not trust his judgment in war or peace, unable to reconcile the solitary long hunter life with that of a family man. The TV show always ended with a tidy resolution of whatever problems Boone and his family confronted. Would that his life have been so simple and free of hardship. He lost a son, James, who was tortured and killed by the Cherokee warrior, Big Jim; a brother, Ned, killed in an ambush that Daniel escaped; and another son, Israel, who died at the Battle of Blue Licks, in which Daniel reluctantly led a division after warning hotheaded leaders of the ambush that awaited them.

His relationship with his wife, Rebecca, was strained by long hunts that took him far from home. Once, after returning from a twenty-month absence, he found Rebecca at home with a new baby girl, which turned out to be the daughter of his brother, Ned. Boone apparently forgave his wife, who stated that she had grown lonely and did not know whether he was dead or alive. Years later, he would use his courage, resourcefulness, and physical endurance to rescue the daughter, Jemima, and two other girls, after they were captured by a band of Shawnee and Cherokee warriors led by Hanging Maw, an acquaintance of Boone's. For all his love of solitude and quest for "elbow room," Boone formed close connections with his family, and he struggled mightily with the loss of his sons. After James's death Boone wrote: "James was a good son . . . , and I looked forward to a long and useful life for him, but it is not to be. . . . Sometimes I feel like a leaf carried on a stream. It may whirl about and turn and twist, but it is always carried forward" (Elliott 74). Even after the deaths of so many family members, there is no mention in biographies of Boone's swearing vengeance on the Indians or of his using tor-ture when he fought them. Many years after the torture and death of his son James, Boone witnessed the killing of Big Jim, who had slain James so bru-tally. As Faragher tells it, Boone "stood watching numbly as the rangers scalped Big Jim and mutilated his body" (252–53). Despite living in a time of brutality and panic, when many died early deaths, Boone was consistent, even-tempered, and cool in a crisis, qualities that kept him alive until his mid-eighties and made him a natural leader.

The presence of such a magnificent and tragic ghost infused our drizzly passage through the rapids with mystery, and the deep, empty woods and high bluffs surrounding the river only added to its historical resonance. Here was land that didn't show much change over the centuries, dark places that still held that sense of the unknown that must have enchanted Boone to keep moving west, toward wilderness, away from civilization. In the fog and mist that seemed to be thickening in the late morning, Randy and I pulled into a narrow creek, quiet and deep like a Norwegian fjord. We stealthily dipped our paddles into the still surface and coasted up to a small, tree-covered island the size of a backyard gazebo. As the creek's current nudged us backward into the Cumberland, we sat still, paddles raised. Something crashed against the limbs and leaves above us; then there was the quiet and darkness of the day-time woods, dimmer than any forest I had ever seen, yet with a dearth of undergrowth that made it hospitable to explorers on foot.

We floated on the main river until we got to one of the rock houses noted in a guidebook as a good place to camp. We sniffed around and within the rock overhang, noting the presence of previous campers, as evidenced by some litter. Water dripped from the outcropping above the roof of the rock, which was twenty feet deep and high enough for us to stand under. We decided to look for something dryer, more open. In the middle of the next shoals, Thunderstruck, we paddled hard for an eddy next to a wide beach on the left bank and landed just a few feet upstream of a canoe-killing rock around which the water sloshed heavily. The beach was thirty feet deep and extended along the bank fifty yards or so. Driftwood—easy to burn, even when damp—lay everywhere. There was a fire ring and a rocky path that led to the site, but it did not look as if anyone had been there for a while. Best of all, we had ringside seats to the river's drama: a wide shoal that gurgled and roared at us as we stood on the soft sand, a perspective much more relaxing than scouting it on the run from a laden canoe. Our only misgiving was that the next morning, when we started out, we would have no time to mentally prepare for the first obstacle; we would have a narrow passage to thread as soon as we pushed off the beach, with no margin for error.

After we gathered driftwood for the fire and got our tents set up, I set off for a hike on Sheltowee Trace to scout the rapids ahead and to see just how far we would have to paddle the next day before we pulled out above the falls to wait for Lara and Randy's friend, Curt, to pick us up. Because of the heavy rain the night before, rivulets trickled down the trail, and streams poured from the cliff sides above. I climbed up a boulder the size of a small house for a look at the river ahead. It bent right and showed the downward incline and flashing water of another shoal, which roared louder than the one we were camped beside. Already I was beginning to notice that the roar of the rapids over rocks was not always a good measure of its difficulty. It wasn't a friendly sound, but not something to panic about. I walked another mile up a trail that climbed the ridge. The dirt path turned to a gravel road that met a paved highway at the top.

Vic Scoggin had told me about an uneasy night near here when a group of men on four-wheelers joined them in camp, friendly at first, then growing hostile and accusing Vic and his crew of breaking out their truck windshield. Vic lay in his sleeping bag, listening to the argument, ready to pull out the .45, but the men finally left. Four-wheelers could get to our camp, but the last quarter-mile of trail, strewn with basketball-sized boulders and cave-ins from the big storms, would be rough on them. If uninvited guests joined us tonight, they would have to go to a lot of trouble.

When I returned to camp, Randy was busy with the fire. This was the first time we had set up camp so early, and now, as I watched Randy, I began to perceive how neat and organized his camping protocol. As I sat on a rock and pondered my next move, he got the fire going; set up a clothesline and hung up his sleeping bag and clothes to dry and air out; hung up the tarp and cleaned off the mud from last night's camp, pouring river water onto it with our bailer, a cut-out plastic gallon jug; tied his hammock to a couple of trees; began to clean out the canoe, then thought better of it, wondering aloud whether an immaculate canoe would make Lara and Curt think we'd had it easy. Perhaps a little dirt would be appropriate, he reasoned. Then, unable to tolerate the mud and sand at the bottom of the canoe, he took our large sponge (which I had filched from my wife's car washing supplies) and wiped it cleaner than I'd ever seen it.

While he was employed with these tasks, I tied a Rooster Tail lure to my spinning reel and cast it upstream in the shallow, swift water. My father taught me how to fish, taking me to Kentucky and Barkley lakes between swing shifts at the chemical plant where he labored for thirty years. Like me, he had little patience for gadgets and machinery that failed, but unlike me, he maintained his gadgetry so that he didn't have to deal with its failure. He lubricated his reels, replaced worn line and kept his tackle box neat and organized. A quiet man not prone to expounding on good habits, he set a good example that I had trouble emulating. Disorganized and sloppy in my fishing habits, easily distracted by scenery or stray thoughts, I spent more time unfouling lines and lures than catching fish. Though I hadn't fished for a while, I retained the bad habits I developed in childhood.

After extracting my lure from a couple of bushes, I got it hung on the fourth cast in a crevice between underwater rocks. Breaking the line, I remembered why I no longer fished; it was hard work, and I was not very good at it. I set about reorganizing the contents of my three dry bags and the kitchen bag, a black, rubber-bottomed, green mesh duffle bag which held our cookery, the stove, the propane canisters, the dishwashing liquid, and other miscellany. It sat between my feet in the boat and got soaked every day; by now the paper labels were disintegrating, and the detergent had leaked onto everything else in the bag. As I rinsed off the contents of the kitchen bag, put the evening's dinner implements on a rock near the fire, and gathered materials for other evening activities, such as reading and writing, I began to perceive the distilled essence of camping, encapsulated in two repetitive activities: *getting things out and putting things up where you could find them again.*

Exhausted by my burst of reorganizing, I sat on a boulder and sipped whiskey while Randy continued to clean and reorganize the wilderness. I needed to rest up in order to prepare supper. We had been taking turns on KP duty, combining ingredients from our packaged foods supply. Two nights earlier, Randy had prepared an excellent meal from a box of rice and beans and a can of okra and tomatoes. The night before that, I had mixed macaroni and powdered cheese, canned mushrooms, tuna, and canned spicy tomatoes into a yellow-red mixture that resembled in color the muddy water that washed past our campsite after the storm. Randy ate it without complaint. Not until I repeatedly complimented my own cooking and asked him what he thought did he acknowledge the concoction's tolerable edibility. The cooking wars had begun. There was talk of a river recipe book, designed for weight loss.

Early that evening, maybe an hour before dark, sunlight seeped through the fog that thickened after the drizzle stopped. The diffuse light from the setting sun transformed the fog into a warm, golden veil, and the muddy water turned amber with flashes of white all the way across to the opposite bluffs, dark indistinct masses that loomed over the river. Randy, who was lying in his hammock next to the river, sprang up and grabbed his camera. We were witnessing a rare convergence of light and moving water, and I tried to sear into my memory the spontaneous and momentary spectacle. It was free and unrehearsed, and the river expected no praise or critique. It was just there, being itself, without pretense or intent.

That night it was difficult to close our eyes to the rapids flashing at us through the darkness. We fed and poked at the fire until after midnight like children wanting to stay awake through Christmas Eve.

The next day would be a run of three or four miles. We pushed off and threaded our way through the narrow passage between the big rock and the bank, and bounced through the first shoal of wavy gravy. I thought this might be the one segment of the river where we would see absolutely no one, but two boys appeared on the left bank in the trees, staring at us without returning our waves. Cumberland Falls lodge emerged from the forested bluffs high above us, by far the most imposing structure we had seen, a monument of stone, cedar, and glass protruding from the steep slope.

By this landmark, I knew we were heading for Slick Shoals, and I tried to soothe Randy's anxieties about us overshooting the landing and catapulting over the falls. A headwind blasted us here, and the rapids ahead looked faster, whiter, and more complex than we had seen. We stayed far right, passing close to a couple of fishermen standing on a boulder, rocking in the waves toward the highway bridge that marked our takeout, maybe three hundred yards from where the river fell off sixty-eight feet.

A ranger at the Cumberland Falls State Park, Al Gooden, had told me that everyone who had gone over the falls, either on purpose or accidentally, was "pretty well intoxicated." He said that a fisherman had fallen asleep in his boat and survived a trip over the falls in 1972. Danny Brown, supervising ranger at the park, said that eight years ago a kid fell asleep in his canoe and went over. They found him the next morning, wearing only a bathing suit, clinging to a cooler. There were also those who jumped. One midnight daredevil, who had already jumped off once, was climbing up for a second jump when Gooden caught him. When he sobered up a bit, said Gooden, he admitted that the current at the base of the falls "almost got him." Brown said they kept no records of people jumping off the falls, that such stunts had been extremely rare since they put up the fences and danger signs next to the rock ledge overlooking the falls. These are incidents, he said, that "we just try to forget."

I never would have believed it had I not seen the stunt on a video, but two Knoxvillians, John Grace and Nathan Helms, kayaked over the falls in February of 2003. Their narration of the feat is almost absurd in its understatement. Grace, who went first, said they had "ditched the cops," since it's illegal to go over the falls. As he negotiated the rapids above the falls, he said he could have easily "eddied out" and forgotten the whole thing: "When I got to the lip," he said, "everything was good, and then I realized I was seventy feet up. I had a pretty good line, . . . but I'm not going back." Helms, who windmilled his paddle on the long descent, struggling with his line, said he "probably won't do it again."

The Lunch Video Magazine DVD which included this stunt was full of wild descents by young people in closed plastic boats the size of teacups, but nothing as rash and irrevocable as the seventy-foot plunge over Cumberland Falls.

The first whites to encounter the falls were Zachariah Green and his hunting party, who were floating down the Cumberland in their dugout canoe in

February 1780, a time of year when the river "had its big britches on," as state naturalist Mack Prichard would say. When they felt a rumble that shook the earth, the men got the boat to shore above the falls, unloaded it, and carried their gear to the base of the falls. One of the long hunters paddled the canoe to the center of the rapids above the falls and jumped out before it plunged down the precipice. Men such as Green were "hardy souls," as Harriet Arnow put it in *Seedtime on the Cumberland,* unimpeded by natural wonders such as a seventy-foot waterfall in the way. Green was once left for dead by his companions after being mangled by a bear, but survived the wounds "alone in the woods save for one faithful hunting dog" (218).

Randy and I pulled out at the Highway 90 bridge, having made the final crossing without serious incident, though the fishermen who watched us probably didn't go home raving about our skills. We were dry and we were happy, thinking that we had survived the most dangerous part of our trip. We unloaded the canoe and laid it and our gear under some brush about fifty yards from the river. I took the cell phones up to the museum, hoping that the ranger would let us charge them. Walking up toward the falls outlook through the quarter-mile-long parking lot, I reeled from the shock: the noise of many voices, increasing as I approached the museum and gift shop complex, the smell of exhaust, the hardness of the asphalt and concrete, the colorful clothes of leisure fashion. A young couple played a version of petanque (the European game of tossing balls at a small target) on a mown lawn near the river. Their white skin glared so luminously in the bright sun I had to look away.

At the museum, I guess I expected the ranger to express astonishment and admiration at my arrival, but she had no comment about where we had started our trip and where we were going. She was gracious enough to plug in our phones behind her desk. Without even peeking at the falls just a few steps away, I noted the snack bar menu included cheeseburgers and hurried back to inform Randy. This would be the beginning of our corruption, this cheeseburger stand at Cumberland Falls.

CHAPTER 4

GETTING SOFT

Zachariah Green would have shooed us away from his dugout canoe. Boone would have escorted us back to the nearest fort. Shamefully, I must admit that, after long and careful agonizing, Randy and I decided to skip the five miles below the falls, which includes some borderline Class III ("Rapids with high, irregular waves often capable of swamping an open canoe," according to the American Whitewater Association). At the "big britches" stage, the river would resemble a giant washing machine on "agitate," not the kind of water for which my flatwater touring canoe was designed. We could have unloaded all of our gear, given it to our helpers, and asked them to meet us downriver after negotiating the five miles in an empty canoe. We also could have rented from Sheltowee Trace Outfitters (STO) a "duckie," an inflatable open kayak in which we had made this run the summer before. On this voyage, we would have had to ask our helpers to load our boat and our gear, take us to STO for the rental, and then wait for us below the rapids. This would be a two-day ordeal for them, which seemed too much to ask. Since we had "duckied" this stretch before, we felt a little less cowardly about skipping it.

Ranger Danny Brown had told me he'd been on the river below the falls quite a bit in rafts but would not run it in an open canoe. "I've seen plenty of canoes wrapped around rocks," he said. "I guarantee you'll turn over if the water's up and you don't have a whitewater canoe." *Guarantee?* Then he said something about "lost" canoes that were never found, and then something else about the rescue squad. "I'm not trying to scare you," he said, "but . . ." He had. And I knew enough about the run to respect his opinion.

In the midsummer of 2002 Randy and I drove the hour and a half from Knoxville to make the run below the falls, which, along with the Redbird segment above the falls, was designated a Kentucky Wild River in 1972. Parts of nine Kentucky rivers had attained this status, recognized for their "exceptional quality and aesthetic character," according to the Kentucky Division of Water. Designated wild rivers are protected from development such as mining, timber harvests, and damming that would damage their status as relatively clean refuges for animals and recreating humans.

At STO, a handsome compound with campsites, cabins, a climbing wall, and a cavernous cedar headquarters, we were shown a video about how to survive a fall into rapids, given helmets and life jackets, had our car keys confiscated for safe keeping, and ordered to sign a form that exonerated STO from anything bad that might happen to us, misfortunes which, it seemed to me, were quite numerous. The most common were drowning, snakebite, and getting clubbed on the head with a paddle. The owner, Rick Egedi, also known as Papa Smurf, gave us the rundown on the river like a burned-out comedian, with deadpan lines such as, "Don't drop your paddle; you may need it."

His business was the sole concessionaire of boat rentals below the falls, and he'd been at it a couple of decades, so he knew the river well and had an excellent safety record. Perhaps because he'd been on so many trips and knew from experience the sorts of disasters that could happen, usually the result of a client's stupidity, he had a sort of river-weary attitude that precluded much questioning or discussion from us pilgrims. Let's get on with it, his tone implied, I got a bunch coming after you guys, and I don't want any trouble or holdups. Add to that his somewhat disturbing demeanor—the bushy white beard, bald head, and squat stature—and he resembled Santa Claus with an attitude (in sandals).

The other employees at STO were more engaging personalities. As we got to our put-in, our guide, T.J., helped his six or eight pilgrims into a large rubber raft, then asked Randy and me if we'd had much experience paddling whitewater.

"Sure," I said, "some," thinking of our most recent capsizing incident on the Little River, diminutive and tame compared to what we were about to take on.

"Have you ever paddled together?" he asked.

"Yes," I said, not revealing that it had only been twice.

T.J. seemed satisfied with that brief interview. A burly young man sporting an eyebrow ring and numerous tattoos, he loaded his six pilgrims in the raft and headed upriver toward the base of the falls, Randy and I following. We idled in the eddy just a few yards from where the 68-foot-high, 125-foot-wide deluge pounded the surface. T.J. told us if we followed the routes that he would take in the raft, we would be fine. The next thing he did was a little puzzling. Grinning like a pirate, he and the other guide, Jake, truly fearsome looking with a nose ring and pointed goatee, rammed our duckie with their raft and proceeded to try to flip us. Under orders, the pilgrims splashed us with their paddles. Instead of struggling, Randy and I just slipped over the side into the river. This was, I understood, a baptism of sorts, their way of initiating us to the shock of the cold water before the rapids. After we reembarked, T.J. warned us to stay away from the "death rock" just ahead. He said go one direction then another to avoid the paddler-sucking vortex below it. "Do not fall in there," he said. "We don't have safety lines on the bank today."

"Did he say go left, then right?" I asked Randy after we were under way.

"I think it was right, then left," he shouted just before the approaching roar made debate irrelevant. We blundered through the day careening off rocks and spinning out of control without overturning the duckie, though we did take on plenty of cold water going through passages such as Center Rock Rapid, Willie Nelson (where the musician himself reportedly took a spill), Surfer Rapid, and more disturbing names, such as Pinball, Screaming Right, Last Drop, and Stairsteps. Despite the names, STO advertises the run below the falls as a "soft adventure."

In this five miles, the river transforms itself into an animal much different from any other segment. The swift water's roar at each passage is much louder and deeper than the shoals we'd been hearing upstream. Created by the narrowness of the gorge and the steep downward slope of the river's bed, the rapids collide with boulders the size of houses, big gray mammoths rounded off from the eternal force of water and wind. Between each rapid the river deepens into calm pools, where paddlers swim or kick back in the raft and relax before the next action. Sheltowee Trace continues alongside this stretch of the river, and despite the proximity of tourists and roads and the trappings of a state park (gift shop, tennis courts, lodge), a hike on it always haunts me. Dark and damp under the thick canopy, its rock houses and overhanging gray cliffs drip cold water on your head in summer and grow swordlike icicles in winter. I transported Maryville College writing classes there three consecutive Januarys, and some of them got the same feeling of ancient mystery, a place where cataclysmic geologic changes had created a hard dim world apart from the region's rolling green landscape. The falls itself, which is gradually eroding and will eventually disappear, had once been forty-five miles downstream, in the vicinity of Burnside, Kentucky, where it was estimated to be five hundred feet high. This was, alas, before the existence of folks who could walk upright and lean on a rail to admire such a drop.

The STO rafting trip takes three to four hours, after which the river is becalmed by the influence of Wolf Creek Dam, over one hundred miles downriver. In the flatwater, the beginnings of Lake Cumberland, Papa Smurf picked us up in the Cumberland Star, a canopied pontoon. He fed us sandwiches, chips, and cookies, and gave us a ride back to the compound in a school bus.

Now, a year later, after a week on the upper river, we devoured our cheeseburgers at the falls snack bar, and smirked at Papa Smurf's camera-toting pilgrims, who lined up at the bathrooms in their helmets and lifejackets before boarding the rafts. We scoffed at the gift shop with its T-shirts, quilts, postcards, key chains, and doilies (though Randy bought something for Lara there). We mocked the patriotic/churchy Muzak oozing through invisible speakers and thought of ourselves as hardened river rats, stopping off from the real world of big water, bad weather, and lurking villains. Our faces had sprouted whiskers. We were voyageurs, not tourists. Others probably saw us as hungry loafers with bad table manners, dirty feet, soiled clothing, and inadequate deodorant. Looking back on it, I'm surprised that someone didn't throw a few coins our way. I contemplated ordering another cheeseburger, but Randy reminded me that Lara was bringing steaks, and the teenage girls working the snack bar had escaped out from behind the microwaves to gossip at the picnic table next to us about the local boys who sauntered past.

We strolled the fifty yards to the overlook before returning to the boat. Though I'd visited the falls four or five times, I stood there, mouth agape, for several minutes, imagining an approach in a canoe, on purpose, with the goal of surviving intact. Like the daredevil Knoxvillians, you'd have to go far left, where the greenish water turned amber and white, gushing deepest between rocks in a channel that made a big "V" before the drop. If you tried anything different, you'd get turned sideways and overturned before the dropoff. Not that it would matter much. Looking long enough at the falls itself distorted my vision so that the white water seemed to fall in slow motion, individual drops suspended like a film on "pause." Below, mists rose and drifted downriver toward the big round rocks. Amber suds floated in the eddies where driftwood, cans, bottles, and plastic wrappers crowded into corners away from the pounding falls. How anybody could survive falling or jumping or kayaking into that water was beyond me. Some had, some hadn't.

The main overlook, where we stood, was a flat rock the size of a tennis court, a chain strung around its perimeter with signs warning onlookers to

stay behind it. Farther down, stairs led to more overlooks for distant perspec-
tives. Groups of men, women, and children straggled from the gift shop to
the overlook to the bathrooms, taking photographs of each other and clutch-
ing brochures. I was glad that people brought their kids here. Plenty of other
natural wonders, such as Niagara Falls, seem incidental to the casinos, theme
parks, golf courses, and other retail that crowds them, while at Cumberland
Falls, the attractions are crass but low key, and the falls retains its own majes-
tic dignity, its roar drowning out the bankside smarm. In the winter, the place
is nearly deserted, more conducive to meditation, solace, and turning thoughts
over in your head. One Maryville College student, a native of the region, ran
to the overlook when she heard the falls' roar, turned back to the group and
cried, "I can't believe I've never been here!" Another, gazing long at the double
rainbow in the mist of the falls, turned to me and said, "Thank you for bringing us to this place." These are unusually earnest comments from even the
most serious of students.

The creation of such an aesthetically pleasing natural wonder took millions of years. Over geologic time, the force of the river cut through different
types of rock, some more resistant than others. At the falls, the river met with
what is known as Rockcastle Conglomerate, which resisted erosion. Below
this hard rock was material that was less resistant, resulting in a dropoff
carved into the soft rock. Over time, the falls moved upstream, from the area
of Burnside, when softer material under the Rockcastle Conglomerate wore
away, and the resulting overhanging ledges broke off. Eventually, as this
process continues, the falls will dwindle to mere rapids.

Humans have inhabited the area around the falls for ten to twenty thousand years, plentiful game and fresh water making it a good place for subsistence. The Shawnee considered it a sacred place, partly because of a phenomenon known as the moonbow, which sounds like the invention of a promoter
with colored lights and mirrors, but is in reality a natural occurrence that adds
to the falls' mystique. A moonbow resembles a rainbow but is white and
occurs as a result of a cosmic conjunction between the moon and the mists
rising from the base of the falls. Twice a year, when the heavens and the moon
cooperate, visitors come from miles around to see Kentucky's moonbow, a
phenomenon that occurs in only one other place on earth: Victoria Falls on
the Zambezi River in Africa.

What spiritual significance the moonbow held for the Shawnee is unclear,
though like most Native Americans, their spirituality came from the land,
their divine beings often taking the form of animals or other natural objects
or phenomena. For a time, the Shawnee were considered the main populace
along the Cumberland. In fact, the river was originally named for them by

the French (Riviere Chaouanons), until Dr. Thomas Walker renamed the river (and the gap) after the English nobleman. The Shawnee, according to James Howard, called it "shkipakithithipi," translated as Blue River (6).

In the seventeenth and eighteenth centuries the Shawnee wandered all over the eastern half of what would become the United States, from the Delaware River region to the Ohio to the Cumberland. They were, R. E. Banta notes, an intelligent tribe, like their "cousins," the Cherokee, but they differed in color, having a "yellowish" complexion "rather than the typical reddish brown of most Indians of historic times," indicating, Banta speculates, "some rather special racial strain" (54). By 1715, the Shawnee were driven from the falls area by Cherokee and Chickasaw, who used it mainly as a hunting ground and not a settlement. Most of the displaced Shawnee settled north of the Ohio River but still hunted in Kentucky, their anger rising when whites, led by Daniel Boone and others, came in and laid waste to the game, saving only the furs and leaving the meat to rot. Although Boone was reportedly more of a conservationist in his hunting, not wasteful or greedy like many other whites, the threatened Shawnee captured him and a group of hunters in 1769 (before the salt-making capture), confiscating their weapons and furs. When freeing Boone and his men, a Shawnee named Captain Will gave them two pairs of moccasins, doeskin for patch leather, and a small trading gun with powder to hunt for subsistence.

"Don't come here anymore," Captain Will said to Boone, "for this is the Indians' hunting ground, and all the animals, skins, and furs are ours. If you are so foolish as to venture here again, you may be sure that the wasps and yellow-jackets will sting you severely" (Elliott 58).

Boone returned, of course, and the Shawnee struggle to hold onto their hunting grounds was doomed. After the Shawnee War of 1774 (also known as Lord Dunmore's War), the tribe agreed to a treaty that established the Ohio River as their southern boundary. Despite wavering Shawnee alliances with both the French and English in the French and Indian War, and with the British in the Revolutionary War, the British left them "high and dry" (Howard 16) without land or a treaty after the shooting stopped and many of their warriors had died. General "Mad" Anthony Wayne defeated a confederacy of tribes, including the Shawnee, at the Battle of Fallen Timbers in 1795, which virtually ended organized native resistance east of the Mississippi. After uniting under the charismatic Tecumseh and his brother, the Prophet, the Shawnee sided with the British in the War of 1812, in which Tecumseh died. Fragments of the tribe ended up in Ontario, Missouri, Kansas, and farther west to Oklahoma and Texas after Andrew Jackson's Removal Act and the Trail of Tears, the journey west that many did not survive.

Like many eastern tribes desperate to hold onto their land for subsistence, the Shawnee were not only fierce warriors who took scalps but also, at times, unmerciful and brutal torturers. Although some whites, such as Boone, were adopted into tribes or set free from capture, for others death came as a relief after mutilation with knives, tomahawks, and red-hot gun barrels, and slow burning at the stake, their flesh pin-cushioned with pine splinters. So contemptuous were they of their victims that the Indians would cut off body parts—fingers and ears—and stuff them into the victims' own mouths. In many of the capture narratives that recount these incidents, whites—whether French, English, or American—presided over the spectacle, which sometimes lasted an entire day, as if supervising the natives as they did the dirty work of inflicting humiliation, terror, and brutality upon their enemies.

As in most violent conflicts, atrocities were not limited to one side. British, Americans, and French were often just as guilty of brutality and treachery, and to an extent, they exacerbated the Indian raids that continued into the late eighteenth century. Banta writes that some whites would fabricate rumors of war just to carry out vengeance on the most convenient enemy. One of these men was Daniel Greathouse, "whose savagery soon came to amaze the savages themselves" (126), writes Banta. Intent upon avenging the death of a white frontiersman, Greathouse and his men invited an Indian family to cross Yellow Creek and join them in camp, where they gave them liquor, then murdered them "in cold blood" (126). They seized one woman, who was pregnant, strung her up by the wrists and hacked open her belly with a tomahawk. From her womb they took the child and impaled it upon a stake. It did not concern Greathouse that the family was Mingo and that his comrade was killed by Cherokee. As Banta puts it, "They were Indians and they thus would serve the purpose" (126).

The family that Greathouse murdered, it turns out, was related to the half-breed Chief Logan, the pregnant woman his sister. This brutal act, which occurred soon after the massacre in which Boone's son James was tortured and killed, created repercussions that prolonged hostilities into conflicts such as Lord Dunmore's War. The violence and treachery of that troubled time seemed to haunt the falls, a hotly contested area, even though there's no knowledge of major battles fought there.

By the mid-nineteenth century, according to falls historian Jeannie McConnell, a Baptist preacher and his wife legally owned the falls. They lived there between 1850 and 1875, when they sold the land to Socrates Owens, who built a large inn near the falls. In 1902, Henry Brunson, from Indianapolis, bought the land and built the Cumberland Falls Hotel—forty rooms and two stories—which his family ran for thirty years. Even in the twentieth century, the falls was not an easy place to get to. In 1907 the first horse-drawn wagon took sixteen hours to arrive from Corbin, a town that is now about a thirty-minute drive away on paved highways. Guests could shower under the falls, do some ballroom dancing on the hotel's second floor, or buy moonshine by picking up a jar at a designated spot under the boardwalk, then leaving money for the anonymous manufacturer. The Brunson Inn would burn to the ground in the 1940s.

Others had more intrusive development plans for the falls. In 1924 the Cumberland River Power Company proposed a dam upstream of the falls as well as a power plant. This project did not come to pass. Vermont Senator Thomas Coleman Dupont, a native of Louisville who had visited the falls for many summers, proposed to purchase the falls and donate it to the state. In 1931, after his death, his heirs bought 593 acres for four hundred thousand dollars and did just that. This land became Kentucky's third state park. The same year, a road was built between Corbin and the falls, and tourists from all over the country began to visit. Also in the 1930s the Civilian Conservation Corps built trails, a water and sewage system, a bathhouse, fifteen cabins, and the Dupont Lodge, the landmark that Randy and I had sighted before our takeout above the falls. The CCC also constructed a walkway that allowed people to walk under the falls from one side to another. Floodwaters destroyed it. The original Dupont Lodge burned in 1940 (arson was suspected) and rebuilt the next year. The bridge above the falls, where Randy and I pulled out, was completed in 1954. Built of steel and concrete, it was faced with native sandstone to make it look like the "ole world bridges" that builder R. R. Dawson, of Bloomfield, Kentucky, saw on his visit to the Rhine River.

No matter how hard we try to make the natural world accessible to all without cheapening or damaging it, there are still reminders that a significant part of humanity does more harm than good. A few yards upriver from the falls next to the parking lot, a sign with big black letters proclaims at the top, "The Message is Clear." What follows is a description that confirmed for us that, even though the river may be cleaner than it was in the mid-twentieth century, we still have much work to do to return the river to the pristine state that the Shawnee worshiped:

> Unfortunately the wild Cumberland River has become a carrier of some of the waste that has been carelessly disposed of by Kentuckians who live upstream from Cumberland Falls. As our population increases so does improper dumping of garbage. During floods or periods of high water, some of this garbage finds its way into the river. . . . The natural currents and eddies formed around the boulders below the falls act as traps for

numerous plastic containers, driftwood and other debris that are washed over the falls. As the river level goes down, an unsightly social message is left for all to see. The message is clear—our water must be protected from the improper disposal of waste. . . . You can help us by encouraging people to dispose of waste properly.

A sad but truthful commentary. I particularly liked how the park service unflinchingly named Kentuckians as the culprits. The description is without sugar coating or euphemism. Although Randy and I had been careful to pick up after ourselves, we'd done nothing to encourage others to dispose of their waste, except to gawk at them with unbelieving eyes, and that was just one poor settlement. The rest of the stuff—cars, appliances, bottles, cans, boats—was probably dumped from roads and pastures under the cover of night, not in broad daylight where a couple of jokers in a canoe could scold and shake our fingers. If only the solution were as simple as encouraging or scolding the offenders.

In her essay "The Memory Place," Barbara Kingsolver describes the conflict between maintaining a clean environment and trying to live off that environment: "Poverty rarely brings out the most generous human impulses, especially when it comes to environmental matters. Ask a hungry West African about the evils of deforestation, or an unemployed Oregon logger about the endangered spotted owl, and you'll get just about the same answer: I can't afford to think about that right now" (202).

When I first talked to Vic Scoggin and we were comparing notes about the Cumberland and the Tennessee, I mentioned that the Tennessee no longer existed as a river but as a series of lakes developed with resorts and industrial complexes. The Cumberland, on the other hand, where it still runs free, has the pollution problems of a living river trying to flush itself clean of the refuse of humans who live on its banks. The trash has to end up somewhere, if not above a dam, as on the Tennessee, then at the scenic falls. From what we'd seen so far, it seemed that the economically disadvantaged lived on free-flowing rivers, where sudden rises could destroy their homes and wash their belongings downstream. On the dammed parts of rivers, wealthier landowners built homes high above the permanent floods created by the dams, and the pollution was perhaps not as visible.

Randy and I carried the canoe and gear up from the river to a picnic area next to the road and napped in the shade, waiting for Curt and Lara. That evening, after showering, we sat at a picnic table and ate steak, salad, and corn on the cob. In addition to Lara and Curt, Randy's friends Bryan and Tammy camped with us. We sat around the big fire and told them stories as if we were wild ancient mariners, and Randy replayed the video recording of the cow invasion. I met a neighboring camper, Virgil, who was taking his wife and kids down the run above the falls that Randy and I had fretted over the last two days. That night it stormed again, but we didn't care. We were high on a ridge, the river far below us. All around us were recreational vehicles, electricity, and running water. I could hear Boone scolding: "Elbow Room!" We would get it soon, more than we wanted.

CHAPTER 5

UPPER LAKE CUMBERLAND
HOIST THE VIKING SAIL!

HOIST THE VIKING SAIL!
UPPER LAKE CUMBERLAND

Sawyer to Wolf Creek Dam.

"They were men enough to face the darkness."

CONRAD,
Heart of Darkness

Gazing up at Kentucky game and fish ranger Stuart Bryant, who stood above us in his patrol boat, I asked him what was the strangest thing he'd ever seen on the job.

From the shade of his canopy he squinted down at us, two sober adults roasting under the sun in a boat without a motor, who had paddled up Buck Creek, four miles out of their way, for the privilege of buying four frozen lunch pizzas from Willie Zink, the proprietor of Buck Creek Marina. Ranger Bryant reckoned that the strangest thing he'd seen on the job was right in front of him in the green canoe.

As Randy snapped pictures of him in his green uniform, his cap off, a youthful man with a deadpan face, dark mustache, and smiling eyes, he started telling us the real stories.

"I saw one guy skiing . . . without a life jacket . . . naked . . . holding a beer in one hand. . . . He sailed right past a dock where a bunch of kids were," said Bryant with disgust. "I put him in cuffs and he laid down in the back of the boat in the fetal position and whimpered like a baby."

He cautioned us about Seventy-six Falls, up Indian Creek, where people lash their big boats together and get naked. "You don't want to go there," he said.

"No, we sure want to stay away from there," said Randy.

"I'm serious," he said, his voice rising. "There's lots of drugs up there. It's dangerous."

As Randy was trying to line up a photograph that would include the ranger and me, Bryant asked, "Do you want me to act like I'm arresting him?"

When we first saw him that day, motoring straight at us in his runabout, I thought he might arrest us, though I didn't know what for. He idled up beside us, and we caught onto the gunnels of his cop boat. We had just seen a sign at Willie Zink's that said, "Five people have drowned in this lake. Zero wore life jackets." The sign worked on us, so when Bryant motored up, we were trussed up and sweating in our vests, which usually lay somewhere in the bottom of the boat.

"What *are* y'all doing?" he had asked, as we bobbed in the wake of his motorboat. We told him.

"Are you *crazy?*" he said. "Why?"

We explained as best we could about our project.

"Please," he said, his voice plaintive, "please don't write about the trash in the river."

⬤

Lara, Curt, Tammy, and Bryan had waved good-bye to us the day before as we paddled away from the boat ramp at the confluence of the Laurel River and the Cumberland. It was early afternoon; we had frittered away the morning at the campsite, then loitered at the falls, where Randy and I devoured chili dogs, a final snack-bar fix, anticipating much hardship on Lake Cumberland, our first taste of flatwater, of which there would be many miles to come.

The first white canoeists in America, French voyageurs, were not so lucky to have chili dog stands; they didn't flinch at long portages and paddling upstream, two strenuous activities that Randy and I had thus far avoided. Though many Americans these days might think French machismo an impossible paradox, these voyageurs paddled their dugout and birch bark canoes up and down the rivers of central North America in the 1600s, *a hundred years before Boone and the long hunters.* These *hommes courageux* went native long before it became fashionable. They made their living off the land, trapping furs, killing game. Their version of the chili dog, I suppose, took the form of buffalo bladders they stuffed with fat and marrow. Another treat, as John Franklin Belue describes it, combined jerky and berries "pounded into mush and coated with suet": pemmican, a far distant ancestor of its modern namesake, identical flat strips of meat packaged in brightly colored resealable plastic bags that Randy's mother sent him via Lara. These voyageurs, tough as they were, often succumbed to the brutalities of their livelihood: ruptured hernias from long, strenuous portages of supplies and meat and canoes; or drowning, as they were "notoriously poor swimmers," says Belue (36–37). Long before Boone's adoption by the Shawnee, many of these Frenchmen were intermarrying into Algonquin tribes and becoming "white savages," rejecting both the strenuous life of the fur trade and European-style civilization for the freedom of the native peoples.

Back on the water, away from gravel-floored campsites and prepared food, Randy and I enjoyed the freedom of the river once more—but only briefly. By midafternoon the wind had risen, pushing in a cool front that would dip temperatures into the midforties come nighttime. Under the influence of Wolf Creek Dam, one hundred miles downstream, the river opened up into a quarter-mile-wide lake and the wind swept across our bow, two-foot waves cresting white and slapping against our plastic boat like an insult. We were shipping a bit of water. After less than an hour of this, we headed for Sawyer, the first campsite, only four miles from where we started out that day. This would be the shortest day of the trip (an average day, up to that point, twenty to twenty-five miles, our stopping time, six or seven o'clock). We felt guilty about it, especially after laying up so long at Cumberland Falls, but I knew that a canoe was no place to be on open water in winds that were gusting up to thirty-five miles per hour, as the weather radio told us.

After our softening at the falls, shouldering the load of our guilty consciences, we pulled the canoe's bow onto the muddy bank and slogged up the hill thirty yards to the nearest site. This was a U.S. Forest Service camp-ground, with a bathroom, picnic tables, and fire rings at the ten to twelve campsites. The bathrooms were locked, inoperable, we assumed. At the site next to us, the only one that hinted at occupation, a tethered tent fluttered for-lornly, the gusts from the lake folding it in half. A fisherman, we figured, he'd be back later that afternoon. We set up camp—no charge here—and I lay back in my tent to nap before supper. The wind whooshed through the trees above us, buffeting my pegged-down nylon tent. The day brightened and dark-ened, the light taking on a brownish color, the sun never quite revealing itself, the clouds never organizing enough to threaten rain. The fisherman's tent bumped against a tree trunk, settled, then rose again like a large, injured bird, its fabric swooshing against the leaves. A man in a muffler-challenged truck drove past twice, gunning the motor each time to create the maximum rumble. I dozed. Randy explored.

He appeared at my tent door. "There's something you have to see," he said.

"What is it?" I asked, irritable after the nap.

"Just come on," he insisted.

We walked through campsites that looked down at a creek. Above us tow-ered the tallest beech trees I have ever seen, smooth-barked grandmothers that seemed a hundred feet tall.

"What?" I asked Randy. "You just want me to see how much better these sites are? We'd just have to move all our stuff farther from the boat."

"Just come on," he said quietly.

We came up on the gravel road that circled the campground, and he motioned for me to wait, as if he were the point man for a platoon planning an ambush. The rumbling pickup truck was parked just around the bend of the road. Randy tiptoed up the hill a few paces and returned. "He's just sit-ting there," he whispered.

We crept up the hill toward the truck and stopped at a campsite that at first glance seemed trashed by a band of revelers. As I got closer to it and the truck up the hill, I contemplated turning back, the goose bumps rising on my arms signaling something further out of the ordinary than I wanted to know about. Randy had charged ahead, and he was standing in the middle of all this "stuff" shooting video. On the picnic table were penciled drawings of scenes from the Bible, scripture scrawled in large cursive, the paper torn and damp, as if it had been there for days. In the center of the drawings a framed portrait of Jesus was propped. It was covered with a pane of glass that reflected our faces when we looked closely enough. This Jesus, portrayed from the chest up, seemed to float in blue sky. He did not smile. Compared with other Jesus likenesses, this one's bearded jaw seemed more pronounced, the brow heavy and disapproving, an older world-weary Christ who seemed more human than divine.

A half-filled gallon jug of water sat on the table beside Jesus. Beyond, a bench and a hand-crafted wooden lectern for the pulpit. Crosses sprouted like wildflowers all around the site. One, made of wood, had been thrust into the rocky soil. In front of it, on flat rocks stacked two feet high, sat a small white ceramic cross, the focal point of the shrine, which included a saucer-sized offering plate with a smatter of change. Red, unlit candles flanked the crosses. Two lines of small stones formed a walkway up to the shrine. On an iron hook (standard for the campsites) near the picnic table hung a heavy purple shirt with what looked like generous blood smears all over it. I hoped it was a dye job gone wrong. I wondered how long since a congregation had been here and when they would return, though I imagined a lone worshiper, a zealot, preaching to the one empty pew. Why would he leave the drawings out in the rain? Did the guy in the truck have anything to do with the site? He wasn't moving.

Though the site was intended, I suppose, to lend spiritual solace, it had the opposite effect on me. I could not help thinking of *The Blair Witch Project* and the baby handprints on the abandoned cabin stairway where the videographers met their demise. And here was Randy shooting video. I did not utter the words "Blair Witch Project" aloud because that and "Deliverance" were forbidden on our trip. I walked back to our own site—maybe a quarter mile away. Randy was not far behind. We couldn't leave this strange place. The wind had us pinned, and it was late afternoon, too late to get far before dark. I didn't feel so uneasy at a respectful distance from the shrine, but gawking at it and shooting video elicited the same sort of uneasiness as staring at the trash-heap people in Harlan County. The shrine seemed private, unknowable, not intended for the eyes of outsiders.

My own spiritual quest had never been so focused, so dedicated, but in retrospect I understood in part what the shrine maker was up to. I'd grown up in the Baptist Church, baptized at twelve. I'd never felt all that close to God in a church, spending most of my time in the back row of the balcony fantasizing about girls and stifling laughter at my paper-wad throwing, note-passing seatmates. The preacher, a pale, distant old man with a mournful voice, whistled faintly into the microphone on his esses, as if he were passing into the spirit world before our eyes. He had a talent for portraying hell as a real place in close proximity, thus terrorizing me and my friends into baptism. By the age of seventeen, when my parents no longer required it, I stopped going. I've tried other churches sporadically but never depended on the sense of community in common worship that others value so much. Give me a mountain, a forest, or better yet a river, and leave me alone in the silence, and there I understand something about God. Like the shrine maker who worshiped near the river under the giant beech trees and the open sky, my spirit felt most at ease, most grateful in places where humans were scarce, where nobody was asking me questions or getting up in my face about sin and righteousness.

Late that afternoon two men showed up at the unpegged tent the next site over from us. One spoke in a guttural voice, with a heavily diphthongal accent seasoned with curses, though I couldn't understand much of anything else. The other voice was higher, plaintive, a younger man getting scolded or just listening to the older man's complaints. After about a half hour, they left the fluttering tent in the same condition as before.

From our campsite we commanded a decent view of the boat ramp, about a hundred yards away. Not much had been going on down there, with the cold front coming in. Then a pickup pulled up to the concrete ramp and skidded to a stop. A man and a woman got on each side of the truck bed and, using sticks, ushered something toward the tailgate. They poked and prodded until the thing fell into a five-gallon plastic bucket with a thud that suggested the weight and mass of a small boulder. They dumped the thing on the riprap slope below the side of the ramp, snapped a photo, jumped into the truck, and roared away. Even through our binoculars we could not determine what it was that had been treated so rudely. I thought maybe it was a snake, but who would go to the trouble of catching a snake, then turning it loose at a place that people frequented?

On the other hand, somebody might rescue a snapping turtle. His shell was as big around as a hubcap, and he lay awkwardly on the rocks, one fore-leg bent under him, facing downhill. When Randy moved around in front of him, he retracted his head, the size of a child's fist. The flesh under his shell was wrinkled, saggy, and tough looking, his eyes heavily lidded, the circles of flesh around them darker than the rest of his khaki-colored skin. The claws at the end of his thick legs were two inches long. When, at Randy's prompting, I prodded the back of his shell with my sandal, he made a quick threatening movement with his head. I prodded no more. I'd heard that once a snapping turtle latched onto you, it wouldn't let go until the next full moon. That's assuming, of course, that he didn't amputate whatever he bit.

The pickup truck couple must have rescued him from a roadside and dropped him off at the nearest water. He seemed stunned, unable to gain his bearings. We decided to let him be so he could sort things out. Later, from camp, we heard a sudden clattering sound over the rocks, like someone dropping heavy wooden blocks down the slope. We trotted down to the riprap to look for him, but he was gone. Having gathered his senses, the turtle could move in a hurry.

To top off an eventful day in camp, the river claimed its first prize from us: a fork/knife/spoon tool that my wife, Julie, had given me. While washing the dishes at the boat ramp, I dropped it into the water and watched it sink into the depths beside the riprap. For a while, I searched with my hands and feet in the cold water among the rocks, and then I started calculating when the next full moon would be and decided to concede the loss, a sacrifice to the river gods.

Our night at Sawyer passed without incident, and the cool front brought us a morning of brilliant sun and a tailwind, the sky deep and blue, with no rain forecast. At the boat ramp, we chatted with a commercial fisherman who was fishing for spoonbill catfish, which he sold to a market in Burnside, downstream. The fisherman seemed abnormally normal for Sawyer, friendly and open, but we instinctively avoided asking him about the religious shrine. The spoonbill itself is a kind of oddity, befitting this part of the river. More accurately known as the paddlefish, spoonbill cats are ancient river survivors, endangered in some states. They have a long snout that they use as a sensory organ that detects food and changes in the current. A relative of the sturgeon (not the catfish), paddlefish have no teeth, and except for the jaw, their skeleton is composed almost entirely of cartilage, causing early scientists to place them in the shark family. Paddlefish can live up to thirty years and may roam over two hundred miles upstream during a month if dams don't block their way. The easiest way to catch paddlefish is to try to snag them with big hooks at the tailwaters of dams, where they idle at the barrier, their mouths agape, fattening up on microscopic zooplankton.

After the fog burned off and the wind picked up, Randy, having heard about the makeshift sail I'd used on the Tennessee River trip, sat up straight and extended his arms, holding up the corners of his black plastic tarp to catch the tailwind. Though a modest breeze, we let it push us forward for a half hour or so, the tarp ballooning like a spinnaker, me ruddering to maximize the wind's power. The next day Randy would modify what we called the "Viking sail." Into the holes at the top two corners of his tarp, he inserted two sticks of driftwood, each about two feet long, lengthening the human mast and increasing the area of the sail. Now he didn't have to hold his arms out straight, crucifixion style, to create a bit of locomotion. I began calling him maestro because he looked like a conductor with the sticks. He played it to the hilt, sniffing the air each time he felt a hint of breeze, raising the tarp with one quick motion to catch the biggest gusts, then lowering it with disdain as the windpower faded, the plastic sail crackling at his feet, where he kept it ready.

We passed the mouth of the Rockcastle River, the Cumberland's second major tributary after the Laurel, and turned up Buck Creek. Walled with sheer tan rock, the creek was a fjordlike passage that twisted and turned a couple of miles before revealing Willie Zink's marina, tucked back into a corner, a high cliff rising behind it next to a concrete boat ramp. Zink had commissioned a man to paint a fresco on the rock wall, an illustration of the marina with boats, blue water, fishermen, crows, and deer. Fifty feet above the boat ramp, this artistic advertisement was hidden behind bushes that had sprung from the rock's crevices. Willie, a German immigrant, repeated what he'd told me about the painter when I had visited a year earlier: "Much talent in the hands, no brains in the head."

Willie had photographs under the glass of his countertop, one of him on a bicycle with two other men, and another of what he said was the world record spoonbill catfish (paddlefish)—290 pounds—caught on Buck Creek. With a grin, I pointed at a photo of a baby raccoon.

"That one," Willie said in his stern accent, "had its head chopped off by a boat propeller."

A spare, strong-looking man not much over five feet tall, Willie had skin that was taut and tanned, like seasoned leather. He remembered Vic Scoggin's swim down the river, and as he had on my last visit, diminished Vic's achievement.

He had a suit that helped him float, said Willie, and fins and a mask and people following along in a boat. "That's not really swimming," he declared.

Vic, who swam ten miles a day for over two months, floating suit or not, later smiled at the summation and noted that Willie had done some long-distance swimming in Europe. It seemed to me a bit mean-spirited to characterize Vic's achievement in that way, but I didn't think it wise to argue with old, leather-skinned Willie, who had food we wanted to purchase.

After heating up the lunch pizzas in Willie's microwave, we took them outside and ate next to his gas pumps under the crisp blue sky. There we saw our first jet skier. Muscled, with a low forehead and a bleach-blond crew cut, he dismounted his steed and said, "Cold out there," in a low, jaw-clenched voice. After gassing up, he puttered slowly through Willie's no-wake zone, then accelerated abruptly so that the crotch rocket leaped forward and carved two big wakes out of the placid water behind him, shattering the creek's peace and quiet. Dams created this recreation. Burning gas, making noise, and going fast would be the norm on reservoirs, and miles of this stretched before us.

Still, Lake Cumberland, at this point, differed from any of the dammed reservoirs I'd canoed on the Tennessee River. Its water was cold and clear in June, and it was lined with rock walls that made it difficult for trash to wash up onto its shoreline. Where there were low places or coves, especially on the outside of bends, driftwood and trash gathered. Sycamores and maples no longer dominated, as they had upriver. Now there were cedars, oaks, and hickories. We jumped our first wakes that day—fishing boat–sized little disturbances that barely troubled the smooth water. And it was a good thing the wakes were small, the traffic minimal, because in this narrow, riverlike section of the lake, a boat's wake bounces off the Cumberland's rock walls and reverberates, requiring unfortunate canoeists to turn their bow and jump it twice. This was not true flat water, not yet what I would call a lake: we still enjoyed the mystery of rounding bends, and though it was barely noticeable, we were benefiting from the current.

We paddled around twenty-five miles and camped at an abandoned city park called Omega Point, where a man and his two sons also camped. That night, we were raided by a large mammal, who sorted frantically through our garbage bag behind the tent, no doubt disappointed at the scanty leftovers. A cocker spaniel mix belonging to our fellow campers, this was our first uninvited nighttime visitor, but far from our last.

A couple of nights downriver, I was asleep in my tent at Conley Bottoms Marina, surrounded by RVs, when I heard a canoe paddle clatter against a tree trunk. Randy turned loose a string of curses, uncharacteristic of him. In a voice clouded with sleep and irritation, he explained to me that he was fending off "two raccoons and a skunk" with his canoe paddle. This odd trio of critters was pawing at one of Randy's dry bags, or so he said. One of them managed a swiping blow that broke through the thick rubber material. Randy is abnormally fond of animals, so much so that he refuses to kill bugs crawling across his skin. I have watched him, in the front of the boat, shuffle a spider back and forth with his feet until he could get close enough to the bank to turn him loose on a leaf so he wouldn't drown. He was elated to discover that granddaddy long legs could walk on water. Imagine what the unholy trio had done to get Randy so angry that he baited them with a Tabasco-soaked cracker. The animals won the battle, and Randy put his food bags inside his tent.

Early the next morning, while Randy recovered from his nighttime battle, I witnessed a gangland war over the boat ramp. The domestic geese squared off against the Canada geese in a savage and frightening skirmish. Each group had pickets that rushed forward with their heads lowered, their necks close to the revered concrete of the boat ramp, hissing as they charged with giant goose steps. It was difficult not to see this as a kind of allegory—our fear of differences, our quick tempers—enacted for my early-morning edification. The white geese appeared to win the battle.

The morning after the cocker spaniel invasion at Omega Park, we launched the canoe into a bright early morning fog that the rising sunlight dispersed.

Wisps of vapor swirled around our paddles like tiny tornadoes, creating whirl-pool wakes on water so calm it seemed frozen. Mornings like this helped me remember why we traveled in a canoe, why we didn't attach a trolling motor to it, as many would suggest to us. Only within the silence and stealth of a canoe could we travel slowly enough to observe the habits of swirling, dying fog. Only in a canoe could we have gotten as close to the many deer we saw on the banks between Harlan and the falls, some of them staring at us as we passed, unafraid, others turning and strolling away unhurried after they had satisfied their curiosity. That morning, so calm, so quiet in the muffled atmos-phere, I felt the weight of the water as I pulled the paddle forward, careful not to splash. A motor separates the boater from such physical engagement with vapor, water, and wind. Only Vic, immersed, had been on more intimate terms with the Cumberland.

We flew the Viking sail to great advantage in a following wind of ten to fifteen miles an hour. Our bow carved the water silently, and we left a gentle but respectable wake as Randy strained with his maestro sticks to harness the breezes. The day would end on a dispiriting note near a town called Burn-side, whose ghostly predecessor, also known as Point Isabel, lay far beneath the water's surface. We had arrived in the land of reservoirs and progress. Burnside now stood on a bluff commanding the construction of a four-lane bridge that we passed under, the modern version with a solid concrete wall that kept drivers safe from the distraction of the scenery below, obliterating the river from their consciousness.

CHAPTER 6

A BURIED WORLD
A BURIED WORLD

Bowling balls float. We learned this downstream of Burnside, where we skirted the riprap shoreline looking for a place to land the canoe at Waitsboro Campground. Among a flotilla of driftwood and trash bobbed a maroon bowling ball. As we rocked in waves blown across the lake, a half-mile wide here, I poked at it with my paddle. It ducked underwater and cheerfully resurfaced. As with cars and other heavy appliances, we wondered what route a perfectly good ball had taken to arrive in this sorry predicament, miles from a road, much less a bowling alley.

Randy speculated that a bowler, in despair over a loss or absence of talent, happened to be indulging his melancholy lakeside and disposed of the ball in the water, thinking it would sink to the bottom so he could forget about the sport he could not master. I imagined an irate wife, sick of her husband's late nights at the alley, marching down here one Sunday morning while he slept off his bowling hangover, and hurling it two-handed into the water, exhaling a litany of curses on the follow through. She spanked her hands together as it splashed, turning her back and imagining its descent to the murky bottom, among the ruins of old Burnside. However it got there, the bowling ball aroused a sense of poignancy that motivated a rescue attempt. Tragically, it was wedged within a thicket of driftwood so dense that I could not maneuver either one of us into position to harvest the ball.

On the Cumberland we would see lost balls representing just about every sport. In eastern Kentucky, the river dribbled abandoned basketballs, some fully inflated. Once we descended into Tennessee, footballs lay fumbled along the banks. We would also scoop a couple of baseballs and see several tennis balls volleyed into the flatwater of West Tennessee. Near Nashville, a soccer ball or two.

At Waitsboro, it seemed that all of the trash we'd missed the past few days had gathered in this outside bend, and that the character of the refuse had changed from everyday household items to the discards of leisure: bottles and cans for outdoor drinking bobbing among the solid line of driftwood festooned with fishing line. The plastic lawn chairs we'd seen so often upriver had changed from white to green or red, reflecting some alteration of taste and socioeconomic class in those whose furniture had been swept away.

We had entered the Kentucky region known as the Pennyroyal, named after a type of mint plant. In the shadow of the Cumberland Plateau to the east, the Pennyroyal or Pennyrile, as it is known, encompasses much of south central Kentucky, with Bowling Green at its center. The Cumberland skirts the southern edge of this region, a hilly landscape where limestone cliffs rise above the river.

On the bluff above the river was Burnside, which had, before the Civil War, been known as Point Isabel, named after a brokenhearted girl who jumped into the river and drowned, according to the legend passed on by writer Harriet Arnow, who grew up there. In 1890, the name was changed to Burnside in honor of the Union Army General Ambrose Burnside, who set up headquarters in the town in 1864. Though unaware of it at the time, General Burnside was a tonsorial trendsetter. His name became associated with the bushy black whiskers he wore from ear to ear (no chin whiskers). Somehow, by the time Elvis and Joe Cocker caught on, the word got scrambled and came out "sideburns." Fortunately for the general, that is the legacy for which most remember him, not for his failures on the battlefield. After twice turning down command of the Army of the Potomac, he finally accepted Lincoln's request and led the Union to a bloody defeat at Fredericksburg. He was relieved of that command and sent to lead the Ohio Department, where he successfully defended Knoxville. Near the end of the war, after he left Point Isabel, he is remembered for another failure under General Grant, when he did not effectively exploit the enemy's disadvantage at the Battle of the Crater in Petersburg, Virginia. In short, he hesitated and missed an opportunity for victory. After Petersburg, Burnside resigned from the army; perhaps, born a hundred years later, he might have been a rock star.

The Big South Fork of the Cumberland, flowing due north up from Tennessee, meets the main river near the place where old Point Isabel rests underwater. Before Wolf Creek Dam was built, the town Point Isabel/Burnside was the Cumberland's head of navigation (River Mile 516), the farthest that commercial traffic could safely navigate. In the early 1800s wooden flatboats and keelboats shipped goods such as corn, tobacco, whiskey, saltpeter (used to make gunpowder), goose feathers, and cedar fence posts 325 miles downriver to Nashville. Most of the flatboatmen sold their goods and their boat, then walked back home, though with the development of the keelboat, crews of men with long poles went upriver as well as down.

Like the French voyageurs in the eighteenth century, the nineteenth-century keelboatmen engaged in commerce that was hard, dangerous work. Mike Fink, the most famous of them, figured in mythic tales involving unlikely physical feats against opponents such as alligators and panthers. As with most myths, there is some truth contained within. Keelboating was an occupation fraught with hazards—drowning, scalping, shooting, tomahawking, or succumbing to venereal disease were just a few of the most common causes of death. Crews who used poles to push off the river bottom and propel a boat full of goods against the river's current had to be tough, and hard work has always engendered a need for hard play. Keelboatmen who stopped onshore for recreation—usually consisting of prodigious amounts of liquor and no-holds-barred brawling—were known to push an entire building into the river if they took offense at some tavern owner or land-based merchant. In his book on the Ohio River, R. E. Banta, in an attempt to balance reality with myth, creates a vivid portrait of these river dwellers:

> [The keelboatman] usually carried upon his person one or more marks of his avocation; most frequently it was a damaged ear, sometimes bitten off, sometimes cauliflowered . . . , or most often simply chawed in a scalloped design around its rim. Or he could have lost the fleshy portion of his nose. . . . If, in addition to any or all of these misfortunes, he happened to be a veteran of an Indian foray in which he had got himself scalped . . . , he was likely to present a rather frazzled appearance; one which could not be rendered attractive even by his red-flannel shirt, remaining hair worn in a shoulder-length bob, wool hat set off with a feather, and skin pants—both skin in material and skin tight in cut. . . . (255)

With the development of the steamboat came the demise of the keelboat. The first steamboat made it to Point Isabel in 1833, intrepid pilots negotiating shoals in an awkward craft with highly combustible engines, powered by a fragile wooden wheel that could be easily damaged by snags and rocks, and a hull vulnerable to puncture. While Point Isabel was considered the head of navigation, no one actually lived there until after 1849. After that, steamboats began to bring luxury items such as rice, coffee, tea, and sugar, then furniture and farm equipment. When General Burnside arrived in 1863, he built roads in order to fortify the area and requested that a railroad be extended from Nicholasville to Point Isabel, a project that was not carried out until after the war. Point Isabel became a processing and shipping center for lumber by river or rail, though the railroad eventually cut into the steamboat business.

Another commercial enterprise that endured a bit longer than steamboating was the transport of timber to Nashville using log rafts. Around the perimeter of a load of logs, the raftsmen would construct a boom, with spikes and cable, to keep the logs in place. Another method, described in Jack Knox's *Riverman*, involved spiking strips of hickory bark into the logs across the width of the raft. Some rafts could be up to 400 feet long and 75 feet across, though after the Corps of Engineers began to build locks for navigation at the turn of the twentieth century, the rafts could only be 250 feet by 75 feet. (These locks had all been blown up by the time the high dams were built.) Except when there was a full moon and a good stage of water (not too high or too low), raftsmen would moor themselves to shoreline trees for the night.

The trip from Celina to Nashville (about two hundred river miles) would take a raft of logs about a week. These loads usually had some sort of shelter built on them, where the raftsmen could build a fire for cooking or warmth. Five or six men steered a raft with long oars and used pike poles and cant hooks to load the logs and chase down the ones that got loose. A cold, wet, dangerous job, rafting required an intimate knowledge of the river without the help of gasoline-powered engines or other navigational technology, such as radar or depth finders. Whiskey was commonly used as a blood warmer, stimulant, and stress reliever. Nowadays, men in air-conditioned pilot houses with big glass windows push buttons and operate levers to guide barges filled with petroleum, coal, gravel, sand, timber, crops, and chemicals both up and down the Cumberland and Tennessee. They drink gallons of coffee and no whiskey. Modern towboats are equipped with kitchens and a full-time cook who lays out gargantuan meals. More often than not, they navigate dammed reservoirs rather than free-flowing rivers. Not that modern commercial transport is any easier, just different: larger loads, often toxic or flammable, extend the consequences of mishaps beyond captain and crew to the greater population that now lives near rivers. With all the gadgetry and improved tools, the tasks of the modern commercial navigator are more mentally complex and less physical than the keelboatman's or the rafter's, and overall, I would say, accompanied by more stress and urgent demands for speed and efficiency, a development one could trace over the centuries in just about every other occupation—from journalist to farmer to banker.

Our campsite view at Waitsboro commanded an expanse of water that only the most stubborn of historical purists would insist on calling a river.

The Cumberland had been "lakequified," and as if to confirm the transformation, across the way was General Burnside Island, a state park with a swimming pool, golf course, and a campground high on a bluff accessible only to those arriving by road. The little brochure for the park was typical, yet somewhat more irritating than the others I would collect. Perhaps it was the jet skiers on the cover, a couple about my age, their faces distorted with manic expressions of joy, hair perfectly in place, sporting spotless canary-yellow life jackets and purple and black wet suits. The woman, standing behind the man, has her arm flung in the air like a bull rider in a rodeo, the man smugly handsome, laughing as he twists the throttle.

What had I done wrong to be paddling a canoe across a lake, my life jacket (dull purple and fading black) lying on the muddy floor of my boat? Why was I not experiencing such ecstasy? Nothing against jet skis or those who ride them. They don't leave much of a wake, and the crotch rockets are, I grudgingly admit, loads of fun. What's irritating to a canoeist is the crotch rocketeer's ability to invade the shallows once the domain of paddlers, their clouding of sacred waters, the stench of their exhaust, the muddying of sweet silent coves with the amplified mosquito buzz of their motors. So yeah, I guess it was the jet skiers that irritated me about the park brochure, that and the sanitized entertainment offerings, designed to make everyone forget that this used to be a river. Here's a sample of the brochure's language: "As the only island park in the Kentucky State Parks' system, General Burnside is truly a unique treasure!"

The dam downstream had robbed the river of its current and its "truly unique!" personality. It had the same cloudy gray demeanor as the lakes on the Tennessee, inscrutable and featureless as you gazed across it looking for some sign of life, a bubble, a swirl, a branch bobbing up and down in the current, a frog or an otter plopping from the bank into the water, all those little events that make a river alive, that make a person riding the river feel alive, all of those things that had been swallowed up by the expanse of water that had obliterated Point Isabel as certainly as if the Union had burned it to the ground. It did not seem like the same river that plunged down the falls, that roared over shoals, whose shorelines grew trees that stretched over our heads and shaded us. It did not even seem like the same river of the past two days.

Paddlers, historians, romantics, and tree huggers like me complain the loudest about what dams do to rivers. In her book *Flowering of the Cumberland*, Harriet Arnow mourns what was lost with the building of Wolf Creek Dam, completed in 1950:

> The back of the Cumberland was not broken until Wolf Creek Dam
> was finished. Never again can a boat go from the upper river to Nashville.

The upper river like most of the lower has, with its lakes and its hydroelectric plants, become a tourist attraction; yearly several million people come to boat and swim and fish on some reach of the cold and silent Cumberland, still now, for most of its length until one is near Cumberland Falls, another tourist attraction.

No one of those enjoying the dead river can ever know what it was when the creeks were dry half the year and flooded the other half, and farmers, with wheat stacked by the riverbank and hungry chickens cooped, listened for steamboats slow in the coming because of low water. The life of the Cumberland, its importance to the people not only on the main river but high up the tributaries, can never be measured by the amount of work it did.

It works still; tonnage on the lower river is high and yearly Wolf Creek Dam, not to mention others lower down, makes a vast amount of electricity. Yet, the old Cumberland was so many things other than work horse. It was for most of us a beloved but completely unpredictable neighbor of whom we never tired of talking and whose house we never tired of watching and of visiting. (388)

Under the heading "Why a Lake?" the Corps of Engineers' brochure for the reservoir has its own explanation for the dam, quite a contrast to cranks like me, or residents with long, poetic memories like Arnow. Note the frequent use of passive voice (italics mine):

Widespread benefits for the entire Cumberland River Valley *are being realized* [by whom?] from the comprehensive development of the water resources of the river. . . . Industrial, commercial, and agricultural development of the region *is being stimulated* by control of these resources. Energy *is produced* . . . at a moderate cost. . . . Economic development *is encouraged*. Other benefits include water quality control for domestic and industrial supplies, conservation, and recreation. [Couldn't all these things exist without a dam?] Dams impound floodwaters, thereby reducing the frequency and severity of floods. These manmade lakes provide opportunities for recreation development, with facilities for camping, picnicking, boating, swimming, fishing, and other outdoor activities. [Why must we have a dam behind which to picnic, camp, boat, swim, and fish?]

I'll give Arnow the last word. In her book *Old Burnside* she describes the pre-dam confluence of the Big South Fork and the Cumberland, a place that produced nothing more important than the poetry of nature:

During summers, when the rivers flowed gently, there were small sandy beaches on the southern side of the Cumberland; above these, willows grew on the steep banks that led up to the floodplains. Cane grew thick and tall on the floodplains while giant beech, oak, hickory, sweet gum, and other trees grew on the slopes of the hills above. The silence was broken only by bird song and the wind in the trees. (5)

As we were beginning to realize, free-flowing rivers didn't seem to fit neatly into economic growth strategies. Indeed, there was only one major river system in the continental United States that flowed unimpeded by dams, levees, and channelization. That was the Pascagoula, in Mississippi, and the kayaker/canoeist team of Scott Williams and Ernest Herndon paddled its length in the spring of 2004 before somebody remembered to dam it up and grow the economy. According to Williams, "the Pascagoula . . . absorbs 11 fine tributaries for a total of nearly 800 miles of magnificent, slow-water, deep-woods canoeing." A hundred years ago, the Cumberland would have been nearly identical in length and character. Of course, nothing is that simple. In the last century, we built an entire culture and economy around dams, and we rely on them to prevent damage to the economic assets that have been constructed on the reservoirs they back up and the towns and cities downriver of them.

CHAPTER 7

OUR INSANITY

OUR INSANITY

"Do I contradict myself?" asked Walt Whitman. "Very well. I contradict myself."

Just so, despite my sadness over the loss of the river and the creation of the tourist-oriented lake, I took solace in the order and neatness of Waitsboro, our first Corps of Engineers campsite. Boxed riprap in square wire baskets defined the borders of each raised campsite. Ditches reinforced with long ridges of embedded concrete drained runoff, of which there would be plenty the next day, and the bathhouse featured immaculate concrete showers, miraculously free of slime and mildew. Our campsite had a layer of evenly spread, finely ground limestone; a fire ring; plenty of driftwood washed up on the riprap wall, where our canoe was tied to a dead tree at the bow, a big rock at stern; solid shade; a concrete picnic table; electric outlets and water spigots; a wooden railing around the site's perimeter; and crossties to reinforce the slope from the site to the road above.

At the site next to us a shiny recreational vehicle sheltered retirement-aged folks who stayed up late smoking cigarettes and feeding their bonfire with imported logs. Earlier that afternoon, they had set up a microwave oven on their picnic table. A few yards from the bathhouse was a van with a serious dent in the side, inside an organ set off kilter among a pile of miscellany visible through the rear window. I'd seen the kid—wearing brown knit pants too short, scuffed leather street shoes, a polyester shirt, and bushy reddish side-burns—when I'd walked up to the pay booth to reserve our site. The van had Wisconsin plates. On his trip to the bathhouse, Randy said he saw a girl at the boy's site. An extension cord ran from their tent to an outlet in the bath-house. I imagined a budding boy/girl duo, she on keyboards, he on guitar, playing quirky duets for hostile audiences. Their journey, in my imagination, held as much adventure as ours.

Just down the slope, Elmer the lonely fisherman unloaded his gear from the back of a pickup parked next to a 1970s-era tent, its damp fabric sagging against the thick aluminum frame. He resembled a disheveled Norman Mailer, with the white hair, round face, and wrinkled forehead, plus the slumped shoulders and paunch of a retired light heavyweight.

"I'm worn out from fishing," he said. "Losing weight . . . whewww!" he added, patting his ample stomach.

For someone who was worn out, Elmer had a lot of breath left for talk-ing. Speaking with the urgency of a man who harbored important secrets, he launched into a description of his elaborate method for catching walleye. Before dawn, Elmer would rig his boat with a blue light and a red light. The blue light attracted shad, which the walleye fed on, then the red light blinded the walleye when they showed up for dinner.

"Don't tell anybody," he whispered, "but this is the best fishing spot for miles."

Elmer needn't worry. Kentuckians prefer to sport fish for the more famil-iar bass and crappie. A member of the perch family, cousin to the sauger, walleye are much more popular and plentiful in the northern lakes than in the South. Long and trim, with yellowish sides and a white belly, the walleye has tiny teeth and is named for its large clouded eyes, covered by a reflective film that helps it see at night.

As a walleye fisherman in Kentucky, Elmer possessed somewhat special-ized angling knowledge, and he had traveled a long way to put that knowledge to use. From Hazard, Kentucky, in the eastern coalfield north of Harlan, he had driven more than three hours to Waitsboro.

Like Mailer, the writer, Elmer had many stories, each commencing with high drama but ending in anticlimax or without a point or resolution. He had met a man afflicted with throat cancer camped at the site above him, waiting for his family to return from an outing on the lake. Elmer, already back from his predawn excursion, began to deep-fry his walleye in grease that was not yet hot, a rare departure from standard procedure. As the grease heated, the fish broke up. Elmer carried some of the pieces to the sick man.

"How did you know this is how I liked my fish?" said the man. "That's the only way I can eat it."

Elmer saw this as evidence for the existence of angels.

The next day, as Randy and I prepared to leave, Elmer grabbed me by the arm. "Just wait a minute," he said. "You've got to hear this one."

"This one" turned into two or three. The first story reached its height of tension when Elmer dropped his sunglasses into the lake, followed by a side-bar about how a friend's wife bought him glasses straps (like I was wearing) and that the old fool wore them under his chin, cowboy style, until Elmer corrected him. The last was a fishing tale that Randy and I could not comprehend. Elmer prefaced the story by calling it a "miracle" because of the way a fish had hooked itself on his unattended rig. He had left it there on the hook for most of a day while he fished from the boat, making us think it was some kind of monster he was afraid of or unable to pull to the surface. Then came the anticlimax. When he pulled it in that evening, apparently without a struggle, it was a "decent" seven-pound walleye.

Elmer was a species who thrived at dammed reservoirs: the lonely retired man obsessed with fishing. Only on reservoirs, where a man could sit in a boat all day without navigating, where certain species such as bass and walleye prospered, did we find men like Elmer, their solitude filled with meditations and memories they poured out to anyone available to listen. When my father told stories, which was rare, they often featured characters like Elmer, who had the leisure to experience the sorts of things that made for good tales. Most of my father's experiences came from work, at a chemical plant in Calvert City, Kentucky. He never talked about his job, but it came home with him as a metallic scent on his clothes. It wasn't long after his retirement that he got cancer as a reward for those long, irregular hours at the plant near the lower Tennessee River. A child of the Depression, fearful of hard times, he worked more than I wish he had, even at leisure activities such as gardening. These long canoe trips that dominated my middle age seemed to him the ultimate in absurdity, like one of Elmer's long, pointless tales. If only he'd had a longer healthy period after his life of labor, I might have convinced him to escort us in his old riveted metal utility boat with the twenty-five-horse Johnson to consider the merits of long, cheap trips without material compensation.

Waitsboro held us for longer than we wanted to stay. And I was in a hurry to leave the next day because I found flat water less demoralizing in the early morning when winds were calm, and the jet skiers and pleasure boaters slept. By the time we had everything packed away, the canoe half loaded, the rain and wind began. Moored twenty feet below the campsite, tied to the rock and the tree, the canoe rocked side to side, waves splashing over the gunnels, the plastic bottom rasping against the riprap, scraping off the green polyprophe-lene that stood between us and the depths.

Randy and I stood in the rain, our identical wide-brimmed hats growing soggy, and stared down at the boat. "I think we need to unload it and drag it up here," he finally said.

What followed was forty-five minutes of stumbling up and down wet riprap with all our gear, then dragging the poor canoe up the slope to our campsite, an exhausting chore. Since we'd broken down our tents, we retreated to the canopy around the bathhouse and waited two hours for the rain to slacken. Listening to an oldies station on the yellow transistor radio, we watched the rock band tent for signs of life. There were none. I wondered if our oldies music tortured them, if they despaired looking outside at what sort would listen to such drivel at this ungodly hour and why anyone would hang out so long at the bathhouse.

By one o'clock, in full raingear, we were paddling through a drizzle and a ten-mile-an-hour headwind. "Randy," I said, breaking the grim silence, "you are crazy for doing this with me."

He paused in his paddling and glanced back with good-natured incredulity.

I explained that paddling even short distances on dammed lakes in good weather suggested mental instability, but canoeing the length of a one-hundred-mile-long lake under a weeping sky of roiling clouds was clearly insane. Paddling the first of a series of flat water stretches that awaited us, we already missed the upper river: the constant variables of current, the rocks and stumps to dodge, the bends that hid what was coming, the need to communicate and work as a team to stay afloat. Now we drifted off into private meditations and aimed from distant point to point, across wide waters. The points, some hours away, seemed like mirages in the soggy atmosphere, not unlike the points to Elmer's stories. Normal people did not do this sort of thing. It was like hiking across a giant parking lot; you had to be seriously obsessed to complete such a voyage. I already knew that Randy, like me, was far from normal, though I wasn't sure until this point, as he paddled through the drizzle without complaint, that he was irrevocably insane.

Upriver, he'd given me hints. During the Blizzard of 1993 (known at the time as the Storm of the Century), where was Randy? Not at home watching the Weather Channel like most of us. He was camping in the Smokies. Alone. Unlike other campers in the area, Randy hadn't been caught unawares by the spring snowstorm; when he'd heard it was coming, he tried to persuade friends to go camping with him. They all declined and politely asked why he would want to be on a mountain, in a tent, during a freakish March blizzard. Randy told them he wanted to take pictures. This he did, not for one day, but for several, as he and other more sheepish pilgrims "camped" at a ranger station. They were drafted to shovel snow to clear a landing area for a helicopter, and stood gazing in sweaty dismay as the chopper flew over their clearing and set down in an uncleared parking area a few yards away.

After two hours of drizzle on the Cumberland, the clouds broke up and the wind swept the rain behind us, as if retracting a lid across the gray sky to reveal a deep blue backdrop and a sun so bright it made us squint through our colored glasses. The fair weather lasted a couple of hours, until we got to Mill Springs, looking for a Civil War battlefield where we thought we might camp among ghosts.

We stopped at a long gravel point at the mouth of White Oak Creek and debated whether or not to camp. Randy didn't like it because it had been used before, a well-worn path leading down to it and a fire ring that mesmerized a swarm of flies. I walked up the path a half-mile to see how close we were to a house or road or battlefield, and stopped at a fence surrounding a sloping green pasture. Satisfied, ready to make a case for staying, I trotted down the path back to the boat in time to see a black bank of clouds approaching from around a bend in the lake/river. It seemed the clouds were blowing perpendicular to the direction we were heading, that the storm might bypass us if we moved farther downriver and took a westward turn, so we proceeded onward toward the darkness away from the flyblown fire ring. Five minutes later a dark curtain of rain began to blow fat drops in our faces. We paddled to the bank, unable to land, and sat in the boat holding onto the rocky shoreline, the rain drenching us for the second time that day. Behind us, upriver, in the path of the storm, the sun burst open the clouds and a rainbow blasted through, its shaft ending on the deck of a boat that cruised toward us.

The rain stopped after ten minutes, and we rounded the bend to discover a marina complex that I had somehow missed on the maps: Conley Bottoms. Becoming spoiled by settled campsites, we paid for a plot at the boathouse—which had a grocery and restaurant—and paddled another half mile around all the slips to the boat ramp near our site. Here we saw our first big cabin cruisers on the Cumberland. Fortunately for us, they were docked, their grills smoking, rock and roll music thrumming from their stereos. We settled in at Conley Bottoms among the RVs, skunks, raccoons, beavers, geese, crows, and buzzards. That night, Randy would turn against the animals he loved so much.

While we were eating breakfast in the marina restaurant the next morning, a tall, thin man walked up to our booth and asked if the air conditioning was too high. We assured him that it was not. After the thin man left, the guy in the next booth told us that was Charley Denney, the owner of this marina and others.

"He's worth millions," said the guy, "but you couldn't tell it."

When Charley came back, we told him what we were doing, and he pointed at the wall above us at a paddle signed by Vic Scoggin, who had swam in for a breakfast break on his voyage down the river. Charley wanted to know all about our trip. Unlike many, who would tell us they admired or envied us, and others who would suggest we were crazy or merely shake their heads, Charley seemed truly happy that we had undertaken such a voyage. Now beyond the two-hundred-mile mark, we were able to afford ourselves a measure of pride in what we'd accomplished. Charley regretted that we'd paid for our campsite and insisted we take a free T-shirt from the marina shop. He gave us a waterproof map of Lake Cumberland.

While we digested our breakfast and surveyed the gusty weather, Charley told us outdoor stories. He'd gone on a day hike along the Big South Fork of the Cumberland, whose mouth we'd passed the day before, near Burnside. The voice of reason among a macho group of middle-aged guys, Charley kept telling the group, in his quiet way, that they were getting too far away from the river and that they were running low on water. After dragging ass back into their campsite hours after they were expected, all were bedraggled and dehydrated, but in particular a close friend of Charley's.

"Here," Charley had said gently, offering a bottle of water, "just sip some of this."

"No, goddammit," said the friend. "I want a Gatorade."

Charley tried once again to persuade him to sip water temperately, but gave up when the fellow got "downright mean." He was given a jug of Gatorade—the red kind—and he gulped a couple of quarts of it. Not long after, he began to vomit, and a photographer, not part of Charley's group, wandered upon the scene.

"That man needs help," he said, looking at the Gatorade drinker spewing the red liquid.

"No, he's all right," said mild-mannered Charley.

"Well, look at the amount of blood he's losing," said the photographer, and Charley patiently explained what had happened.

All of Charley's stories had a common theme: people either underestimating the outdoors or overestimating their ability to "conquer" it. Charley said he admired what we were doing because we were learning about the entire river; so many people who came through here, he said, only knew the river a few miles upstream or down, and thought they knew it all, confirming my theory that dams not only blocked current but also knowledge of river systems.

I told Charley about Randy's battle with the four-legged axis of evil the night before, which he appeared to believe, though I remained skeptical.

Charley said that another marina owner had once said he wanted to import some of Charley's Canada geese to his place.

"No, you don't," Charley had said. He explained that the geese were aggressive and messy, tending to congregate in packs that battled with the domestic geese, a scene that I had witnessed that morning at the boat ramp. Charley also told us that beaver were wreaking widespread destruction on the trees in the area. Game and Fish officials had encouraged him to trap the beasts for relocation. "A lot of people think of a beaver as a cute little character," said Charley, "but some of ours are as big as small bears."

When we'd first pulled up to Conley Bottoms, I'd had a hostile attitude, with all the big boats and the money they represented. We hadn't been treated rudely at that point, but I remembered being turned away from campsites/marinas similar to this one in Alabama, on my Tennessee River trip. It only takes one civil person to obliterate negative preconceptions. You'd think such a wealthy guy like Charley would want to tool around in a yacht and brag about his wealth, but here he was spending his entire morning with a couple of smelly canoeists, telling us stories of hikes and canoe trips and giving us information about campsites downriver. With regret, we left Conley Bottoms around noon.

When we asked Charley about portaging a narrow strip of land around which the river curved, he informed us first of all that it was a high ridge and second that it was "*Deliverance* country."

There was no escaping it. Like it or not, *Deliverance* had become a part of the American psyche. Tell somebody from anywhere in America but particularly in the South that you're taking a long canoe trip and wait for the *Deliverance* allusions to surface. At Maryville College, I was directing a student's thesis on why the myth of *Deliverance* had endured so long; she (Ruthie Cartlidge) rafted the Chattooga, the river where the movie was filmed, as part of her research. The guides, she said, didn't like to talk about the movie. A literary river rat named John Lane would soon publish a book on the Chattooga called *Descending into the Myth of Deliverance*. A former teacher of mine at the University of Alabama, Diane Roberts, captured the complexity of *Deliverance* when, in an *Oxford American* article, she described the character Burt Reynolds played, one of the ill-fated canoeists, Lewis, as someone who was "able to tap into his inner redneck, recovering that primitive self that is willing, even eager, to kill." Her ominous description of the locals haunted me as much as the book and movie itself: "The gaunt, pale mountain people with their skeletal eyes and moss-colored clothes, their high, alien voices and their elemental violence are the worse nightmare of the urban, affluent New South. They are what the South once was, what it could revert to" (145).

Perhaps *Deliverance* was within us as well as all around us. As the lake grew wider under a low gray sky, the points that we aimed for more and more distant, our canoe seemed to shrink in the expansive landscape. I couldn't get a clear station on my transistor radio. The canoe would not cut a straight line across the channel when we tried to shorten the distant curves of the reservoir. Wind and current conspired to push us sideways. On top of all this, Randy's paddling began to irritate me. He leaned back with his feet on the gunnels (imagine that on a seven-hundred-mile trip!), and in this position pulled his paddle through the water at a slant. His relaxed paddle stroke made it necessary for me to constantly correct our course with what is called a "J-stroke" to counteract the direction in which he was unwittingly pushing the front of the boat.

Back around Williamsburg I had first broached the rather delicate subject. "Randy," I said, breaking a long, fuming silence, "if you paddle like this," I said, demonstrating a short forward stroke with the blade straight up and down, "it will keep the boat straighter."

He had glanced back at me and nodded, but after about thirty minutes he was back to his old habits. Now, a week later, on the lake, the angled stroke, along with the wind and current, seemed like a grand conspiracy in my quest for efficient progress. At one point, exasperated with endless J-stroking when all I wanted was to reach a point of scrubby cedars miles away, I stopped paddling and let him keep dipping and pulling until the boat almost turned about.

"Oh," he said mildly. "I must not be paddling right." Then he straightened up in his seat and paddled strong and steady for a half hour or so.

I had offered repeatedly to switch ends with Randy, but he seemed to like it in the bow. I think that both of us liked the routine of taking our designated seats, plus he had the Viking sail responsibility. Thinking back on it now, if it had been me in the bow, and some guy like me was giving instructions from the stern, his eyes on my stroke every day, I might have to mutiny. I might have to use a perpendicular stroke against the side of his head. Randy seemed not to mind my peevish instruction. He even laughed when, soon after, I started in on a frantic jag of "propeller paddling," furiously striking the water as hard and fast as I could for five minutes or so, just because . . . just because.

A couple of hours before dark, we disagreed on where to camp. He was sick of paddling, as was I, but he wanted to settle for a narrow slope of rocks on the main lake, the first place we'd seen for miles where we could actually land the canoe. Not liking how exposed the site was and noting to myself that this was below the jeep trail that Charley had called "*Deliverance* Country," I convinced Randy to paddle two more miles to the channel between Lake Cumberland State Park and Cowgap Island, where Charley had suggested we might find a good site. After another hour of paddling, we arrived at the channel, where the banks on each side were too steep for landing the boat, much less camping. Finally, at the end of the channel that flowed into the main lake was a long, relatively flat point, a couple of small trees sprouting up through the rocks. This would be one of the few times that my instincts about campsites trumped Randy's. I didn't say, "I told you so," but he didn't say, "You were right," either.

While we were setting up our tents, two children came skipping and chattering down a path from the woods. When they saw us in the clearing, they stopped, transfixed, as if in the presence of monsters. Their parents followed. To my relief, they were not equally horrified.

"We're letting them burn off some energy before bed," said the father, leading the kids down the shoreline away from us.

Later, on a short hike up the hill where the family had come from, I found power lines, a group of cabins, and a deer grazing on the mown grass next to the paved road, part of the state park where we were squatting for free.

That night, I was unable to sleep. The tree frogs in the distance sounded to my inflamed imagination like a massacre. I had read about massacres along the Cumberland in Harriet Arnow's books, torture and mayhem and murder on both sides of the wars between settlers and native Americans, mostly Cherokee, Shawnee, or Chickamauga, a mixture of tribes led by Dragging Canoe, who had refused to acknowledge the treaty at Sycamore Shoals that purported to give whites the right to settle much of East and Middle Tennessee. On paper the treaty might have seemed clear and proper. In practice, the settlement created skirmishes in which captives were burned to death, scalped, slowly skinned alive, that sort of thing; women and children often were not spared. The worst of it lasted about ten years, toward the end of the eighteenth century, the area around Nashville one of the most contentious.

A long time ago, all that, far downriver from our campsite. Still, the faint chirruping of the frogs sounded like wailing, and I could not help thinking of the family at the top of the ridge, could not stop the horror movie scenes that bloomed in my brain. Such, at times, is life in the outdoors, at night, away from the facile influence of television and electric lights. I wondered what Dragging Canoe and early white settlers such as John Donelson and James Robertson dreamed after witnessing and participating in so much bloodshed. Though we'd like to think we can control or program everything these days, dreams are one part of our lives beyond our direct influence. They embarrass or horrify us, sometimes reflecting what we'd rather not acknowledge: the mayhem within, a capability for cruelty or cowardice so debased that we dare not speak of it in daylight. It is a blessing that most dreams are forgotten in the moments after we awake. And yet, these dreams, the ones that horrify us, are the most likely to persist in our waking lives as an image or two, pictures that, oddly enough, take hold of the imagination more than the odd wish fulfillment about flying or winning the lottery. On the river, I invited such dreams to reveal to me what I didn't know about myself, and lying beside open water on a long point, cold smooth stones beneath your back, is the best way to receive such knowledge.

The next day we had twelve more miles on Lake Cumberland, and then we would be back on a free-flowing river, where perhaps my waking mental state would improve. One more obstacle blocked our path: Wolf Creek Dam. It had no navigational lock, and we had no ride to take us around it. Time to turn on the charm.

CHAPTER 8

GOOD SAMARITANS

Before the trip, I looked for books devoted to the entire Cumberland River. One, published in 1973 as part of the Rivers of America Series, rattled off dates and figures and historical events about the Cumberland region but lacked immediacy, detail, and firsthand knowledge of the river. Another, *Adventures along the Cumberland*, was written by Wisconsin native Warren S. O'Brien, a commercial photographer who had become infatuated with the Cumberland from vacations he'd taken there. The point of view is a little quirky, O'Brien inventing the personas "George" and "Jane" to represent him and his wife, resulting in strange passages in which he describes the "beliefs" and "thoughts" of the couple as if they were characters in a novel and he were an omniscient narrator. Still, the account describes long stretches of the river at a time when it snaked through areas much more isolated and "unspoiled," as O'Brien says, than they are now.

O'Brien (George) recounts the canoe trip he and his wife took in 1954, soon after Wolf Creek Dam was finished, and flashes back periodically to another trip, in the 1930s, when he accompanied his friend Sam Hicken, a Paducah, Kentucky, native, up most of the river in a small boat with an outboard motor. Wild man Sam, a river rat and nature boy whose permanent residence is a houseboat near Smithland, acts as George's guide into the mysteries of the river and Cumberland culture, introducing him to moonshine makers, doing handstands on high bluffs above the river, skinny dipping, and generally making George wish he could live free off the land and walk around half-naked full time. There's one photograph of Sam wearing sort of loin-cloth, a lean, well-muscled guy who holds a five-foot snake (dead, I assume) up to his mouth as if preparing to bite into a corn on the cob. George is bulkier, square-headed and crew cut, wearing dark swimming trunks and a wife-beater T-shirt, the kind of guy, who, in order to satisfy his curiosity, accom-panies federal agents on a raid of moonshine stills, despite Sam's vehement disapproval. There are black-and-white photographs of stills, the whiskey makers' faces blurred out, but George's revenuer friends don't bust anybody.

George is the undisputed authority on the run with his wife in 1954. In between lectures to her (and us) about canoeing and camping and fond remembrances of his friend Sam, George notes the differences between the river above the dam and below it. At times, he describes the dam and re-sulting lake in a neutral tone, as if writing a script for a Corps of Engineers documentary:

> The lake was new but they [George and Jane] had noticed considerable activity along its shores. There were a number of floating docks and house-boats already completed but many more were under construction. Other business establishments were going up and resorts for vacationers were seen. It was apparent there would be plenty of all types of boats available to fishermen who would be drawn to the good fishing in this lake. . . . [O]ne farmer who had already started renting boats to the public said he also was able to sell his corn crop to the fishermen by bringing it to them "in bottles." (29–30)

At other times, George describes, without much ardor, how the dam has diminished the river's beauty: "Now they were on Lake Cumberland, formed by water backed up by the New [sic] Wolf Creek Dam. They believed this would be the least interesting part of the journey because the river here was a sprawling lake with new shorelines made by man and not yet corrected by nature to conform to the beauty of the older sections" (17).

George would get a little more worked up about the dam when, while canoe camping below it, he is unable to recognize landmarks, now submerged, and cannot predict the water's power-generating rises at his campsites. In one photo, he's shoveling sand with his paddle to construct a dike; in another, Jane is shoveling to "reinforce" his embankment. When Jane hurts her back and then suffers from an apparent inflammation of the appendix, George, who barely hides his irritation, has to call off his adventure at Celina, just a few days downriver from the dam.

Randy and I would have our own troubles on the same stretch, but for now, we had twelve miles to paddle on the most "recreated" part of the lake, though we were fortunate that it was Thursday and not a weekend. Maybe it was the weather—bright, sunny, temperatures in the 70s, little wind—or maybe it was the fact that we had a short paddle before we would say good-bye to the lake, but our spirits had lifted. We stayed close to the north shore, where our takeout would be, and although we passed a few houseboats forty feet long, none of their wakes disturbed us because they were so far away. One houseboat came up behind us, passed us on the port side, then cut about thirty yards in front of us at full speed to turn into a cove.

"What's he doing?" asked Randy, finishing up his morning suntan lotion slather. "Can't he see us?" His voice escalated off the top end of the musical scale.

"He doesn't care about us," I said, trying to prepare Randy for the four reservoirs to come, where the status of canoeists in the food chain of boats was at plankton level.

"Fire the cannons," he shouted, gesturing at the houseboat.

"Man the oars," I said, as the wakes approached.

We met the waves bow first and surfed over the first big-boat wakes on the Cumberland River, these medium sized, the jolts about like riding a bike down concrete steps.

On the Tennessee River lakes that Jasper and I canoed in 1998—Ft. Loudoun, Watts Bar, Chickamauga, Nickajack, Guntersville, Wheeler, Wilson, and Kentucky—I laid down in my tent each night and felt the earth undulate beneath me, residual muscle spasms from jumping boat wakes all day. Nothing hurt me more than my tailbone. I expected the same on the Cumberland's reservoirs, but so far boat traffic had been sparse and docile.

Lake Cumberland was cleaner and colder than any reservoir I'd been on in the South, and because of the magnificent gorges the lake had flooded, it was also the deepest I'd floated. David Treadway, of the U.S. Corps of Engineers, Nashville District, said that the lake is, at normal pool, 205 feet deep at the back of Wolf Creek Dam, with a capacity to hold a 240-foot pool. Elsewhere in the channel the lake averages 90 feet deep. This kind of depth meant that the water released below the dam, already cold from its free-flowing origins in the mountains, was further refrigerated, having come from the bottom of a dark abyss. This cold water, flushed from the lake's bottom for power, would change the life on the other side for many miles. Cold water made a trout hatchery viable, but the creation of the habitat also made life impossible for the warm water fish that were there before the dam. For an idea about just how cold the water was in early summer, as of May 13, 2004, the water temperature at Lee's Ford Marina, above the dam near Somerset, was, as the Corps reported, 73 degrees at the surface, 72 degrees at 5 feet, 67 degrees at 10 feet, 63 degrees at 15 feet, 60 degrees at 20 feet, 59 degrees at 25 feet and 57 degrees at 30 feet.

From five miles away we could see the horizon that the dam formed, over a mile long, its length extended by riprap lining the built-up road (Highway 127) that crossed the dam. In spite of my opposition to the philosophy of dam building, I have yet to approach one by water and not be impressed with what human engineering can accomplish. And we were looking at the up-stream side, where only forty feet of the structure protruded above the water. Not until we would get to the other side, below the dam, could we see that it was 258 feet high, and at the time it was finished (1950) the largest earth-fill (or embankment) dam in the United States. The original purposes of the dam were to control flooding through water storage and to generate electric-ity by letting water pass through the dam's penstocks, large corridors with turbines that the force of the water turns to create power.

Treadway said that the Flood Control Act of 1938 and the Rivers and Harbor Act of 1946 authorized construction of Wolf Creek Dam to prevent catastrophic floods such as those in 1913, 1936, and 1937. The Corps built no lock at Wolf Creek, he said, because the lack of commercial traffic above the dam would not justify the cost and because the lock would have had to be far higher than any that exists in the world—250 feet. Each lockage would require such a large volume of water that it would "impact" the communities downstream. The farthest we would be dropped in a lock on this trip would be sixty feet at Old Hickory Dam. On the Tennessee, I was dropped the far-thest inside Wilson Dam lock—ninety-three feet—the second highest lock in the United States and the third highest in the world.

Because of heavy rains since February, the dams on the Cumberland had been storing and releasing water in order to balance high water on the reser-voirs, which had flooded recreation area parking lots, campgrounds, and mari-nas, with potential flooding of towns and cities downstream of reservoirs. In late February, the *Times-Journal* of Russell County reported that as a result of Wolf Creek Dam's storing floodwaters from heavy rains, Lake Cumberland's level had recently risen twenty-five feet. As a result of the high lake level and the expectation of more rain, the Corps opened the dam's floodgates to release some of that water downstream. The floodgates, which release 553 cubic feet per second, had only been opened about half a dozen times since the dam was finished. Gulls swarmed the man-made waterfall and fed on the small fish being flushed through.

Even as late as May, when Randy and I started out, the Tennessee and Cumberland river systems were backed up, the damkeepers busy releasing and holding back water. According the *Nashville Tennessean* on May 9, water held back by Percy Priest Dam, on the Stones River, and by Old Hickory and the other dams upstream of Nashville, prevented flooding there, said Jim Upchurch, chief of water management at the Army Corps Nashville Office. "This is exactly how the system was designed to be operated," he said.

Around noon we pulled the canoe up into the shade of a big sycamore next to the parking lot at Holcomb's Landing. A family—father, mother, daughter, and son—fished from the bank around the bend from us, the children running from parent to parent for help untangling lines or baiting hooks with nightcrawlers. An old man who spoke with what sounded like a garbled English accent held a pole under the shade tree where we'd landed our canoe. We said, "Excuse us," and he said something strange and bitter about his luck that day. Randy and I pulled the boat out of the man's fishing hole onto the grass next to the parking lot and consulted about what to do next. A portage of boat and equipment to Kendall Campground on the other side of the dam—a mile or so away—would take at least four trips each, we figured, eight miles of hauling gear. But who among these Kentuckians would take time out of their allotment of leisure to haul our gear—and us? In spite of Good Samaritan John Holbrook back in Bell County, I was skeptical of more free help.

Most people at this boat ramp were hurrying to drop their boat into the water and take off onto the blue lake, or they were loading their boat to zip away home. A frenzied group of workers were assembling the rails and canopies of a sixty-foot houseboat in the parking lot. Nobody was paying attention to a couple of canoeists, standing in the shade with a pile of gear and no motor vehicle. Can-do Randy walked up the embankment to the road to further survey our situation. I had already resigned myself to portaging on foot, not wanting, as my grandmother would say, to be beholden to anyone. After the short pleasant paddle that morning, I tried to convince myself that the grueling portage would be good exercise. Randy, though in much better shape than me, was intent on exhausting more practical possibilities before submitting himself to such physical torture.

While I sat in the shade brooding about the portage, Randy stood by the side of Highway 127. He tried to flag down a cop, who turned out to be a security guard for the dam. When the guy drove on past him and stopped on the roadside ahead, Randy started walking fast to catch up. Then the cop car started going forward again, and Randy stopped and said, "Well, damn you," pretty loud. The car stopped abruptly and backed up to meet Randy, who was worried that the cop had heard him.

"Did you want me?" asked the security guard. After Randy told him our predicament, he said he couldn't help us because his trunk was full of diving equipment and other paraphernalia. "I'll try to find someone who can help you," he said and took off toward Kendall Campground. That someone turned out to be Casey, a trout fisherman that the security guard, Curtis, pulled over on a side road that led to a put-in below the dam. Casey, a college student who had driven two hours from Bowling Green to fish for trout, was hauling his canoe in his pickup truck, making him an obvious target for Curtis, who thought a fellow canoeist might be inclined to help two hapless voyagers without a land vehicle. When he saw the blue lights in his rearview mirror, Casey thought he had been caught speeding.

Curtis walked up to his window and said, "Do you feel like doing a good deed today?" and Casey wondered what the cop was up to. He agreed to help us, but before he did so, he had to drop his friend off at the river so he could start fishing.

When Casey arrived at the parking lot to pick us up, he helped us shove our canoe in the bed of his truck next to his red canoe and load all the gear in the space around the two boats. A lanky, good-looking kid, Casey wore his bib waders and clearly was anxious to get into the water soon because the river level below the dam fluctuated so unpredictably that the fishing sometimes varied by the hour. He waited patiently as I paid the campground manager at the entrance to Kendall, drove us another half mile to our site, and helped us unload our gear. Like the Good Samaritan at Four Mile, he would accept no money for his time and trouble.

Randy and I now had the entire afternoon free at a civilized campground that included a laundry, bathhouse, snack bar, and playground. We were lucky to get a site at Kendall. Over the weekend, an influx of parents and children would fill up Kendall's eighty-three sites to compete in a kids' fishing tournament, tempting the released trout with corn, salmon eggs, nightcrawlers, spinner baits, skittles, red hots, gummy bears, and other leftover candy. It was a good thing we would be forced out because Kendall was a paradise of convenience and ease, the kind of place that might distract us from our goal. The laundry was only a few yards away. Since we didn't have detergent, Randy suggested we use soap from the dispenser in the men's room. I waited for my load to fill up with water to assure myself that the machine wouldn't explode with soap suds or clog up, then I lay down in my tent for a nap. About the time I drifted into a sweaty doze, Curtis, the security guard, pulled up in his undercover police car.

We thanked him again for engineering our portage with such speed, skill, and diplomacy. He was near the end of his shift and, it seemed, in need of a break from maintaining dam security. Seeing him and his vehicle up close with no state, county, or town affiliation, I asked Curtis as circumspectly as I could manage just what sort of cop he was. He explained to us that he worked for an independent contractor, employed by the federal government to patrol the area around the dam. As we paddled toward the dam, he said, there were quite a few eyes on us, some of them mechanical. Curtis said he didn't worry as much about terrorists of Middle Eastern descent as he did about the homegrown kind, along the lines of Timothy McVeigh. Security around dams since the 9/11 attacks had not affected the routine of the navigational locks, said Curtis, but new restrictions kept people from getting close to the dam on land. There were no more visitor tours of a dam's inner workings.

Curtis had been a policeman in Indianapolis for fourteen years, and he had stories to tell. First came details about recovering bodies, a chore he helped the local rescue squad with. He told us what people looked like after they'd been in the water a few days. He'd helped retrieve the body of a suicide victim from a remote cave on the man's property. Recently, Curtis said, barely pausing between episodes, he had helped recover a new vehicle from the lake and helped question the owner.

"Guy said he stopped on a slope, going uphill, to take a pee. Left the vehicle in neutral and it rolled into the lake. Now what's funny about that?" He waited. "If he's standing there, with the door open, taking a piss, the door's going to knock him over. No way it happened like that."

"Insurance scam?" asked Randy.

Curtis nodded. He gave us a tour of his car, a Crown Victoria that he'd purchased himself, at a great bargain. It had an Interceptor engine, a siren, which he turned on for us, a police radio, and a flashing light, but there were more gadgets he needed to fully equip the car. He opened the trunk and showed us his diving equipment, a multiuse tool he'd recently bought (knife, flashlight, pliers, screwdriver), his global positioning system, and his bulletproof vest. Randy asked about the tear in the vest. "I self-tested it," said Curtis.

Randy later joked about Curtis's self-testing, and we argued about whether he was wearing the vest when he tested it. To me, self-testing a bulletproof vest, particularly if you bought it at a yard sale or an army surplus shop, seemed like a good idea. Just how he carried out the test was of mild interest to me, but I assumed Curtis knew what he was doing.

Having shown us everything in his trunk, Curtis got on his radio, confirmed to us that he had been relieved from his shift, and started the Crown

Vic's powerful motor, which purred quietly. Lowering his tinted window, Curtis, Good Samaritan number three, wished us luck and departed.

Randy and I were getting warm, fuzzy feelings about the river and its inhabitants. Everyone seemed benevolent and sympathetic to our quest. This feeling, which we falsely extended to the river itself, would put us off guard for hard times ahead.

CHAPTER 9

LONG RAIN, HIGH WATER

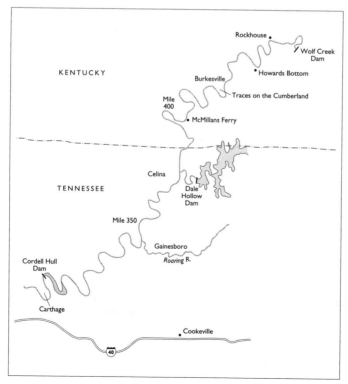

Wolf Creek Dam to Carthage.

After a restful night at Kendall, we were faced with one of our longest portages from campsite to water—about three hundred yards—the last fifty down a steep, muddy slope that had been underwater the evening before. First we carried the canoe to the water's edge, then rushed back to camp for another load, unsure of when the dam would begin releasing water, potentially setting the boat adrift. We would hear varying reports from fishermen all morning, but the first news quickened our pace considerably. A trout fisherman from Louisville said he expected the water to rise starting at eight-thirty, in half an hour. We had at least three more trips to the campsite and back in order to get all of our gear into the boat.

The fisherman, who had his son with him, added that we did not want to fall in here; the water was so cold that you could not survive in it for long. He said that a man had drowned on this stretch a few months earlier. The victim had been dragging anchor to fish, and when the water began to rise, his anchor got hung, the boat got swamped, and he fell into the frigid river. The water below the dam averaged about fifty degrees this time of year.

Randy and I embarked hastily after the frantic portage, already exhausted though the day had just begun. The dam was at our backs about a half-mile away around a bend, and the current sluicing through it swept us past fishermen in boats about every twenty yards. The day was calm and cool, a thin veil of fog rising from the river's surface. We could see through the water to the bottom as we passed over gravel shoals and patches of grass waving ghostlike in the currents. Fishermen wading out from the bank whipped fluorescent lines over their heads, snapping them forward to plop a fly upstream, poised to set the hook as the current carried it toward them. In five minutes, we saw one man catch a trout from a boat, and another man pull one from the bank, each a keeper. A few waved at us, but no one talked; only the whiplash zing of the lines and the sluice of water against rock broke the silence.

This was the perfect tonic after the doldrums of lake paddling. The day before, the sun beat down on us in a boat suspended above ninety feet of water; the wakes of distant cruisers, sloshing against the side of the boat, was the only relief from the monotony of our steady paddling. Now we shivered in air supercooled by moving water, our progress charted by the gravel bottom that rushed past us, the trees passing above our heads. As the day brightened, we had brief, murmured conversations with fishermen and hardly paddled, letting the river determine our pace. Mainly, we tried to steer clear of the fishermen, who became more and more numerous. At one bend, we passed a group of fifteen or so strung out on the edge of a gravel bar casting their lures onto a deep eddy on the opposite bank, no more than thirty feet away. We saw about fifty fishermen (two women) in the first ten miles of our float. Later we would find out that this was the first good day to fish in a long time. All the recent rain had made the water too high and too muddy to catch trout.

We kept glancing behind us as if for a tidal wave, anticipating the dam's release of water. I thought one guy said the generation would start at nine and end at eleven, but Randy heard something different, and in the swift current there was no time for a "Come again?" without asking the man to shout as he receded in the distance. The next informant said that the new water would reach us (eight miles below the dam at this point) at one-thirty and crest at seven o'clock.

When we told one fisherwoman about our trip, she immediately offered to cook us breakfast at the cabin that she and her husband owned.

"We'll let you fish," said Randy, "but thank you."

"I'd really rather cook than fish," she said.

We declined as graciously as we could, the moving water more intoxicating than the offer of good food. The water was high enough that we had no shoals or rocks or broken trees to steer around. It was the easiest paddling day of the entire trip, requiring little mental or physical effort. Creeping up on me was a queasy feeling that things were going too well, that the day was almost too beautiful, but I did not speak of this aloud to Randy, who deserved to be spared my darker musings, though I suspected he shared them, despite his upbeat demeanor. Thus far on the river, we had come to expect alternating stretches of hardship and good fortune. Too much of either meant that the pendulum would swing higher when it came back.

Besides awaiting the surge of water from the dam, another sense of foreboding struck us as we scanned the banks. The trees growing at the top of the fifteen-foot-high embankment had watermarks on their trunks, a distinct border where the wood had grown pale underwater. If those marks indicated the point to which the river rose routinely during power generation, we would have to camp far off the river and carry the boat to the campsite with us. It would be our most blatant trespass so far.

When O'Brien's George and Sam canoed this section in 1933, the water was so shallow they often had to get out and drag the boat, and they frequently stopped to see Sam's friends along the banks. Seventeen years later, George barely recognized the river below the newly built dam. It was faster, deeper, and too cold for swimming. A boy he met called it the "mean old river." George mourned the absence of fishermen, boats, or anyone else enjoying the Cumberland. In the fifty years since then, people had adjusted to the colder, swifter river below the dam and the calm waters above it, recreating with a passion that would have amazed George. Feeling the need to justify its drastic alteration of the river, the Corps details the dam's "value to the nation" on its Web site, tabulating with statistics three separate categories of benefits: "Social," "Economic," and "Environmental." Under "Social Benefits" are over four million visits to the river in 1999, subdivided into boaters, campers, picnickers, and so on. These four million visits, in turn, created jobs and infused the local economy with millions of dollars. Environmental benefits include an increased area of shoreline, where the lake was created (1,085 shoreline acres) and 591 acres reforested.

Though the numbers are impressive, I can't help but wonder, like George, what was lost that we can't get back. Such drastic alterations of the landscape leave me uneasy. Constructing grandiose dams, canals, and superhighways show off human ingenuity, even a kind of imagination, in the ability to envision a drastically altered landscape. Such revisions of nature also indicate a lack of humility about our place in the world, a shortsighted optimism about problems we think we can solve with technology and stubbornness. But of course I recognize the good intentions of people who see the world differently than me, a man who resists change in even the smallest details of his life. I hope that those with the power to set such drastic changes into motion proceed at a deliberate and thoughtful pace, with a sharp and vivid sense of the past.

Around noon we stopped at Rock House Natural Bridge, about fifteen miles from the dam. Vic suggested that we camp under the high roof of the cave, open at both ends so that it resembled an arch. According to O'Brien's George, the opening on the cave's river side was 60 feet high and 150 feet wide, while the distance from one entrance to the other was about 100 feet. George thought that where the arch stood was an old riverbed, and that the force of the water had washed away the softer stone beneath the harder rock that remained.

Inside was evidence that people visited often and felt compelled to leave their marks. Graffiti listed names and dates and unlikely braggadocio. One girl, Amanda, seemed quite popular. On one wall, some sap proclaimed his love for her; on the opposite another called her a slut and listed her phone number. On the ceiling, a high flier had written his initials with the date 1943. How the artist had accomplished this task was a matter of debate between Randy and me. I thought maybe a long pole, with a paintbrush taped to the end. Perhaps, said Randy, the water had flooded to that great height during that year, and the painter had been in a boat.

George and Jane had the good sense to camp under the arch and wait out a rain. Randy and I, with considerably less sense, did not. After lunch at the Rock House, we paddled onward, forced to seek a landing for the night when the sky began to darken and the air to thicken and exude that expectant damp aroma with which we had become all too familiar. We were at Howard's Bottom, we calculated, about twenty-five miles downriver from the dam, when we pulled over at a short concrete ramp that led up to a cow pasture. Though we had camped in the domain of cattle before and would again, this pasture was far from optimal. Damp cow pies blotted the ground at frequent intervals, and weeds grew in stiff clumps so numerous we had to stomp them down under the ground tarps. A few scrubby trees lined a small creek that trickled between bare, muddy banks about fifteen feet from where we spread our tarps. Remembering the water marks on the trees, we pulled the boat up the ramp next to our tarps.

While we were setting up camp, it began to rain softly. After a half hour, my waterproof jacket was soaked through. Why we stood there in the rain waiting for it to stop, I do not know, perhaps because it seemed such a light, friendly rain, without thunder or lightning, and after the idyllic day, we expected the heavens to shower us, and then offer the sun to towel us off, with a rainbow thrown in as an amenity, no charge. Randy rigged a tarp over the canoe in an attempt to set up a "kitchen." When the wind tilted the tarps and the droplets spewed in our faces, we retired to our separate tents. There would be no supper tonight except what we could slap together from our private stashes. For me it was peanut butter and tortillas, which had also been my lunch.

I sought comfort in Basho's *Narrow Road to the Interior*, the one book I'd brought. In a temple at Hikarido, surrounded by statues of Buddhas, jeweled doors, and gold columns, Basho writes:

> Fifth-month rains hammer
> and blow but never quite touch
> Hikarido (20)

I dozed. I studied the map by flashlight. Dozed some more. Dreamed. Stared at the ceiling waiting for dawn. Peeked out the door at the black river. Craned my neck to see how far the creek beside us had risen. Dozed. Organized things. Mopped water from a corner. Wished my clothes were dry. Peeked outside to check on the boat. Waited for the rain to stop.

Thirteen hours later it did. It had poured steadily, without pause, for fifteen hours. Across the river a forty-foot dugout canoe floated silently through the fog. Poking my head out farther through the soggy tent vestibule, I rubbed sleep from my eyes and squinted: not a dugout, but a fully grown sycamore, its leafy branches twirling in the heavy current. From the clear, cheerful stream of the day before, the river had been turned into T. S. Eliot's "strong brown god." Trees, bushes, and heavy trash rode on a deep brown gush that bubbled and swirled and gurgled, its current a heavy, insistent push. Ten feet from our tents, the once trickling creek roared, its muddy banks filled to the top. The river flowed only a few feet from where we had pulled our canoe, and the farmer's concrete ramp was completely submerged.

We squatted beside the boat and discussed our options. I was in no mood to hole up in the soggy pasture for another day. Howard's Bottom, so aptly named, was so far my least favorite campsite. Randy was hesitant to set out on the big water, and I didn't feel very confident either. He couldn't decide whether it would be better to stay in the middle of the river, away from newly submerged obstacles near the banks, or to chance floating near land, where if we fell out, at least we'd have better chance of making it to shore in the strong, cold current.

Complicating the decision, we were to meet my wife, Julie, that afternoon, seventeen miles downstream at Gar Whicker's boat storage facility, Traces on the Cumberland. Julie would be leaving from work in a couple of hours, so we would need to let her know if we couldn't make the rendezvous. No way could she find us at Howard's Bottom. There was no road nearby, nothing but an abandoned shack up the slope a ways and a forlorn little cabin across the river. *If I were alone*, I thought, *I'd already be on the water.* With another paddler, the stakes were higher.

Why was I open to taking such a risk? Did I need to see my wife that badly? It is true that I missed her, for the usual reasons a man misses his wife, and that I knew she was bringing fresh lemons, gin, tonic, ice, and other more essential supplies. It is also true that I looked forward to talking to someone about subjects beyond wildlife identification, weather, and the relative merits of Kenny Chesney versus Johnny Cash. I liked Randy, but a break would be welcome, as would my wife's sense of humor and her uncanny ability to expose the absurdity of my obsessions, such as arguing about Johnny Cash over Kenny Chesney.

Still, there was the decision. Kneeling and angling my line of sight close to the river's surface gave me a better idea of the current's speed and power. Looking at it created a hollow spot in my gut. "If you don't want to go," I said, "I understand. We can stay here another night."

"I don't know," Randy kept saying. He was unusually quiet that morning.

Two hours later, at about one o'clock, we were on the water, trussed up in our lifejackets, gear tied up tight. I steered us into the middle of the deluge and we dipped our paddles cautiously, as if packing a load of nitro. Paddling was superfluous; the river carried us about eight miles an hour, and forward strokes needed to be strong and quick to stay ahead of the river's speed.

Old-time travelers, Harriet Arnow writes, accepted the vagaries of the weather as a matter of routine. As Kentucky and Tennessee were being settled in the early nineteenth century, there were few houses, fewer inns, and no trailside shelters. Anybody who wanted to get somewhere took a horse and hoped for a cave or tree cover for shelter. Instead of nylon tents, long hunters would use tree bark and twigs to build lean-to's, then stop up the cracks with moss, grass, and leaves. People were used to living outdoors, and as Arnow points out, everyone suffered when the weather turned bad.

> Lawyers such as [Andrew] Jackson traveled from one end of the state to the other, and though his horses were undoubtedly better than those of Davy Crockett, a flooded creek or a sudden violent thunderstorm wetted each, for such was life; no amount of money could entirely shield any human being from the discomforts of the weather. (*Flowering of the Cumberland* 88)

In our place, Jackson or Crockett would have had enough gumption to stop at the Rock House and get settled in for the long rain. They probably could have forecasted it by sniffing the wind. If we had camped ten miles upstream under the arch, we wouldn't have been cooped up in our tents, we could have cooked a decent supper, and we could have watched the river rise from a safe height and spared ourselves the shock of peeking out our tent doors the next morning. We could have easily made up the distance today in the powerful current that the rain had created. Sometimes stupidity leads to adventure.

That the river was slowly receding that day did not ease our fears once we crept onto its back. The afternoon seemed like early morning, with the fog spreading a shroud over the water, so much colder than the air after the big rain. There were no people in boats or on the banks. We rode the brown beast without talking, and I steered clear of any swirl or bubble that hinted of an obstruction beneath the surface. I have to admit a fascination with high water that I came by naturally. My mother, who grew up in southern Indiana near the confluence of the Wabash and Ohio, remembers Grandma Lena and the children cowering in the back seat of their Studebaker as Grandpa Esco powered it through waters that covered the narrow country roads and rose above the skinny tires, apparently unworried that the floodwaters might choke his engine. As I remember him, with a white crew cut and a deadpan face, Grandpa was an inveterate prankster who loved going to the Evansville Zoo, where with an arsenal of creative noises, he raised the rancor of nearly every species. In short, he liked to get a rise out of people and animals, and enjoyed a good rise in the river.

I thought this a little strange, but I'd known Esco long enough to understand that he was unusual, prone to behavior that set more conventional heads to shaking. When my mother told me about the drowning of her older brother, ten-year-old Melvin, it further complicated Esco's fascination with floods. Though he'd been warned to stay away from the floodwaters, Melvin ventured into the Ohio River alone one afternoon in July 1931. A fisherman found his body the next morning, arms locked around a floating willow log. My grandma, Lena, accepted the tragedy as God's will. She told the children that God needed Melvin in heaven. Esco gathered no such solace from religion. Melvin's death "just about killed him," said my mother. After such a tragedy, how to explain Esco's continued fascination with raging rivers, his driving through big water to incite panic among the family? He had not an evil bone in his body, so good-natured was his teasing. He was generous to a fault and had a soft, welcoming heart. I believe that Esco held two things in his heart that did not mix, like the confluence of the Ohio and the Mississippi, where green mingles with big muddy: he held fascination and fear together, and indulged them both on the high-water car rides.

This I sometimes shared with him. I doubt I was any less nervous than Randy, but under the nervousness was a fascination for the river's power to lift trees and earth and carry them as far as it pleased.

The night of the long rain, Randy later told me, was the low point of the trip for him. I had heard him on the phone with Lara, talking low, but I couldn't make out what he was saying for the noise of the rain and the river. The inactivity of those thirteen hours was much more difficult for him than for me. Randy liked to be busy, and in the long rain, there was little we could do except sleep or read or eat from our stores. For me the time passed like a blur. Other than the threat of the river rising to tent level and washing away the boat, I didn't let the hibernation bother me. It made me that much more ready to keep moving once the rain stopped.

The Highway 90 bridge at Burkesville emerged from the fog downriver long before we expected. Loud chirping noises from the right bank startled us. In the dead limbs of a sycamore tree, sixty feet overhead, were seven great blue heron nests made of twigs, their shelter as big as a human infant's crib. The roosting birds clucked as they fed their young regurgitated food. The great blue heron was one animal that we would see down the length of the entire river, no matter the elevation, the vegetation, the human population, or whether the water was still or moving. We would see them standing on one skinny leg in the shallows, waiting like lawn ornaments for the chance to snag a fish in their beak, necks poised in an "S" shape. Or more often, they would lift off from the bank as we approached. Their wings, with a span of about four feet, beat the air with great whumps as they flew downriver for a more secluded fishing spot. Besides fish, the slate-blue bird also ate pocket gophers, ground squirrels, and field mice. We saw at least one just about every day of the trip, even through Nashville, and though they were a common sight, I always got a thrill out of the comical squawks and the great whoosh of their wings as they beat the air. I'm not sure they regarded us with the same amiability because we continually disturbed their fishing as we followed them downriver.

Ten minutes after the roost, we passed under the Highway 61 bridge and angled toward the boat ramp at Traces of the Cumberland. We'd floated seventeen miles in about two hours.

CHAPTER 10

RIVER PEOPLE

"My last thought," Gar Whicker told us, "was 'this is really going to hurt.'"

An instant later he crashed his powered parachute into the tallest tree on the bank, a maple fifty yards from the doorstep of his riverside house. Having realized that a tangled line hindered the steering of his flying machine, which includes a three-wheeled landing gear, Gar, soon after taking off, was trying to descend to earth and straighten out the problem. As he approached the field next to his house, the machine lurched left and hurtled him toward the tree. He had a choice, he said, of landing in the tree or in the river below. He chose the tree.

When I'd seen him the year before our trip, he was sitting in a wheelchair in the office of his cavernous gift shop. Much had changed since then. The gift shop was closed, as Randy and I found out, after walking up the wide gravel drive the half-mile up from the concrete ramp past the 250 aluminum boat storage units. To my great disappointment, the snack bar—which had served bratwurst, hamburgers, grilled cheese sandwiches, and milkshakes—was also shut down. Also gone was the canoe renter, a local man, Harold, who had shuttled me on a seventeen-mile paddle with Jasper from Burkesville to Cloyd's Landing. Gar, now up and about, spotted us wandering back to the boat ramp and gave us a ride down the long driveway to his house/office, where he introduced us to Brenda, his wife, a tall, energetic redhead. She was sitting in front of a computer, doing coursework to finish her nursing degree.

In the accident Gar had broken his leg so badly that doctors feared he might lose it. He also had severe lacerations on his head. But he had recovered without losing his dry wit or genteel good looks.

"People ask me," he said, "whether I will ever fly again, and I ask them if after they had a car accident whether they would ever drive again."

A former pharmacist, Gar, with Brenda, moved here from Indiana in 1991, and opened Traces on the Cumberland in 1996. River rats, they had piloted their nineteen-foot cruiser from Wolf Creek Dam to the end of the river, at Smithland, and beyond, exploring up the Tennessee River a ways. Gar used the powered parachute to take aerial photos of the Cumberland and nearby Dale Hollow Lake, the dammed Obey River, a tributary of the Cumberland where, Gar told us, the water was clean enough to drink. He was working on a fishing handbook for the eighty-mile stretch of the Cumberland from Wolf Creek Dam to the Tennessee state line. Now in print, the book, called *Fishing the Lower Cumberland River*, includes detailed maps, aerial photos, fishing strategies, and specific directions to prime spots for rainbow and brown trout and striped bass.

Gar, who wore a dress shirt with the words "Captain Gar" sewn onto its pocket, told Randy he could camp anywhere he wanted, no charge, on a strip of mown lots next to the river that Gar had put up for sale. Even after the long rain night, Randy didn't want to accompany Julie and me to a hotel in Burkesville. I'm sure that Gar's flat, manicured lots, fifty feet above the water, looked inviting to him after the previous night's soupy pasture. Randy ribbed me mercilessly about the hotel night, but he seemed to understand that Julie was not a camper and that squatting on Gar's land with our two dogs might be testing the limits of his hospitality.

When I asked Gar about Harold and his canoeing business, he shook his head and said that Harold couldn't afford liability insurance and that he hadn't worked real hard at it anyway. Now a fellow named Bob was leasing the building that used to be the snack bar to rent rafts, Harleys, and jet skis.

When Bob first approached Gar about the venture, he said that he thought a rafting business would do great here, considering the white water below the dam.

"There isn't any white water below the dam," Gar told him.

"Sure there is," insisted Bob, from Virginia Beach, Virginia. He had visited his in-laws in Burkesville for many years. "There's strong current down there."

"Strong current, yes," said Gar, "when they are generating. But not white water."

"Well, I've got these rafts," said Bob, his enthusiasm undampened, "and people can jump out and get back in easily. Kids will love swimming on these rafting runs."

"Have you felt this water?" asked Gar.

Bob admitted he hadn't for a while.

"It's very cold," said Gar. "I doubt people will want to swim in it."

While Gar took a break from telling us stories, and Randy tidied up his campsite, I walked up to Bob's wooden building. He jumped out of his truck bed, where he was working, and handed me a Coke from his cooler for a dollar. His vending machine, he said, was malfunctioning. He admitted that business was slow, but blamed it on the wet weather and high water.

When I told him we were canoeing to the end of the river, he said it sounded like a great trip. "So you're going all the way to Nashville," he said.

He was the third person in the last two days who thought the river ended in Nashville. I told him we were going considerably beyond Nashville to the Ohio River, where the Cumberland ended, and I hoped I didn't sound like a jerk. Having canoed almost three hundred miles of the river, I was beginning to feel a bit proprietary, as if it were my duty to educate people about the river, though there would be, of course, much more for me to learn.

After his recent divorce, Bob said, he'd jumped on his motorcycle and headed west toward Alaska. In Iowa, he paused because of the cold weather and got the idea for renting watercraft in Burkesville. He turned his bike around and headed back to Kentucky.

"I'm not trying to get rich," said Bob, who resembled the rock musician Joe Walsh ("Life's Been Good to Me, So Far"), with the bushy mustache and ponytail. "I just want to make enough to live on."

He recommended a bar called the Sawmill as a place where Randy and I could meet women. When he heard my wife was coming, he said, "Oh," and told us about a few restaurants. Gar later told us that Bob had been hit over the head with an axe handle at the Sawmill in an altercation over a woman. Bob spent the night in the hospital, it seems, but was still up to recommending the Sawmill as a place for interesting diversion.

Bob said the former owners of the snack bar had tried to get too fancy with such a wide variety of foods. When he reopened it, he planned on offering only barbeque, what he called simple, down-home cooking.

"When people come through here," he said, "they're looking for the Clampetts. They want to see the Beverly Hillbillies." Bob said he was going to do his best to live up to the stereotype that people expected, though his accent and his manner branded him as an outsider from a relatively sophisticated city.

Randy and I visited Bob a few hours later for another Coke, and he was preparing to go for a jet ski ride. "Is business good?" Randy asked innocently.

"Hell no," said Bob.

A few minutes later Bob perked up at the sight of a visiting sales rep, a slim brunette wearing tight jeans. "Come on back to my S and M room," said

Bob, retreating to the back of the one large room of his establishment. We wished Bob luck and headed back to the site for more Gar stories while we waited for Julie.

The strangest thing he'd seen on the river, said Gar, was a ninety-foot houseboat pulling up to the bank beside his house, the captain leaning out and shouting, "Which way to New Orleans?"

He said he had helped the man pilot the big boat up to Wolf Creek Dam, only possible, said Gar, when the water reached the present level or higher. The river, he told us, rose eight feet the previous night; the water's temperature here was about 57 degrees. The marks we'd seen on the trees indicated the level the water had stayed for a couple of months during the floods of late winter and early spring. It took a lot more than a fifteen-hour rain to raise the water that high.

We told Gar that other than the trout fishermen the day before, within ten miles of the dam, we had not seen many on the river, none at all today. He said that many locals feared the river. When he was building his boat ramp, he directed the bulldozer operator to make a cut several yards out from the bank. The dozer operator told Gar that he wouldn't go out that far, that the current would wash him and the machine away.

Gar said, "No, it won't." He hopped aboard the dozer and made the cut into the riverbed himself. I wondered where Gar had learned to drive a bulldozer and what sort of guarantees he made on the man's expensive machine, but I didn't want to ruin a good story. I could tell from his confident attitude and from the well-kept boat storage compound that Gar was a man of many talents, not afraid to take chances, and that driving a bulldozer, even in swift current, would not intimidate him if it were required to complete the job.

Julie arrived about six o'clock, after a five-hour drive from Knoxville. With her were Jasper and Brushy, our dogs. Jasper ignored me at first, as if angered that I hadn't taken him on this trip, but after five minutes or so he was back to himself, jumping up on me and rollicking around the campsite, glad to be out of the house. Forgiving Randy for taking his place in the bow, Jasper gave him a high-five and pranced around while Randy tried to pet him. I warned Gar about Brushy, the irascible small terrier mix that Julie had found on the side of our road in Blount County. I named her after the federal prison at Brushy Mountain in Tennessee. Brushy hated most men and often sank her needlelike teeth into their ankles. Soon after I realized that a long canoe trip would jeopardize Jasper's health, I considered taking Brushy, whose size—about ten pounds—was ideal. I even enrolled her in Diane's School of Canine Charm, in Knoxville, and she passed the three-week course with honors, learning how to sit, stay, come, etc., though she graduated just as mean and stubborn as before. After Brushy bit an FBI agent who visited our home doing background research about a neighbor, I decided that if I took her, she could get me killed.

Brushy was a sort of an anti-Randy. While Randy had much in common with Jasper—good looks and a winning personality—Brushy was rough and unrefined, her coat coarse and multicolored, feet scrawny and hairless like a chicken's, one eye cocked. She had a dark, aggressive side with no fear of the odds, lacking the wisdom to back down from a stronger opponent. Brushy lacked tact and diplomacy. She was cagey but no genius. Only after Jasper nearly ripped out her good eye did she stop messing with him.

Julie broke out the gin, tonic, lemons, and a can of mixed nuts, and we had a tailgate party next to the river. While sipping our cocktails and popping nuts into our mouths, Randy and I spread out the other supplies we had requested. This included some food items such as the usual granola bars, raisins, and canned mushrooms, but also a whiskbroom and large sponge, which coming as a request from me, puzzled Julie. These items, I explained, were requests from Randy, who liked to keep the canoe mud-free, the ground tarps free of sand. I did not let on to Julie that the other big sponge that had been lost was taken from her car wash bucket. I also did not reveal that I'd dropped the eating utensil she'd given me in the water at the haunted campsite in Sawyer. In addition to the requested items, Julie brought an abundant supply of wet wipes and small, single-use dispensers of toilet paper set up on their own little rollers.

Randy agreed without hesitation to accompany us to one of the restaurants that Bob had recommended, the lodge at Dale Hollow Lake State Park. After a thirty-minute drive, we weaved our way down a long driveway through a maze of recreational possibilities—including a golf course and swimming pool—and entered the dining room of the Mary Ray Oaken Lodge, shivering with delight in the air-conditioned atmosphere. Distracted by the presence of so many people in close proximity and the dazzling choices on the menu, I took time to note the dimensions of the dining room. The vaulted wood ceiling, supported by steel trusses, was three stories high, and an A-shaped glass wall faced Dale Hollow Lake three hundred feet below us. If you stayed at the lodge, you had a dizzying array of activities to choose from: golfing, skiing, fishing, swimming, scuba diving, hiking, horseback riding, mountain biking, picnicking, and oddly enough spearfishing, though you are only allowed to spear "rough fish," which would include, I think, carp, gar, buffalo, and the like. From the dimensions of the customers at the dining room, it looked as if one of their main activities was dining, though I had no room to talk. Randy and I gorged ourselves at the buffet, which included, of course, fried fish, and just about every casserole, vegetable, meat, and dessert that a Kentuckian could conceive of, "all that you cared to eat." While Julie ate like a normal person—using her knife, fork, and napkin—she stared as Randy and I shoveled food and said little beyond periodic grunts of satisfaction.

Our manners made the large raccoon skulking on the lodge's patio look finicky. He was nibbling on some handout that he held between his paws. Most thought he was cute, though Julie, a veterinarian, wondered aloud about the possibility of rabies. Randy and I, having already experienced the marauding raccoons of Conley Bottoms, were less than charmed by the overweight beggar.

At 10 the next morning, rested and restored, we prepared to launch once again. Gar, who had been engaged in an animated conversation with Julie about professional school, had strolled to the ramp to shoot photographs of us. Julie shot photos of Randy and me standing next to the loaded canoe, and Randy shot a photograph of Gar standing next to his maritime mileage sign, a post nailed with placards that listed the distance to locations such as Nashville (231 miles) and the Ohio River (415 miles), two destinations that Randy and I hoped to reach. To paddle on to New Orleans by water, it would be 1,337 miles, just a little farther than Chicago, at 1,027 miles, though Chicago would require much upstream traveling. It was odd, I thought, that London, England (7,465 miles) was closer than Anchorage, Alaska, which, at 7,896 miles, was the farthest destination Gar had bothered to figure.

Randy and I, unconscious that we were being scrutinized, went through our sunscreen application ritual. Gar cracked, "The Indians didn't have sunscreen."

After we pushed off, Jasper barked and jumped up and down at the water's edge as Julie held his leash. It broke my heart to leave him there, but I knew it was for the best. As soon as we reached midstream, Julie told me later that Gar, watching us, had murmured, "I envy them," and wouldn't repeat it when she asked what he'd said. We'd heard this same phrase or something like it from others, such as Richard Haynes, our librarian guide through Harlan, and John Holbrook, who helped us around the low dam in Bell County.

Today we had strong current, the river was high but within its banks, and the brief return to civilization had energized us. Gar had recommended an island for camping, warning us that most of the land along the river was private property. We didn't bother to point out that we were veteran trespassers, not out of disrespect for the law but out of necessity. At Gar's Traces, the pendulum had swung back toward the good fortune side, poised there, I hoped, for a few more days before it descended.

CHAPTER 11

MCMILLAN'S FERRY NIRVANA

MCMILLAN'S FERRY NIRVANA

It was one of those moments that you know will stay with you to
the grave: the sweet pie, the gaunt man playing the old music, the
coals in the stove glowing orange, the scent of kerosene and hot
bread. . . . The music was so heavily romantic we both laughed. I
thought: It is for this I have come.

WILLIAM LEAST HEAT-MOON
Blue Highways

They come without warning, these moments. The traveler learns to pay attention and receive them like gifts.

Here's one in Monroe County, at Turkey Neck Bend, a hundred miles
north of Heat-Moon's country store in Nameless, Tennessee: it is twilight,
the very cusp of a day, and with the rising fog and falling darkness, the faces
of the men on the ferry below us are difficult to distinguish, the river beginning to blend with the sky, the trees and the moist air rising from it. A large
man built like a defensive end nimbly dismounts a shiny blue touring motorcycle and dances across the ferry deck, holding in his hands an imaginary
banjo, which he plays furiously. From the bike's stereo comes fast, clear banjo
picking that flows through the air with a virtuoso power as irresistible as the
river's current. A ferry worker closes the gate with a clang, and the towboat

attached to the side of the ferry pivots and moves across the current, the banjo ringing crisp and clear as if Earl Scruggs himself had materialized. Ferry and passengers fade into the fog.

We were camped on a patch of mown grass beside a shack built for the workers at McMillan's Ferry. Below us was the concrete ramp where vehicles drove onto the steel deck of the ferry and rode across the river to continue on Highway 214, which took them west to Thompkinsville, Kentucky, where, we were told, a new Super Wal-Mart had opened.

It had been a day of strong current and variable weather. The sun seared us until a midafternoon storm blew up the river and soaked us as we held onto the limbs of a tree in an eddy on the outside of a bend. Basho comments:

> A rolling cloud—like
> A dog pissing on the run— (160)

The sun came out and dried our flesh, clothes, and hair. We were like beasts in a field.

I had suffered a small tragedy earlier that day: the river claimed my micro-cassette recorder. I'd had it in the mesh pocket of my life jacket, below my ribs, and because I was having a lot of thoughts that day, I left the zipper open as I paddled. After one stroke, close to the vest, as it were, I heard the splash, a ker-plop, and I knew immediately that my talking machine and my thoughts of the past few days had settled at the bottom of the river. It was as if I'd lost a chunk of my brain. After a round of cursing, I got to the bank, sat down with notebook and pen, and got busy piecing together the past, my mind traveling upriver.

The high water complicated our search for a campsite. We spotted a few flat spots on top of the high bank, but could not find a suitable place to land the canoe out of the strong current at a place where we could unload it. There were no beaches, and most of the banks were not only steep but mushy from the rain. A coyote stared at us from a field above, and we considered joining him there, but by the time we concurred on the decision, the current carried us past the spot, and we hadn't the heart to paddle upstream. By seven o'clock we became concerned. Fog began to rise on the shady side of the river, creeping across as the sun sank. Breezes swept up the chill of the river and huffed it into our faces like the breath of a ghost.

"What is that?" asked Randy, pointing straight ahead.

Fifty yards downriver a long, low structure, shrouded in fog, seemed to block the entire river. *Barge*, was my first thought, and I may have said it aloud, though I knew better than that this far upriver. For the first time that day, I glanced at the map and put my finger on McMillan's Ferry. The tow's engine was inaudible from this distance so that its passage seemed as ghostly as the frigid breezes. In five minutes, we paddled to the right bank, where the ferry had landed. The two workers, one in the pilothouse, the other opening the gate for cars, gave us a look, and then returned our waves. We asked the gate tender if it would be all right to camp near the ferry landing. He said that it would, but the only flat spot was a gravel area filled with clumps of high weeds and deep rain puddles.

We asked him if he knew of a good place to camp downriver. He did not. Eagle-eyed Randy pointed at the ferry landing on the other side of the river, fifty yards wide here, where a small shack squatted on a knob of grass. "Could we camp over there?" he asked the gatekeeper.

He said that we could and encouraged us to use the phone and the bathroom inside the shack. We paddled hard across the river, aiming upstream so that we wouldn't be swept below the landing. Going straight across the river with the current passing swiftly across the bow gave me vertigo, so I focused on the shack and dug deep against the current. There was just enough room to set up our tents in the grassy area beside the shack. When people pulled up to wait for the ferry, they glanced to their right and were startled to see us camping there on state property, on the river side of the shack.

One man, who was dropped off by two others, stood and glared at us before getting into his pickup. The gatekeeper, about halfway across the river on the ferry, shouted, "Don't pay any attention to that old man!" We tried not to, but it looked as if he were muttering curses at us and would shoot us like snakes if he had a gun. Later, the gatekeeper told us that the old man, when sober, would give you the shirt off his back, but drunk you couldn't tell what he would say or do. He might come up here and tell you he owned this land and to get the hell off, said the gatekeeper, a stout man who talked to us with a soft voice, his words clearly enunciated, accent rounded off and slight.

The ferry worker who had been piloting the towboat walked up the hill and said we might consider pulling our canoe farther up the ramp, closer to where we were camped.

I asked why.

"Somebody might shoot a hole in it," he said, his eyebrows raised under the bill of his cap.

"You really think we should move it?" I asked, weary from the long day.

"Naw," he said, tugging at his cap bill. "They probably so drunk, they'd miss."

The workers didn't get a chance to chat long. In five minutes a family in an old pickup truck waited to be loaded onto the ferry. While the ferrymen boarded and opened the gate, the driver considered our boat and campsite, smiled, and said, "God be with you." He had the gaunt look of an Okie on his way to California, but the truck's engine purred smoothly in spite of its age and battered body.

Randy prepared our supper from vacuum-sealed bags of dehydrated meat, rice, and vegetables that his mother had sent, and I sat in the door of my tent taking notes, facing away from the ferry landing road, toward the creek below us. That's when I heard the bluegrass music, so clear and amplified that it sounded like a band playing. Instead of looking, I tried to imagine who would be playing such music, at this place. I figured out that it wasn't a band but a stereo and pictured a rusty old flatbed truck, the easy stereotype.

Somebody turned down the music. "Good sound system," said Randy to that somebody.

I stood. Randy was talking to a motorcyclist, who wore jeans, a blue tank top, and a baseball cap. "Thanks," he said, and then turned to talk to a family that pulled up in a car beside him.

He turned back to Randy. "You want a Pepsi?" He reached into the compartment behind his leg and held up a beer, dripping with cold water.

Randy said we had plenty of Pepsi. The guy drained the beer in one long gulp and said, "Ahhh . . . first of the day." He tossed the empty into the back floorboard of the family's car, where a couple of kids were sitting.

"Mommy," said one of the kids, "I want a Pepsi."

The motorcyclist told us he was the one who towed the ferryboat from Louisville, Kentucky, where it was built. When the ferry was ready, he sputtered down the ramp, parked his bike, and started playing air banjo.

When they came back to our side of the river, the workers returned to talk about the ferry operation and their jobs. They were working the afternoon shift, from three to eleven. After eleven, said the gatekeeper, Terry, traffic would slow down and we could get some sleep. The other guy, Leon, smoked and spit and talked with suspenseful pauses between thoughts. Under the bill of his cap, his eyes squinted with amusement, as if the world were a passing spectacle of jokes. Leon had his pilot's license from the Coast Guard. Terry, without a license, could pilot the towboat but only if Leon was present.

"What was the strangest thing you've seen on the river?" asked Randy.

Both men were silent for half a minute, their eyes focused on the concrete ramp at their feet. We stood on the grassy hillock five feet above them, forking chicken and rice from plastic bags.

"Last Friday night," said Terry softly, "a woman pulled up her blouse and showed me her titties."

"How did they look?" asked Randy.

Terry waited a beat to recollect. "Well used," he said without smiling.

That seemed to open the floodgate through which the stories flowed. After eating, we rode back and forth on the deck of the ferry. Leon let Terry pilot the boat because he was the one who loved telling tales the most.

They ran down the list of bad behavior on the ferry boat. Drunken ferry passengers seemed always on the verge of falling into the river. Some, prompted by the sound of the rushing water, acted upon the urge to urinate, women included, some letting it flow right through the ferry's grated floor. Others, like the hippie girl in the 1970s, got the notion to jump off the ferry and swim beside her car.

"She pulled her dress over her head, jumped over the side and swam on across," said Leon. "When she came up out of the water on the other side, she looked over at the gatekeeper and said, 'Pretty day, isn't it, Mr. Davis?'"

"It *sure* is, ma'am," said Old Davis.

On another occasion, Leon said he noticed that a boy who was riding shotgun next to his girlfriend was wriggling in his seat. "He stripped down to his shorts," said Leon, "jumped into the johnboat on the side of the ferry, then hopped into the river." Leon said he put the engine in neutral when he couldn't find the boy in the water, but when he saw him at a safe distance behind the boat, he gunned the motor and pushed him a good distance downstream. "I saw him get out way down the bank," said Leon, laughing, "and he had to wade through the briars to get back to the ramp. He had these little flip-flops on and there were scratches all over his feet. Said he wouldn't do that again."

Taking the exam for his pilot's license in Nashville, Leon could not resist playing the fool. After Leon turned in his test, the Coast Guard official said he wanted to ask one more question, just out of curiosity. He wanted to know what Leon would do if a man fell overboard off his ferry.

"Now, I knew the correct answer according to Coast Guard regulations," said Leon, "but I looked at him a minute and said, 'It being Monroe County, depends on who it was fell in the water.' He made me tell it to the receptionist. Her name was Delma Dunphy. I'll never forget that name."

Riding back and forth on the ferry, we leaned against the railing next to the little cabin that was furnished with two cots. Randy said, "I like your office," and Leon grinned, then got serious. He said that the ferry was the main tourist attraction in Monroe County, but that the state was threatening to close it down and build a bridge because it was so expensive to operate and the population of the area was increasing to the point where the ferry couldn't handle all of the traffic.

(Talking to local farmer Johnny Brewington the next summer, I found that not all residents of Monroe County are so fond of the ferry, particularly when they're in a hurry.)

Also known as the Cumberland Ferry, this was one of two operating ferries in Kentucky, the other on the Kentucky River. The state bought it from Cleo Finley in 1968. According to the Monroe County Chamber of Commerce, this ferry is "the only means of crossing the river for thirty miles" and makes "several hundred trips each day."

"I got another story where I scared him," said Leon, nodding at Terry, who was solemnly piloting the tug, not laughing at Leon's stories, which he had probably heard a thousand times. Leon prefaced the story by saying that folks in a nearby restaurant asked him to tell this one over and over. Terry looked away, concentrating on the river.

Leon had helped his mother-in-law in her garden on a hot day, and then had to come in to work that night on no sleep. It was a slow night at the ferry landing, so he and Terry were able to nap on the cots in the little cabin. "You know how when you're real tired, you'll have nightmares? Well, I dreamed this rabid dog was after me and I was running across a field with no trees to climb. After a little bit, I got so tired I decided to just let the dog have me. So I stomped my foot on the floor of the cabin there and yelled, 'Get outta here' at the dog in my dream. Terry jumped up out of a dead sleep and busted down the door getting out of the there."

The ferry ran back and forth without much pause, and the ferry operators not only knew most of the passengers but also where they'd been and what they'd been doing. Nodding at a pickup cab crammed full with three big men, Leon said they were just getting back from fishing at the "rental pond."

Leon found humor in what others considered a crisis. Standing on the bank one foggy night waiting for a shift change, Leon said he heard the motor quit on the crossing ferry, and the pilot, known for being high strung, snapped to his coworker, "Get your shit together, Stanley. We've had it."

For others, drifting downriver out of control was no reason for panic. One man, known for his nervousness, was returning from the grocery with his wife when the towboat motor died, and they were at the mercy of the river. The wife was reading the paper and hadn't noticed. He stared at her for a few moments to see if she'd look up and see what a fix they were in. Finally, he could not resist: "Have you noticed that we're drifting downriver?"

She put down the paper and said, "You reckon that ice cream will melt?"

While Leon took over the pilothouse for a trip, Terry quietly told us about his life. Growing up, he said, he never spent much time on the main river, mainly on nearby creeks. Now he had a cabin on the river, with a pond. Said he used to grow corn and tobacco but since working on the ferry he now just "runs feeder cows."

Turns out that Leon and Terry knew Bob, the raft/jet ski renter at Traces on the Cumberland. Terry said, "Oh yeah, that's the guy from Virginia." They knew about his collision with the axe handle at the Sawmill and said that one day the repo man came looking for Bob.

When it was time for the next shift to take over, we introduced ourselves to the new guys and turned in. The ferry ran back and forth all night, through a heavy fog. According to historian Harriet Arnow, steamboat pilots would also run all night, rarely tying up to the bank. On foggy nights—just about every night around here—the pilots would estimate their distance from the bank by how long it took their boat wake to hit the shoreline behind them. They could also yell and judge the location of the bank by the echo.

I slept soundly in probably the most public place we would camp the entire trip. The ferry was reassuring in its link to the past, to the days of rivermen and their stories, and the way the ferrymen accepted us without question as people who knew and loved the river made me think that after close to three hundred miles of paddling, we were beginning to earn some respect.

Vic Scoggin told me we wouldn't see any "normal" people until we left Kentucky. The next day, we'd be doing just that, leaving Kentucky. As a native of the Bluegrass State, I would constantly remind Randy, a Tennessean, of Vic's words, and we would grapple with what it meant to be normal, and how the relative normality of the folks we met would either help or hinder us. Perhaps we weren't the best to determine normality: two guys who rode a ferry back and forth across the river half the night and camped a few feet from a busy road.

The bow-headed billboard baby taunted us repeatedly on the drive from Knoxville to the headwaters in Harlan, Kentucky. Photo by Ian Joyce.

Friends Murray Browne and Ian Joyce dropped us off on Martins Fork near Harlan's floodwall, just downstream of the Wal-Mart. Photo by Mack Prichard, Tennessee State naturalist.

Where we launched, on Martins Fork, one of three tributaries that form the Cumberland, the navigable channel was narrow and the water barely deep enough to keep us afloat. Photo by Ian Joyce.

Harlan County resident and children's librarian Richard Haynes, in the canoe behind us, accompanied us on the first day of the trip. In the background are tunnels drilled through Ivy Hill, part of a flood control project to divert waters from Clover Fork.

We passed under this iron railroad bridge early on the first day of the trip, and that night we would camp uncomfortably close to the tracks and the rumbling freight trains.

More than on any other segment of the river, in Harlan County people lived near the banks in small houses and mobile homes.

Typical of the upper Cumberland were mornings that we squinted through the fog to spot fallen trees or rocks to avoid.

The river claimed craft of all sorts, including this pinkish-colored speedboat, no doubt an object of envy in its day, but now just another large obstruction for us to steer around.

On the third night, somewhere downriver of Barbourville, we camped high above the river on a shelf below a pasture. After dinner, we endured our first big thunderstorm.

Some Kentuckians disposed of their cars in the river. This one had inhabited the bank long enough to gather soil and sprout weeds.

John Holbrook, a high school biology teacher, took time out from his fishing to help us portage around a low dam near Four Mile, Kentucky. He saved us at least a half day's work.

Just within the Daniel Boone National Forest, near Redbird, Kentucky, a delegation of cattle visited our campsite after a night of hard rain.

One of our favorite campsites on the trip was a wide beach just a few miles above Cumberland Falls, where the rapids flashed at us all night.

At Cumberland Falls water was running high and amber-colored over the sixty-eight-foot dropoff. The fishermen on the rocks to the lower left were trying to lure large fish with live bait.

An elaborate religious shrine, with offering plate, pulpit, and drawings, made Randy and me, the lone occupants of the campground, uneasy at Sawyer.

Near the boat ramp at Sawyer Campground, a couple in a pickup truck dropped off this granddaddy of a snapping turtle, having rescued him from a road, we guessed.

Kentucky Fish and Wildlife ranger Stuart Bryant was quite concerned about our sanity and safety after we confessed to him, under intense interrogation, that we were paddling the entire river.

On Lake Cumberland, one of the river's cleanest reservoirs, debris tended to congregate on the outside of bends. This was at Waitsboro Campground, where we spotted a maroon bowling ball floating among the driftwood and plastic.

Charley Denney, one of the owners of Conley Bottom Resort and Marina, told us river stories and gave us T-shirts and a good map of Lake Cumberland.

On Charley Denney's recommendation, we camped at Cumberland Point and paddled a few miles to Wolf Creek Dam the next day.

Preparing to leave Kendall Campground below Wolf Creek Dam, we anxiously loaded the canoe in anticipation of the dam's daily power generation, which would cause a rapid rise in the river.

On the morning after the long rain—fifteen hours—we awoke to a muddy, swollen river and a canoe half full of water.

Gar and Brenda Whicker's Traces on the Cumberland boat storage facility featured a sign with nautical mileage to everywhere from Anchorage to London, England.

Terry Tooley, operating the gate, and Leon Crawford, at the helm of the towboat, were our hospitable hosts at McMillan's Ferry in Monroe County, Kentucky.

The weather radio recommended that Jackson Countians seek immediate shelter indoors as a storm approached on Cordell Hull Lake near Gainsboro. Winds gusted to at least sixty miles an hour as we held on in the mud under the canoe.

To draw attention to the Cumberland's environmental concerns, Save the Cumberland founder Vic Scoggin swam the length of the river in 1996, tracking ten miles a day for over two months. Photo by James E. Mims.

Lockmaster Pat Lampkin dropped us fifty-nine feet and opened the lower lock gate of Cordell Hull Dam for us to continue our journey.

Lampkin closed the gates behind us as we paddled toward Carthage, the hometown of Al Gore. Note the Corps of Engineers' Charts open in front of me.

We stumbled upon this furnished cave just in time to escape from a rain that came upriver on upper Old Hickory Lake. Both of our tents fit under the roof of this overhang, where we stayed dry.

At Indian Ladder Bluff on Old Hickory Lake, Randy persuaded me to paddle into this cave. An owl flew out of the cave's mouth as we approached.

Approaching downtown Nashville, Randy took advantage of a strong tailwind to power us downriver using his ground tarp as a sail. He'd lost his maestro sticks—used for extending the area of the sail— a couple of days earlier.

Just before pulling off the river at Bicentennial Park in Nashville, we passed under this newly constructed bridge, where a welder was working.

Tennessee State naturalist Mack Prichard provided us with food, drink, refuge, and river wisdom at his riverside home in Nashville. He leaned against a massive cottonwood after helping us haul our gear from the river to his basement.

Near the mouth of Whites Creek, we made our way out of Nashville, heading toward West Tennessee. Photo by Tennessee State naturalist Mack Prichard.

Near Clarksville, Tennessee, the Ocie Clark passed us with a load of empties, which ride high out of the water and complicate the tow pilot's job on windy days.

The ferry workers at Cumberland City had no idea about McMillans Ferry, upriver in Monroe County, Kentucky. Downriver puff the smokestacks of the Cumberland City Steam Plant.

Atop the Corps of Engineers' 89.1 mile marker, osprey built a nest the size of a bushel basket and complained loudly at our passage below them.

Below the Dover bridge, Rhonda Frattarelli showed off an eight-pound largemouth bass she'd caught earlier that day. Her husband, David, said he was proud of her and welcomed the competition.

From here at Fort Donelson Confederate gunners decimated Admiral Foote's gunboat fleet on Valentine's Day, 1862. A few days later, Confederate General Simon Bolivar Buckner would surrender the fort to General Ulysses S. Grant at the Dover Hotel.

After a short day, we set up camp on Barkley Lake in a swampy clearing where Randy found a copperhead and other precious keepsakes.

On the beach at the Corps of Engineers' Eureka Campground, we removed all of our gear to clear the boat of muck.

Locking through a dam in a small boat typically takes about an hour. At Barkley Dam, where we were interviewed by a Corps of Engineers' media relations man in a push boat, it took a bit longer.

Part of the reception party that awaited us at the boat ramp in Smithland, this group includes my wife, Julie, far right; my sister-in-law, Candi Outland; Randy's mother, Elaine Russell, wearing the shorts; and my mother-in-law, Kay Outland, with the stroller in the rear, which contains Will, Candi's son.

Jasper, who canoed the length of the Tennessee River with me in 1998, rode the honorary final two miles to Mile Zero, at the tip of Cumberland Island. Photo by Julie Trevathan.

CHAPTER 12

NORMAL PEOPLE

After our social success at the ferry, we hoped to visit an Amish riverside community and listen to them tell us stories about their lives. I thought they would be astounded at our arrival from the river to buy vegetables that Terry said they sold. It was my turn to cook that evening, and to soundly defeat Randy's bag of dehydrated chicken and rice, I hoped to prepare a vegetable stew with tomatoes, green beans, squash, corn, maybe some hot peppers, and okra.

Because Terry hadn't visited the Amish by water, he could not give us exact directions, so we scanned the right bank for evidence of farms that looked Amish, though neither of us was sure of what the Amish look consisted. We began to see small wooden platforms built out from the bank, some, though unpainted, elaborately constructed for fishing and diving from. Beyond one of these platforms, a two-story house peeked through heavy brush, its siding a dull gray. From a clothesline stretched across the backyard fluttered garments of all kinds and sizes. A baby bawled. Randy climbed out of the bow and crept up through the weeds toward the house. I stayed in the boat, holding onto the platform against the current. After peeping around for a few minutes, Randy returned to the boat.

"What's wrong?" I whispered.

He shrugged. "I didn't see anybody outside."

Feeling like intruders, we moved on. We continued to scan the banks, hoping for some kind of reception. Whatever these people were doing, they weren't gazing at the river looking for canoeists, even though the platforms and the swinging ropes indicated some use of the river. Cows, horses, pigs, and goats grazed above, but no one appeared to be tending them. Somewhere in the distance a tractor engine belched to life. I have never seen so many signs of industry and productivity with such little noise or activity. Even the animals were quiet. Finally, we floated below a young couple working outside their house, built with the same gray material as the others. On the porch, the husband, wearing suspenders, wide-brimmed hat, black pants, and gray shirt, cranked back and forth on something like a winch, putting his back into the motion. His wife wore a gray dress with a small white cap covering her hair. She looked up and said hello sort of sternly, then went back to her work. We decided not to bother them.

Ever since the success of the film *Witness*, which came out in 1985, Amish culture became a subject of fascination for tourists and counterculturalists. The Amish, whose greatest population is in Lancaster County, Pennsylvania, use limited technology for farming. Known for driving the horse and buggy for transportation, they are noted as skilled craftspeople who make and sell handmade products such as quilts and leather goods. They shun the consumer culture that most Americans cherish and strive to live plainly without finery or excess.

Descended from Swiss and Germans who immigrated to America in the eighteenth century, the Amish live for the good of their communities and conform to the principles of their religion and culture. They strive for self-sufficiency and are reluctant to leave the sanctuary of their slow-paced, quiet communities. Despite our good intentions, we were a threat to that sanctuary, paddling up to their back doors ravenous for fresh vegetables. Ironically, our trip was intended as a vacation from American obsessions with complicated technology, speed, and monetary gain. We certainly weren't making any money on the river, nor were we spending much of it, and our canoe, while remote from the Shawnee dugouts, approximated the simplicity and quaintness of a horse and buggy among automobile traffic. We didn't need gas or oil for our mode of transport. Fuel us with a cheeseburger and a few cans of beer every now and then, and we were happy.

Soon after the Amish sighting, we found our own sanctuary: McFarland Creek, a shaded tributary of turquoise water that stained the brown Cumberland. The farther up the creek we paddled, the clearer the water became. The gravel bottom, seven feet below us, looked like we could reach out and touch it. We had lunch on a gravel bar in the deep, quiet shade, away from the

Cumberland's steady push. We could have paddled farther up the creek, but three hundred yards ahead was a bridge, which meant a road, the end of the creek's silent stretch.

Folklorist William Lynwood Montell's book *Don't Go Up Kettle Creek* explores the culture of the Upper Cumberland through oral history. The book takes its title from an incident involving a steamboat pilot coming up the river at Celina, Tennessee, where the Obey River flows into the Cumberland. The pilot, John Stone, navigating at night near the bank, as he had been instructed by the senior pilot, John Claunch, turned the bend above Celina and was alarmed to see that the bank had closed in dramatically on both sides. Claunch, who was a light sleeper, awoke and immediately discerned the problem. He ordered Stone to stop and back up immediately. Having had his headlights "cut short," Stone had turned up the narrow Obey River going full speed ahead.

"Now don't go up Kettle Creek," he ribbed Stone, referring to the next tributary on the upriver right.

That's exactly what we did, just after crossing the Tennessee state line. We were sure it was Kettle Creek because, unlike Claunch and Stone, piloting in the early twentieth century, we benefited from a brown Corps of Engineers sign that announced the name of the creek and the mile marker—384—which meant we'd paddled 312 miles. Kettle Creek's cool silence magnified a waterfall's slow trickle across a wide shelf of dark rocks.

The character of the Cumberland changed after our descent into Tennessee. Past the mouth of the Obey, in Celina, middle-class homes had shaded lawns that sloped down to the riverbank. These were not vacation homes or fishing shacks, but solid brick houses built to last, empty now during the day because their occupants were working. To our sore backs, the closely cropped lawns looked like campsites in heaven. Willow and walnut and catalpa trees crowded the banks. The catalpas grew platter-sized, heart-shaped leaves, their clusters of white blooms big as dinner rolls. Randy, the bird enthusiast, scanned the skies for herons, egrets, geese, ducks, songbirds, and buzzards. Near Celina, a turkey flew low across the river, pumping its wings with great effort, it seemed, to clear the water. We'd never seen a turkey fly such a sustained distance.

A couple of days later, we would see our first beaver, other than the dead one Randy had spotted at an overlook below Cumberland Falls, where cigarette butts were scattered around its corpse. This one, apparently a nonsmoker, was very much alive, lazing about in a pile of floating driftwood next to a golf course at Gainsboro. Although we paddled up to within a few feet of him, he exhibited no fear or shyness. While I ruddered back and forth to keep us in place and Randy took photos, the beaver swam, floated on his back, schlepped over logs, and snorted softly, showing off the fine claws of his forepaws and the big black tail he used as a rudder, once a culinary delicacy for fur trappers. A few times his powerful webbed hind feet surfaced.

From Kentucky's Pennyrile Region, we had now entered what is known as Tennessee's Highland Rim, an elevated plain that forms a sort of horseshoe around the Central Basin of Tennessee, an oval-shaped depression with Nashville at its center. We were still in the shadow of the Cumberland Plateau as the river, for now, paralleled the ridge's northeast-to-southwest course. Passing through Clay and Jackson counties toward Nashville, we were in a subregion of the Highland Rim called the Northeastern Hills, where the Cumberland and its tributaries carved out deep valleys through the limestone, chert, and shale.

Another Seven Sisters Bluff, this one named by Daniel Boone himself, rose high above us in Clay County. As we floated past, we craned our necks to see the top, one thousand feet above us, vertical outcroppings tall as four-story buildings jutting out over the water. I do not know what brought Boone to this place, but I felt his presence above us, surveying the pure water of the river below and the empty land beyond it, his Kentucky rifle cradled in the crook of his arm. God-like from that perspective, Boone also did the divine work of naming, and he must have named a lot of places, considering the territory that he covered on foot, on horseback, and by boat.

When he was nearly eighty, he hiked from Missouri, where he lived, to the Yellowstone country at the headwaters of the Missouri River. There he trapped all winter among mountains vaster and taller than the bluffs that dwarfed us, and wonders such as geysers and grizzly bears. This was a 600-mile trip across rugged, uninhabited land—by an eighty-year-old man afflicted with rheumatism! When he had to, a younger Boone could travel fast, leaving little trace of his passing. When he escaped from the Shawnee at the age of forty-three, he covered 160 miles in four days, what biographer Elliot called "one of the most remarkable journeys of the frontier era" (128). Our little trip, in comparison to Boone's long hunts and flights, was brief and leisurely, though I like to think that we traveled with the same wandering, questing spirit, with the same sense of curiosity about the natural (and unnatural) wonders of the country.

Our first campsite in Tennessee was at Big Bottom Bend, on a shelf of wooded land below a cow pasture, where the cattle had thinned out the weeds in their trots down to the river to drink. One hundred yards across the river was busy Highway 53, which ran from Celina to Gainsboro. The setting sun hit the flat sheer rock wall of the highway cut and turned it gold just before dark.

The site seemed like some kind of raucous meeting place for a multitude of species. All night long a cow moaned, a high-pitched mixture of pain and rage that seemed human in its abject misery. Randy had raccoon nightmares so vivid he woke up at one point and shouted, "Hey! Get outta here!" nearly giving me a heart attack. I didn't sleep enough to create such vivid nightmares. I listened to a sort of punk-rock animal band: whip-poor-wills, coyotes, and tail-plunging beavers backing up the howls of the raging cow, a protégé of Patti Smith ("Because the Night"). The next morning, a cow with a broken horn came to the river for a drink, and I wondered if it were she who had moaned all night.

That day, we planned a gravy run of about eight miles to Roaring River Campground near Gainsboro. Our plan was to set up camp early and stake down for the storms that the robot weatherman predicted for the afternoon. I loved the name Roaring River and anticipated dramatic scenery with showers, picnic tables, electricity, maybe a bathhouse for shelter if the weather got too severe. In spite of my shameful night at the hotel in Burkesville (and Randy's on Gar's lawn), we hadn't camped at an official site since below Wolf Creek Dam, at Kendall, six days earlier.

Around noon we turned into what I insisted was the mouth of the Roaring River. It was not roaring, but there on the Corps of Engineers Navigation Charts, which I'd begun using the day before, was the narrow opening from the main river and the highway bridge crossing it. Randy, who had inherited the *Tennessee Gazetteer*, dared to doubt me, but I overruled him. Not until we'd paddled to the bridge and through the narrow culvert, which had only a few inches of water in it, could I admit that I was wrong. I'd turned up Hurricane Branch. Randy resisted saying he'd told me so.

We turned up the mouth of the Roaring at one o'clock. It, too, did not roar. Perhaps it once did, long ago, before Cordell Hull Dam was built, but for now it was just a big bay with a boat ramp, a swimming area, and few picnic tables. Today was the first day we'd noticed the pooling effect of Cordell Hull, fifty miles downstream. After paddling a half mile across the bay and speculating about the location of the campground, we tied up in the shade next to a picnic table. We walked across the mown grass past the swimming area, where a couple of mothers and their children splashed river water on each other. Up the paved road we walked, past the bathrooms, looking for someone official to tell us how far upriver the campground was. In the gazetteer it looked to be about a mile from the mouth on the left bank, but we'd already paddled a half mile and looking through binoculars saw no sign of it. Up came a man in a golf cart. He wore sunglasses and a hat that said "U.S. Navy" on it.

"We're looking for the campground," I said.

"Don't have camping here," he said.

"It's on our map," I said, showing him the spot, clearly labeled.

The golf cart guard said there might have been a campground upriver a ways, but it had been closed for a long time.

I explained that we were canoeing the length of the Cumberland, that this was our seventeenth day on the river. Couldn't he allow us to camp in the picnic area, right down by the river?

"Can't camp there," he said. "Ranger would come down here and run you off."

"Do you have his phone number?" I asked. "I'd like to call him."

"Wouldn't do any good," he said. "You could go up to Salt Lick Creek. There's camping there."

"That's twenty miles away," I said.

"It's only fourteen by road," he said.

"We're in a canoe," I said slowly, "without a mo-tor."

He mentioned another campground—*upriver*—near Celina, on the Obey.

Trying to control my voice, I told him we wouldn't be going upriver in our canoe. Randy mentioned in a casual tone that it was supposed to storm in a few hours. The golf cart guard said, "Ah, don't believe anything the weatherman tells you. They're always wrong."

In an open boat without a motor, cynicism about weather reports was not a luxury we could afford. Instead of arguing with this expert in the navy cap, I turned around and left him there in his golf cart. Randy and I ate lunch at the picnic table and railed against the official stupidity of disallowing camping in a place where nobody would visit on this, a Tuesday, with big storms rolling in. What were they afraid of? That we would frighten the women and children? That we would somehow taint the picnic area?

We heard the hum of his golf cart coming down the hill toward us. I figured he was making sure that us Visigoths would be on our way soon. While he sat above us, staring at us through his opaque sunglasses, I savagely spurted Easy Cheese onto Wheat Thins and let Randy answer the questions. As if he'd had a delayed response to our journey, now he was down here wanting to know all about it, such as how far we traveled on a typical day, where we'd come from, etc. In the true spirit of a flunky bureaucrat in the age of Homeland Security, he wanted to know what we did for a living, incredulous that we could take a long trip like this without sustaining ourselves as righteous American consumers.

"I teach school," I said, "and he's a freelance photographer."

Despite the curtness of our answers, he was still up to dispensing advice. "There's a dam downriver and other campgrounds," he told us with great authority.

I told him that we had planned on Roaring River as a destination for many days, that we had nowhere else to go today. I was hoping that guilt might persuade him to bend the stupid rules.

"If I were you," he said, "I'd paddle on up the Roaring and camp where that other site used to be."

We'd already decided against paddling upriver; we'd be just as likely to find a decent primitive site on the Cumberland. As we paddled away from Roaring River and toward the gathering clouds, I apologized to Randy for carrying along a gazetteer that was seven years out of date. Randy, as was his habit, laughed it off.

●

Three hours later we were auditioning for a Weather Channel storm video. Randy and I crouched under the canoe, one end of which rested on the ground, the other propped on a tree limb. While Randy videotaped, I held onto the thwart (wooden crosspiece) of the canoe as sixty-mile-an-hour winds tore through the narrow band of trees and threatened to sweep up the boat and carry it into the next county. About forty-five minutes before this, we had pulled off at a little gap in the solid wall of brush along the river, cringing from the dark clouds gathered above us for the storm that the weatherman had accurately predicted. Into this snaky little cove we paddled the boat, brush surrounding us on all sides, small trees closing in above. A small passage, a critter trail, led to a cut-over cornfield, an adequate place, we thought, to ride out an ordinary thunderstorm. We unloaded our gear, ducking under low vines and tearing through briars for the carry from canoe to campsite. As soon as we got our tents set up and pegged down, I turned on the weather radio. Immediately we were greeted with the intermittent buzzer alarm that announced the approach of severe weather. Our friend the robot weatherman warned the people of Jackson County "to take immediate shelter," that a severe thunderstorm with hail and "lethal lightning" was coming our way—*in fifteen minutes.*

Randy didn't think it a good idea to hunker down in the tents, in the open, as we had in earlier storms. I think the "lethal lightning" part concerned him the most. While the wind began to pick up and sprinkles peppered us, we threw all of our gear inside our tents to weigh them down, and then tore our way through the vines and briars to the canoe, which we emptied and upended against the tree. The worst part of the storm lasted about ten minutes, but while it lasted, we got a taste of what it felt like to be outdoors at a time when most were in their basements or bathtubs. It turned out, though, that where we pulled off was strategically placed. The line of trees and brush where we squatted acted as a buffer against the winds that came from the other side of the river (northwest). If it had come from the direction of the cornfield, we might have had to harvest our tents from the trees, or worse, we might have been flying across the river with the canoe on our backs. In any case, it was a storm to remember, made worse by the fact that we were unprepared for its suddenness. We wondered if the golf cart guard worried about us.

After the winds slackened, we got into our tents to wait out the rain that continued in the wake of the front. This, I hoped, would be the worst weather of the trip and the golf cart guard the last of the inhospitable rule enforcers.

CHAPTER 13

"DIE, REFRIGERATOR FISH!"

Despite the wild storm and the vocal wildlife, we were entering the fringes of civilization as we invaded Tennessee and followed the river southwest toward Nashville. Airplanes soared overhead, cars zoomed by with greater frequency, and barge terminals protruded from the banks. After Lake Cumberland and now Cordell Hull Lake, we were beginning to discern differences in lake and river culture. The closer we got to a dam, the more people we saw on the water and on the banks. With people came dwellings, roads, and development. As development increased, so did the prosperity (or credit) of those using the river: the fishermen and skiers had finer boats, the campers larger, newer RVs. Barges loomed in our near future, their commerce indicating an active economy. As the river turned to reservoir, we tried to paddle hard enough to hit a Corps of Engineers campsite every day. We might be rewarded with showers, picnic tables, fire pits, electricity, and people with whom to socialize, or we might paddle a long way to a Corps site and be bitterly disappointed, as we would find out more than once on Cordell Hull and Old Hickory lakes.

Exactly where the river became a lake was debatable. The Corps of Engineers charts do not bother with such trivia; the *Tennessee Gazetteer* changes the designation "Cumberland River" to "Cordell Hull Lake" at McClure Bend, only twenty miles upriver from the dam. The Corps brochure on Cordell Hull Dam says it impounds a seventy-two-mile-long reservoir. Since the dam is at Mile 313, that would put the beginning of the reservoir at Mile 385, right near the mouth of Kettle Creek, a few miles upriver of Celina. For me, the river ended near Seven Sisters Bluff, where the current no longer pulled at the twigs and leaves of low hanging tree limbs.

We paddled away from our storm haven—the cornfield—and planned a short day to get to the Corps' Salt Lick Creek Campground by early afternoon. Here, Vic Scoggin, he who swam the Cumberland, would meet us. Salt Lick was a welcome sight, vacant campsites lined along the water's edge, a grassy shoreline that sloped right down to the waterline, making it easy to land and unload. We stopped at the first site and set up our tents on the shaded white gravel. We walked a mile to pay the campsite manager. As we strolled back leisurely, discussing how we would spend the rest of the day, a man at an RV (like everybody but us) asked us if we'd heard a weather report lately.

Why no, I said.

"A storm with sixty-mile-an-hour winds is due here in five minutes."

Without taking time to bemoan our luck, we broke into a run. As if on cue, the sky darkened, the wind ruffled the surface of the river and the treetops roared and swayed. We ran past a campsite where an obese old man was gruffly ordering three young boys to move two full-sized refrigerators under the canopy that extended from his RV. *Two full-sized refrigerators. For a camping trip. Maybe they stayed there all summer*, I thought, as the first fat drops splatted like bombs on the pavement. We threw everything into our tents, made sure the stakes were driven into the gravel as far as possible, then sprinted to the bathhouse just as the rain started in earnest. This storm threw down heavy rain and pebbles of hail. It rocked the bathhouse with thunder and lightning, but the wind, we judged, did not reach the velocity of the evening before, though that perception might have had something to do with the fact that we were waiting it out under a sturdy structure of concrete and wood and not squatting in the mud under a canoe.

Rather than sulk and complain about stormy weather, as is our tendency these days, the Shawnee viewed thunder and lightning with respect and wonder. Thunderstorms, they believed, were caused by cosmic battles between thunderbirds and giant snakes. The rumbling we heard was the beating of the giant birds' wings, the lightning the flashing of its eyes. Thunderbirds, which were believed to have human faces, guard the gates of heaven.

Oblivious to cosmic battles in the sky and basic common sense, I raised the cell phone to my ear to call Julie. Randy, glancing at the sky, suggested I might want to wait for that call. After an hour, the rain stopped and the thunderbirds rested, the gates of heaven secure from evil giant snakes.

Next to our site were two medium-sized RVs, home for two families camping together for a week. The men had a bass boat and a ski boat, the kids had their bicycles, and the wives tended their makeshift kitchens under plastic awnings.

"It still beats working," one of the men said as we commented on the frequent rains.

Both had full beards and nearly identical potbellies. They offered the use of their kids' bicycles to us as we set off for another mile-long trek to the campsite Laundromat. We considered it, but politely refused.

I had talked to Vic Scoggin on the phone and emailed him many times, but had never met him in person. The only image I had of him was a photo on his Web site from 1996. He was in water up to his chest, wearing a dry suit and tinted swim goggles pushed up on his head. He had a mustache and was smiling. His face had a kind of fleshy innocence about it. When we met him at the camp manager's station, and he descended from his vehicle to shake hands, I was a little taken aback. Not that he was a particularly big person, but he towered over Randy and me, both on the short side, and he had a presence about him, underlying his low-key friendliness, that suggested he was a person with whom you did not want to trifle. He had his hair cut in a military style, shaved on the sides, with a narrow strip of black hair covering the top of his head. There was an intricate network of scars across Vic's scalp, some four or five inches long. He wore a green camouflage long-sleeved T-shirt, shorts, and heavy black boots. Though his arms were thick and muscular, something bad had happened to his right hand and wrist. I guessed that he had been burned.

I don't know why I was so surprised about Vic's commanding appearance: this, after all, was a man who swam ten miles a day for over two months. I was beginning to learn on the river not to judge by appearances, and to be frightened of Vic at this point, as he invited us into his sports utility vehicle and asked us where we needed to go, would have been foolish. First, we had to go back to the campsite, because another big blow had kicked up, and the rain was slanting sideways from the river. When we got to camp, the potbellied men told us they had held down our tents and supplies so that they did not blow away. They had also unplugged my phone, which was charging at the outdoor outlet, and put it where it wouldn't get wet.

Vic drove us fifteen miles to the nearest store to buy propane and junk food, though he asked that we not fill up on chips. Then we pulled up to a tropical-themed bar in a place called Hogtown, where we bought beer to go and Randy videotaped me with no shirt, no shoes, no belt, and a six-pack of Corona under my arm. The women working the counter were greatly amused by this, and Randy aimed the camera at them and asked a few questions about Hogtown, to which they giggled and snorted and muttered profanities in a haze of cigarette smoke.

Back at the campsite, where it continued to drizzle, Vic removed from the back of his truck a twenty-gallon propane tank and an outdoor stove bigger than I've seen in some homes. From the roof rack, he pulled down a large plastic bag of raw chicken. He put it up there when he left Nashville, he said, so it would thaw. He started flouring up and frying the chicken. He had salad. Fried potatoes and onions. For breakfast, there would be deer sausage, eggs, and pancakes. He brought us a baggie of fresh cherries and a couple of apples to prevent scurvy, the malady that afflicted sailors on long voyages across the ocean.

I told Vic I hadn't expected him to feed us. It was the least he could do, he said, calling us "river brothers." He said he knew what it was like to travel long distance on a river, where good food was hard to come by. As if good fortune were pouring down on us like the rain of the last week, the potbellied guys brought us a large plastic baggie of grilled barbeque chicken and pork. This we put into our cooler.

Vic, who grew up near the river in Cheatham County (downriver from Nashville), said he got the idea to swim the Cumberland in a dream. He had shown his fiancée, Julee, the places on the river that had meant so much to him, where most of the milestones of his life had occurred, and he began to see the river through her eyes, realizing how polluted it had become. He wondered what he could do to help the river. Then he had the dream. He called Julee and told her his idea. She didn't seem so concerned at first, until Vic figured out she thought he was merely going to swim *across* the river, not down its entire length.

Vic's swim had a goal: to make people aware of the river's pollution. Swimming, he would see it up close; he would smell and taste it. As Vic's launching date approached, he began to doubt whether he could actually pull off such a feat, but he had told so many people and gotten so much publicity that he could not back down. His brother, a Navy Seal, told Vic, as he was on his way to Harlan, that such a swim could not be done.

"You'll get hypothermia," he said.

"Why did you wait until now to tell me that?" asked Vic, who had a dry suit which helped with flotation, gloves, a mask, and a hood.

In spite of the suit, he said that he did get cold, that during the first week, he camped in the rain and could not get dry. At one point that week, he considered quitting, but he kept on, ten miles a day for sixty-five days. He swam the rapids below Cumberland Falls. He swam the frigid water below Wolf Creek Dam, so cold it made the bones in my legs ache after wading in it for a minute or two. He swam through Nashville. He survived a confrontation on an island in western Kentucky, where two rowdy drunks threw fish at him and Julee and threatened much worse. Though proud of his accomplishment, Vic said he would never do it again.

"It was not fun," he said.

His video of the river—up-close shots of appliances, eddies full of trash, oil-blotched water—spurred people to action. One group in particular, the Cumberland River Compact, was formed in response to the problems that Vic's swim had revealed. He and Julee wrote the organization's mission statement, which focused on cleaning up the river without compromising to other interests. Since then, they had had a falling out with the Compact, which had changed the original mission statement and become more moderate, focusing on education more than confrontation.

Though he supported the Cumberland Compact approach, Vic was more inclined to confrontation. He preferred action to meetings and talk. For example, he had exposed the pollution of the river by his own employer, Ford Glass, and managed to keep his job. He said he was ready to embark on another trip down the river, this time by boat, to confront those who were trashing it. He liked being a lone ranger in his crusade because, he said, he doesn't want someone telling him what to say or do.

"This is what I call an environmental meeting," said Vic, as we sat at the picnic table and watched the day fade on the water. While I washed dishes, Vic told Randy about the motorcycle accident in which he nearly lost his hand and about his decision to stop drinking a few years back. He was on his second alcohol-free beer.

I dug my little lantern out of the bottom of a dry bag and set it on the picnic table, the first time on the trip I felt civilized enough to illuminate a campsite. Next door, the kids were diving down a slope full of mud and water that one of their fathers had created with a water hose. I didn't know how the campground manager would feel about this, but I liked seeing the kids squealing and wrestling in the mud instead of playing a video game or whining about wanting to go to Wal-Mart. Before their wives returned, the men loaded the kids into the back of their monster truck to "hose them off" at the bathhouse. We heard no more kid noise after that: by design, one father said, we let them wear themselves out in the mud. The other father came over to our site with a lantern.

"I could fart on a match and get more light than that," he said, referring to my lantern, which I'd spent an hour finding and illuminating.

He hung his on the site's iron hook and cranked it so high that it seemed we were onstage sitting in a spotlight. Nothing else beyond our campsite was visible; all was oblivion but our circle of blinding light. Though I wanted to take the thing back over to him, I thought it best to acknowledge his good intentions and turn it down so we could see that we were camped beside a river.

Vic's breakfast swelled our stomachs before we embarked on the twenty-one miles from Salt Lick to the Corps' Defeated Creek Campground. We paddled into a strong breeze under a hot sun, exerting much effort in water that widened and slackened. Going without a shirt or hat that day, I soaked in too much sun and got slightly delirious. I remember paddling backward for a while, then standing up in the boat or doing other paddling experiments to see if Randy would turn around and notice that I'd loosened up in my monitoring of proper paddling technique. Upon sighting the dreaded refrigerator fish in its natural habitat, on the outside of a bend, we attacked. "Die refrigerator fish!" I said, jabbing it with my paddle. It did not react. The sun glinted off its silver door handles, its metal still white and unrusted.

Weak with delirium and sunburn by the time we reached Defeated Creek, we already knew that we would likely be defeated in our attempt to camp there. Julie had called ahead to reserve a site for us and found that the campground was booked the entire weekend for a bluegrass festival. Randy and I, imagining some kind of Woodstock scene, theorized that we might be able to share a campsite with some hip campers who might already be set up. We envisioned long-haired boys and girls in their twenties, kayaks propped against the trees, hiking boots and paperback guidebooks strewn around the site. They would let us camp for free just to hear us recount our battles with thunderstorms, refrigerator fish, and golf cart security guards.

The first bad sign was the abundance of jet skiers in the large bay that was the mouth of Defeated Creek. They zigged and zagged, as if devouring their own wakes, not venturing out of the bay. Randy, my ambassador on land, hopped out of the bow at the landing and ventured forth to see what he could find. My job was to guard the boat and steady it against the incessant waves created by the motor-powered craft in the bay. I lay back in the shade and dozed. Randy returned with disappointing news. The woman at the cashier's booth told him there were no campsites available, which would not have been a surprise, he said, his voice getting shrill, had he not walked past dozens of empty sites. He estimated that two-thirds of the campground was empty. It was five o'clock on a Friday afternoon, and the concert was to begin the next day. The cashier suggested we try the Defeated Creek Marina, up the creek a ways (and also part of the campground compound). When I asked Randy whether he thought some folks might let us pitch our tents next to theirs, he laughed. There were no tents, only RVs, and practically everyone was over retirement age. Although Randy's parents owned an RV and had retired, he recognized that it was unlikely we'd get to share whatever small patch of grass was left over from the bulk of an RV, its canopies and accessories, and the frequent horde of children and grandchildren swarming these compounds. We just didn't fit in. But we paddled around the bend toward the marina anyway because we were tired, sunburned, and didn't see much potential for camping on the bank.

We passed the swimming area, where no one swam, and started to round the bend that led to the marina. Suddenly the water exploded with a school of bass boats, their star-spangled hulls reared high out of the water, their motors churning at full throttle. The nearest were maybe twenty feet from us, and they were in tight formation, about fifteen of them, the pilots' eyes riveted straight ahead at distant coves full of lurking largemouth. One of the captains swiveled his head at us and angrily shouted, "Go back to the no-wake zone!"

We had arrived in truly alien waters, where people had no clue what we were doing, nor could they have cared less; they were incapable of even conceiving such a preposterous project. I'm not sure exactly what this guy was thinking, with all his high-tech gear and two-hundred-plus-horsepower motor, out to catch a fish with a brain the size of a pea, but I guess he thought we were a couple of campers who had put in at the swimming area for a paddle before dinner. We didn't get the chance to inform him that we'd paddled almost four hundred miles of the river and that we didn't need the likes of him telling us where to go. The combined wakes of his squadron were barely enough for us to justify turning our bow. We just didn't want to get run over, and we certainly didn't want to slow them down in their quest for the elusive and crafty largemouth bass. It was all I could do to suppress a free bird. And this was only the beginning of our trials at Defeated Creek.

We pulled up to the marina, a small one with a modest array of boats, and went inside the store to find out about the campsites the cashier had told us to check on. The woman in the store knew who we were as soon as she saw our canoe because she remembered Julie's phone call. The store woman said we needed to talk to the owner, a blonde woman who was aiming a metal wand at the sidewalk, pressure washing it.

She turned off the rumbling machine at our approach. No one was allowed to camp at the RV hookups near the marina, she said, and she couldn't allow us to camp anywhere on the marina grounds. This information she relayed to us pleasantly, in a friendly voice.

Randy asked, "What about the yard of that big house we passed?"

"That's where I live," said the marina owner, her pleasant voice leveling out, "and we do not allow campers in our yard. There are no bathroom facilities or *anything* there," she said.

So that was it. She feared that we would poop in her yard or pee on the bank, never mind the oil and gas that her marina leaked into the river. Never mind the crap she was flushing from the sidewalk into the river, the cigarettes her clients routinely tossed onto the surface of what they considered a giant ashtray. Never mind that we were members of a species that had evolved to the point that we could walk upright, our knuckles above the ground, to use the campground toilets a half mile away.

Still polite but firm, she pointed out the log cabin–sided restaurant where we could eat, but said she was sorry she had no place for us to pitch a tent. "There's a big bluegrass festival tomorrow," she said with great urgency, "and we have to get ready for it." She cranked up the pressure washer.

We thanked her and turned to walk back to our boat. I don't know what got into me, perhaps the sun, the bass fishermen, or the bathroom facilities remark, but I had to be a smartass.

"Well, Randy," I said, loud enough for her hear over the pressure washer's rumble, "I guess we'll have to lock through the dam tonight."

She shut off the nozzle of the metal wand. "You can't lock through the dam tonight," she said, horrified. "You have to call them twenty-four hours ahead."

We knew this and had done so. We nodded, smiled, and kept walking.

From the marina's machines we got a couple of Cokes and sat on the picnic tables before beginning our search for a campsite on the bank. This was no big deal. We had expected this. We just needed a little rest before we set out again. Before we could even finish our Cokes, the owner charged around the corner, having just hung up her portable phone, and said, "We've found a campsite for you."

We thanked her and headed back to the original cashier whom Randy had talked to hours ago, the one named Ruth, with whom the owner had been talking on the phone. Ruth told us that yes indeed, they had discovered an empty site, but it was off the river a ways. We took a look at it, probably two hundred yards from the nearest place where we could beach the boat. Randy, fed up with the runaround, wanted to move on downriver, but I convinced him to stay. Back at the pay booth, Ruth said, "We found you a campsite on the river!" She pulled out a campground map and showed us its location, on the other side of the peninsula.

We paddled another thirty minutes to this site and threw our gear onto the ground, astounded now, at seven thirty, to be surrounded by a row of empty sites, all of them right beside the river. They would remain empty that night. By now, we were exhausted and puzzled about why Ruth couldn't have told us about this site two hours previous, when we first arrived. Randy and I walked our sunburned selves back over the hill to the marina to buy beer and ice. The marina cashier, with a manner just as friendly as the owner, had this to say as she propped her fuming cigarette on an ashtray and took my money.

"Let me ask you something," she said. "How long have you been planning this trip?"

I thought she was a potential fan, curious about our project, so I launched into a long-winded account of my Tennessee River voyage, about how I'd researched for this trip starting two years ago and recruited Randy as a paddling partner. She stood there spewing smoke, letting me go on and on.

"Well," she said, "the reason I ask is that it seems like you could have planned ahead a lot better." She said her husband had done a long river trip in his nineteen-foot cruiser, and he had to plan every place he was going to stop for gas and where he was going to drop anchor.

I told her we couldn't adhere to such a plan in a canoe, at the mercy of weather and other intangibles. What's more, we couldn't cover enough miles to hit an official campground every night.

"Well, you can't just camp on the bank," she declared.

Randy chimed in. "Oh yes, you can. We've been doing just that."

All she could come up with was this: "Well, a shower now and then is a good thing, guys."

I needed to leave before I said something I might regret, and besides, the beers were soaking through the paper bag, and I did actually want to shower. Randy and I sat on our picnic table and tried to sort it all out. We were glad to have the site, no question, but we wondered why it hadn't been available when we asked the first time, why we had to paddle an extra two miles, walk at least a mile, and practically beg to camp at one of the many vacant sites. Arriving by canoe, not by RV, I guessed we were scaring people. They didn't know where we had come from, and they didn't want us scaring their regular clients, the ones who paid for the hookups. But then, after we mentioned locking through the dam at night and sat at their picnic table drinking Coke, looking forlorn, they found us not one site but two. Had someone suddenly canceled a reservation? We thought not. Whoever had our site reserved might still be arriving the next day, and, we thought, the campground manager was afraid we would refuse to leave.

The more I thought about it, the more the cashier's condescension irritated me. She was right, in a sense. We hadn't planned everything; we had to be flexible because, unlike her husband, we didn't have a motor to power us a hundred miles a day. We also had no desire to know where we were going to be each night. This desire for certainty on a vacation is typical. It was the reason that people booked cruises with meals and activities programmed in by someone else. They didn't want to think, and they didn't want to resolve problems or come to terms with uncertainties, especially when they were spending a lot of money. Our trip was fraught with uncertainties and little puzzles. We were constantly consulting each other about what to do next. And I guess we really weren't on a vacation.

As soon as Randy and I figured out whose turn it was to cook, a boy and a girl in their early teens walked over. Oh boy, I thought, now the RV folks will be giving us advice.

"Is that your canoe?" the boy asked. He wore tight wranglers with his shirttail tucked in, a NASCAR cap, and work boots—the kind for working in, not for show. The girl wore shorts and a T-shirt with no distinguishable sponsor or brand. Both were slim and tall for their age. They had good posture.

I said that it indeed was my canoe.

"Where y'all from?" asked the girl.

I explained that we were from Knoxville but that we'd paddled the canoe from Harlan, Kentucky.

"That's really something," said the boy. "I bet that's fun." He understood immediately and even knew the location of Harlan.

These two reminded me of kids from another generation, like characters on a friendly animal show, such as *My Friend Flicka* or *Lassie*.

When I told them about my other trip and my book, their mouths dropped open. "That's really neat," they kept saying.

I could hardly believe what I was hearing. I had nephews and nieces, and they were smart and polite, but they didn't talk like this, nor did they stand before me and ask questions, then listen intently to my long-winded, rambling answers.

Kyle and Katie, cousins, were joined by another girl, Kayli, also a cousin. I told them about the storms of the last two days, and Kyle said that he and Katie had also been caught outside in the rain while doing chores at their grandfather's farm. On the four-wheeler they had ridden into the barn for shelter.

"I don't do chores," bragged Kayli. "Me and Katie sit inside the house and watch TV at Grandaddy's farm." She was short and stout, with a big voice.

Seeing our preparations to cook dinner, the kids ran back to their RV across the road, where the women were busy preparing a massive meal. Thirty minutes later the three kids came back with hot food: fried chicken, green beans, boiled new potatoes. We protested weakly that we had supper, gesturing at the saucepan, which held some sort of rice concoction I'd thrown together.

"Miss Sue and Nana said they would just throw this away if you don't eat it," announced Kayli in her big voice.

I gave Kyle a copy of my book to look at, and they went back across the road with it.

This was the best fried chicken I have ever eaten, and my Aunt Robbie is the champion of fried chicken. As soon as we'd eaten our fill, they came back with slices of chocolate pie.

Kyle said, "So you camped illegally in one place?" He had seen a photo of Jasper posing in front of the Watts Bar Nuclear Plant cooling towers at a picnic area where we had camped without permission. "And lost your cell phone," he added.

The kid had apparently read five or six pages in the few minutes I'd lent him the book. I would have given it to him, but Randy was reading it.

"I want to know where to buy this book," said Kyle, "and I want to know when the next one comes out."

By then, Miss Sue and Mr. Freddy Scruggs, the grandparents, had come over. "I have to ask you something," said Miss Sue. "Why are you doing this? Just to prove that you can?"

"They're going to make a bunch of money," said Freddy.

The kids took a lantern to the shoreline and fished, while Freddy sat at the picnic table and told me about his life in Macon County. He was in the textile business, once owning four factories that employed 350 workers. He was down to 25 employees now, and, he said, "about out of business." His farm was more of a hobby than anything. Kyle and another grandchild, Ben, showed registered Limousine cattle, and this summer they were raising a crop of tobacco. He wasn't surprised that I found the children unusually well behaved. He said he envied our journey, and if he were younger, might join us.

Freddy and a couple of other locals I asked thought Defeated Creek was named after the defeat of the Indians by white settlers, but the reminiscences of General William Hall, an early settler and Indian fighter, tell a different story. In 1786 five white men, out on a hunting and surveying trip, camped on an island in what would be called Defeated Creek. While playing cards that night, they were ambushed by Cherokee, led by Hanging Maw, the same warrior who had captured Daniel Boone's daughter, Jemima, in 1776. The whites bolted, leaving their horses and surveying instruments, four of the five wounded but all surviving. A year later, when one of the men, John Peyton, sent word to Hanging Maw that he wanted his horses and surveying equipment returned, Hanging Maw said that because Peyton had run away and not put up a fight for his property that he would not return any of it. What's more, Maw had broken the "land-stealer"—Peyton's compass—against a tree.

Despite this incident, Peyton was no coward. In 1779–80 he had accompanied James Robertson overland from East Tennessee to what would become Nashville. His wife, who accompanied Colonel John Donelson's part of the expedition, which traveled down the Tennessee and up the Cumberland with a fleet of flatboats, gave birth to a child during an Indian attack near present-day Chattanooga. She survived but the baby did not.

Though a warrior who resisted white encroachment, Hanging Maw had a soft spot for whites. While he had Boone's daughter captive, biographer John Mack Faragher reports that he was quite taken with her, and that she was not exactly repulsed by the attraction. He was fascinated with Jemima's raven hair, which hung to her knees, and made her let him undo it and put it back up again. He also asked her to dress his hair. Listening to the story many years after the ordeal, one of Jemima's nieces expressed her disgust at this and said she wouldn't have done it. Jemima said yes you would if it would delay their flight. The whites' biggest fear was that the Indians would rape captured females, and Boone descendants emphasized that nothing of the sort was even attempted. Hanging Maw also called Jemima "a pretty squaw" and "real handsome," and a "fine woman" (Faragher 139). Sounding like her father, Jemima said the Indians behaved honorably and she refused to hate them. After hostilities calmed, Hanging Maw became leader of the Cherokees and a friend of the white settlers, prompting Governor William Blount, namesake of my county, to say of him, "If there is a friendly Indian, in the Cherokee Nation, to the United States, it is the Maw, and he is a very great, beloved man."

However Defeated Creek was named, score a victory for the canoeists. We got our campsite and left with stomachs full of free food. We headed for our first dam lockage at Cordell Hull, then five more miles to Carthage, where Julie, my wife, and Lara, Randy's girlfriend, would meet us.

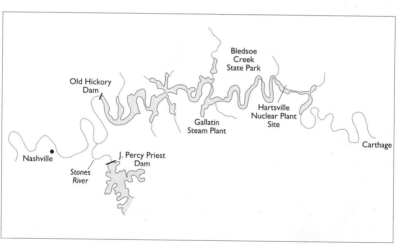

CHAPTER 14

BETWEEN REALMS

BETWEEN REALMS

Carthage to Old Hickory Dam.

To the Olmec, both canoe travel and spirit travel led to communication with one's ancestors and the transformation of the flesh into
spirit and back again. The trader's journey outward from the known
world corresponded to the shaman's journey to the Otherworld, the
land of the dead. Both voyagers mediated between realms, returning
from a Beyond—from death—with valuable goods and information.

CHRIS SHAW
Sacred Monkey River

I had hoped, on this trip, that my father, Ben, would appear to me in a dream
and tell me something practical I could use. When he was alive, he gave me
much advice that I rarely heeded. Before my Tennessee River canoe trip, he
warned me, with eerie accuracy, that I would be "like a cork in the ocean" out
there in my small boat. I thought that on this trip, being outdoors, near a
river, away from the distractions of everyday life, I would have better access
to the spirit world and that taking another ill-advised canoe trip would
prompt an appearance from Ben.

My father's advice to me during his lifetime struck me as dismissive of my
grand plan: soaking up as much "experience" as possible in the form of hanging out with shady characters; self-medicating for the sake of experimenta-
tion, escape, or transcendence; collecting college degrees; roaming the world
and holding a series of odd jobs—house painter, landscaper, window washer—
without any clear purpose other than vague plans to make a living as a writer.
He would never let me forget that I forsook the doctorate program in English for which I'd finished the coursework at the University of Illinois. "When
are you going back to finish that doctorate?" he would ask me every now and
then for fifteen years after I left the program. And when I did things such as
raft Utah's Green River one summer beyond my thirtieth birthday, he asked,
"What are you trying to prove?" I didn't have a good answer. I only knew, as
he did, that the questions he asked irritated me to the core. I didn't care that
he was just trying to protect me from aimlessness and misfortune, much as a
fellow canoeist might warn me about a fallen tree around the bend and suggest a path around it.

Since his death, in 1999, my father continued to advise me in vivid dreams,
and we had argued, as we had while he was living. Often, we'd argue about
the directions to some destination; in the last dream I remember he badgered
me about fixing the broken windshield wiper on the old Saab I was driving,
and I continued to contend, as I did while he was alive, that buying bottles
of a product called Rain-X was just as effective as a working wiper. I regret
now that our disputes were always over trivia, and that we never got to the

heart of the matter—what differed about us as men—and more important, what we held in common.

Boone often dreamed of his dead father and considered Squire's demeanor to portend good or bad fortune. If he quarreled in the dream with his father, which was rare, Boone kept his guard up for catastrophe. In the fall of 1769, on a productive long hunt in the Bluegrass Region, Boone dreamed that his father walked toward him and refused to shake his extended hand, the refusal a sign of disapproval. The next day the Shawnee Captain Will and a war party surprised Boone, confiscated their considerable cache of deerskins, and warned him to stay out of Kentucky (Faragher 63, 79).

Though my dreams on this trip had been mundane and incoherent, that would change in the hotel room at Gordonsville, near Interstate 40, where we stayed on our stopover near Carthage, the hometown of Al Gore. Oddly enough, Julie and I fell asleep watching a rerun of *Saturday Night Live* in which the Gores synchronically appeared and replayed the passionate kiss that had heated the 2000 presidential campaign to a mild simmer. Though Al and Tipper had the good taste to stay out of my dreams, and though my father kept his silence, the river flowed right into the caverns of my unconscious, just as the Tennessee River had in hotel rooms during that trip.

My river dream pattern: I'm somewhere between asleep and awake, and though I'm not sure if my eyes are open or closed, I "see" the hotel room—window, door, ceiling bed—but below me is water, and that water is flowing fast, much as the Cumberland did below Cordell Hull Dam, which Randy and I had locked through that day. I'm focused on the strip of wall between the hotel window and the door as if it were a narrow passage through which we must navigate the canoe.

I had a similar dream the following night. It was as if the river were laying claim to my spirit and imagination as I tried to escape it for a couple of days. In this liminal state—between waking and sleep—there was a strange co-mingling of the two worlds that I inhabited: the mundane setting of the hotel room where my physical self resided, and the river that flowed swift and dark around the bed, the watery world that I had inhabited for over two weeks and four hundred miles, invading my dreams to make sure I didn't forget its grip on my imagination. My father Ben, a habitué of reservoirs, refused to take part in the river dreams, which always featured strong current, flux, and exhilarating fear.

I'm not sure what dream-advice I expected from my father; I had donated the Saab to a charitable institution, and the Buick that my mother sold me, for all its faults, had working windshield wipers. Voyagers always look for enlightenment at milestones, and at this, around the halfway point, I was trying too hard to elicit a vision. The river, like my father, refused to cooperate with my wish for explicit news from the spirit world. It snaked silently through the hotel room, resisting analysis, its muteness an eloquent antidote to the electronic babble that is modern humanity's constant companion.

Though fears of narrow passages emerged in my dreams, the routine of locking through a dam was nothing new to me. Randy, cameras cocked and loaded, sat on the edge of his seat, his first time. Normally boaters pull up to the end of the two-hundred-yard-long concrete guide wall and pull a cord, which triggers a buzzer that alerts the lock operator. This time we didn't have to pull the cord. Pat Lampkin, the lockmaster, was expecting us. I'd called him the day before, as required for Cordell Hull, where traffic is light, and I'd phoned him again when we were within a couple of miles of the dam. When we closed in to a quarter of a mile, the two gates of machined steel, high as a five-story building, began to slowly open from the middle outward. By the time we got to the guide wall, they were fully open. This was the maritime equivalent of the red carpet treatment. The green traffic light above the lock came on, and we were cleared to enter the chamber, which Lampkin had raised to the level of Cordell Hull Reservoir, the lake from which we were descending down to Old Hickory.

On top of the wall above us, Lampkin asked, "if we didn't mind" paddling to the far end of the lock—four hundred feet—and tying off on what is called a mooring bitt, an iron peg that slides up and down with the fluctuating level of water in the lock. As soon as I got the rope around the slimy bitt, on the left side of the lock, I looked for Lampkin above us. Locking through a dam, I always like to maintain some sort of human contact with the people who are in charge of our fate. Lampkin appeared above the right side of the chamber wall, visible from the waist up, bouncing along maybe ten miles an hour. It was a Looney Tunes moment, where you rub your eyes and do a double take. We finally figured out that he was riding a bicycle, which we couldn't see at our angle of vision. Behind us, the upstream gates that we had come through were closed tight, and valves opened up somewhere below, slowly draining the water inside the lock to the level of the river below the dam, what would eventually become Old Hickory Lake. The gates in front of us shed sheets of water as they emerged from the depths. The concrete walls were clammy, scum clinging to the darker recesses, pigeons loitering around the gates, redolent with dead fish that had been trapped in the stagnant waters of the lock. Randy, taking photos, said the dam, from this perspective, was "intimidating." He said, "It makes you feel small."

After about half an hour, Lampkin had lowered us fifty-nine feet. He opened the lower gates, a gaping jaw that revealed our new world, the Cumberland come back to life. I felt as if I had escaped the belly of a great beast. While Randy continued to shoot photos, I paddled out of the lock into the current next to the riprap that always lines the banks below dams, away from the powerhouse turbulence coming from the other end of the structure. We floated with few paddle strokes the five miles to Carthage, past the mouth of the Caney Fork River, arriving at the designated boat ramp about noon, several hours before we expected Julie and Lara.

We hid the boat and gear in the shoreline bushes below the ramp and walked the mile into downtown Carthage with no particular agenda except to kill time and look for vestiges of Gores. I sat on a bench in the court square and read the local paper. In nearby Lebanon an eighteen-year-old boy had shot and killed a twenty-two-year old. It seems that the alleged murderer had just made a rap CD and was selling it on the court square, when somebody challenged him to an impromptu rap contest. It is unclear how this led to a murder, though the victim was the son of a high school wrestling coach and had apparently questioned the budding rapper's talent. Thirty to fifty people were gathered on the square at the time of the shooting.

Randy and I were the only two in the Carthage square that early afternoon. Across the street was the Gore-Lieberman shop, which was connected to a store that sold work clothes such as Red Wing boots, coveralls, and jeans. In the Gore-Lieberman shop were glass cases full of political buttons featuring not only the store's namesake but also Clinton and Bush Jr. Behind the counters stood a life-sized cutout of JFK, Clinton, and the "Dubya," a strange confluence of power in that quiet little town. I wondered what they would say to each other if they suddenly came to life. I've often felt that political leaders, particularly those who work together, should take a long canoe trip to learn about each other's talents and weaknesses. Jimmy Carter is the only president I've seen in a canoe, though Teddy Roosevelt, the first conservationist president, surely paddled. I see Bush in a bass boat, Clinton a cozy houseboat, JFK sailing, of course.

Because we could think of nothing else to do, we decided to eat a late lunch. Main Street Pizza offered an eclectic décor that included surfboards, motorcycle regalia, and a TV that played bluegrass music videos. The owners, Tim and Kathy Henry, were from Long Island, New York, via Florida. They had moved to Carthage to "escape the rat race" and to take advantage of low taxes and a low cost of living. Tim, who took our order and returned to talk, was a slight, energetic man with a well-trimmed red beard. Kathy, a blonde with a big smile, stayed behind the counter and prepared food. Both wore red plastic clogs. Tim had surfed most of the beaches down the Atlantic Coast, and he explained the merits of the surfboards that hung on the wall, one wooden, one plastic. He loved to ride his motorcycle on the back roads around Middle Tennessee and shied away from the organized rallies and busy roads popular with other bikers. He told us about a town named Bugtussle, an hour north of Carthage just over the Kentucky line. A guy had come in one day wearing a black cap with a graphic illustrating the town's name: two wrestling dung beetles. Tim ordered the cap on the spot.

In New York City, Tim worked as an engineer for the Four Seasons Hotel. He was in charge of managing the hotel's physical plant, making sure that, among other things, the heating, cooling, refrigeration, and plumbing were in good working order. He quit, he said, when management decided to transfer him to the Bahamas. Randy and I reacted to his reluctance to move to what many think of as an island paradise, but he shrugged it off. He wanted to talk about Carthage.

"You want to know what this place is like?" he asked. "Watch *Green Acres*."

I expected a litany of complaints about local incompetence and lack of sophistication, but Tim complimented the simplicity of life in Middle Tennessee. He liked being able to trust people, and the spacious countryside relaxed him. He did admit that he and Kathy had started the restaurant because they couldn't find any "good food" in the area. The biggest transition to small-town life for Tim was learning what he called "a different language." He constantly had to translate terms.

"Here, they call a water hose a pipe," he said. "What do you think when somebody says 'tile'? Ceramic stuff you put on a wall, right? Wrong. Here, it's a sewer line."

Randy ordered one slice of New York–style pizza, then another. Kathy prepared me a salad with olives, ham, cheese, cucumbers, tomatoes, and fresh lettuce. We sat in the restaurant, the only clients for a couple of hours, refilling our drinks and listening to Tim. He didn't have much to say about Al Gore Jr., but he said that Al Senior, a former U.S. senator, had style. He walked around town in a straw hat, conversing with everyone and telling "Little Al" stories.

We'd left our canoe and equipment hidden beside the boat ramp for over three hours. Tim, the New Yorker transplant to *Green Acres*, said, with his face squinched up, that it would *probably* be okay. Even booster Tim wasn't ready to concede that the area was free of thieves. After walking back to the river, we carried boat and equipment to the top of the ramp and sat in our canoe seats near the portable toilet waiting for Julie and Lara. On the other side of the ramp's parking lot was an abandoned concrete water tower about fifty feet high. Before going into town, Randy and I had climbed up the rusty steel steps that wound themselves around the tower. The graffiti included swastikas, "KKK," and ungrammatical opinions about nonwhites. Around twilight a car pulled into the parking lot, left when the driver saw us, then returned. A father and son got out of the car and leaned against the trunk, drinking beer. The grandson stayed in the car, occasionally honking the horn and cranking up the radio. We wondered if this black family knew about the graffiti; they were staring directly at the tower. They didn't pay any attention to us, but after they left, and other cars arrived full of occupants clearly in party mode, we decided to move our canoe and gear to a less conspicuous place, on the grass under the trees, several yards away from the parking lot. We put the bright blue, yellow, and green dry bags full of gear behind the canoe. It was not so much that we distrusted Carthagians, just that we didn't want to tempt them, and sitting there with all our stuff and no vehicle, we had nowhere to go if someone decided to harass us. More youngsters arrived to use the portable toilet and sit in their cars drinking at the ramp above the river. They barely glanced our way.

When Julie drove up in her car, Lara following in Randy's truck, Julie yelled out, "Hey Huck and Tom," seeing us sitting in the dry-docked canoe. I think she meant it as a phrase of ridicule, but I was flattered by the allusion. Having read *The Adventures of Huckleberry Finn* repeatedly had probably led to these long river trips. I wanted what Huck found on the long river trip with his sidekick Jim: escape from unresolvable conflicts on land and a peace and simplicity in the outdoors that approached religious ecstasy.

Julie, I think, meant we looked kind of forlorn and simple, though not in a good way. The first thing both women noted was our haven's stench and the overall tawdriness of our situation. While we had commented to each other earlier about the dead fish smell and the attendant flies, we had merely moved upwind of it and enjoyed what we thought of as a nice shady spot in the trees. To the women, we looked like vagrants, which we were. Perhaps their vociferous disgust about the boat ramp was intended to underscore their role as rescuers, as civilizing influences on their men, whose senses had been blunted by their own stench. As we loaded the canoe and put gear into Randy's truck, the party central parking lot filled up, and we basked in our familiar roles as negligent and irresponsible mates, enjoying every minute of good-natured complaining from the women on the ride to the hotel.

The two days we spent off the river rejuvenated our spirits and eased Julie's and Lara's worries. They could see that we were in decent spirits and getting along with each other. Julie and I drove aimlessly through the countryside the next day, she peeling the landscape for antiques, me looking past the antiques at the landscape. After a brief stop at an auction, we headed north to Bugtussle, in search of Tim's cap. We arrived there at almost the same instant that we passed it. I hit the brakes hard, and Jasper stumbled forward from the console where he likes to perch his front paws and stick his head out the sunroof. Brushy started to bark from the floorboard and Julie hissed, white knuckling the dashboard. It was probably the most action that Bugtussle had seen in a while.

We pulled into the empty gravel parking lot in front of the general store. Inside were two Indians, a beautiful Hindu woman behind the counter, and a man, her husband, we assumed, sitting at a table eating from a plateful of food. It was three in the afternoon. Walking down the concrete aisles, we scanned the shelves for a Bugtussle cap. What we noted was a sparse but eccentric array of groceries, hardware, and clothing. Hanging on pegs were price tags for sale. In the hat section were the following models: American flag, camouflage, and reflective hunter orange.

We asked the woman if she had Bugtussle caps.

"We are sold out," she said. "We will have more in ten days."

"Is there another store that might have them?" asked Julie.

"No," she said, laughing softly, her voice lilting.

"Are you from India?" I asked stupidly.

"Yes."

"What city?"

"Bombay. Have you been there?"

I said I hadn't, and wondered why she asked, though I guess it was a reasonable question, seeing how inquisitive I'd been about her origins.

"What brought you to *Bugtussle*?" asked Julie.

The beautiful woman smiled. "I don't *know*," she said, the lilt in her voice one of wonder, as if pondering for the first time the strange fate that led her from a city like Bombay to a remote hamlet in Kentucky named after a conflict between vermin. We waited a few seconds for further explanation, but it was clear that she either didn't have one or didn't want to launch a long, complicated story. How, indeed, did anyone end up where they did? What were the odds of Julie and me visiting this town we'd never heard of until my unlikely canoe trip down a river that no one canoes? Perhaps, like Tim, the Hindu family was tired of crowded city conditions and searching for a quieter place.

Randy and I left land late Sunday morning, pausing at the ramp for a barrage of photos from Julie and Lara. In all the excitement of loading and posing and trying to keep the dogs from rolling in fish guts, I dropped the *Tennessee Gazetteer* into the water, rescuing it before it got soaked beyond use. The women found this amusing. Jasper whined from the bank as we paddled away.

On the transistor radio we tuned to WSM in Nashville, an AM station that played classic country and "today's" country. WSM would accompany us down many miles of the Cumberland, a companion that sometimes irritated us (We heard the 9/11 lament "Have You Forgotten" so many times that we wished we could forget.); sometimes amused us with classics that were deservedly "lost," such as "Common Man" (in a common van); and often inspired us to sing along with the likes of Merle Haggard's "Big City" ("turn me loose and set me free"), Patsy Cline's "Crazy," Johnny Cash's "Folsom Prison Blues," Waylon Jennings's "Amanda," Jon Anderson's "Seminole Wind," Porter Waggoner, Conway Twitty, Bill Monroe, Willie Nelson, Loretta Lynn, Tammy Wynette, Dwight Yoakam, all of the Kenny Rogers ballads, and Dolly Parton's new song, "These Bones," in which she impersonates a cackling old woman. I'd had about enough of the latest wonderboy in western wear, Kenny Chesney, but I tried not to harp on it because Randy's Lara had just paid to see him in concert and he was a near-Knoxville native. Randy loved this song by one of "today's stars" called "Front Porch Looking In," about a guy who lives on a farm, but instead of admiring the panoramic view, twangs about his wife and kids schlepping around inside the house. I cringed every time he referred to a "sippy cup of milk" in the refrain. To torture me, Randy sang this line with particular gusto every time it came on, which was roughly every half hour, it seemed.

Other recently released music seemed uninspired next to the classics: overwrought love songs like the newcomer who kept begging his ex to "stay gooooone" so he could heal his soul ("I don't understand that one," Randy kept saying), and the generational epic that included the line, "Cut the cord/Thank the Lord/That completes the circle of Looove . . . Louuhuhhuhuuvee." Yecch. I regretted Willie Nelson's singing a duet about vigilantism with flag waver Toby Keith, but I couldn't help but sing along with Willie's part and the catchy chorus, "whiskey for my men, beer for my horses." Even Merle Haggard's redneck anthem, "Okie from Muskogee," seemed quaint and harmless on the river (was my neck not red?). I liked the lines about not making a "party out of loving" and not wearing those "Roman sandals" on the streets of Muskogee.

Country music just seemed right for the canoe trip. Until we gathered in WSM's strong signal, Randy had to wear the radio on his head under his hat in order to ground it and get the country stations. Other music stations—rock, R & B, jazz, classical—seemed too urban for an outdoor adventure. Noncountry clashed with the surroundings. If anyone asked, we had country on the radio, we certainly supported our troops, and God Bless America and whoever was running the country. Never mind that we looked like tree huggers in our green canoe, especially with Vic's "Save the Cumberland" decal. We really hadn't thought about terrorism that much, though we ranted for a while about the earnest non sequiturs in the Darryl Ward song, "Have You Forgotten?" then, having memorized it, we sang along to every word. By Nashville, when we'd heard the song fifty or sixty times, we began making up our own lyrics.

The first night away from our women and the hotel put us physically and psychologically back into the river's world, the one that wipes out daytime logic and the solid facts of everyday life. On a low muddy bank near Beasley Bend, a mystery we have not yet solved spooked us. It wasn't the long dark rat snake that paraded through our campsite; nor was it the live animal trap (empty) that we discovered after we set up our tents at this dark and weedy place. This phenomenon occurred after I'd fallen asleep, sweating in the heat on top of my sleeping bag. It was rare for me to fall asleep before Randy. Usually it was I who woke him up to say, "What's that noise?" or "Hey, what are you doing?" This time Randy patted the roof of my tent, and I opened my eyes to his silhouette outlined by a bright white light on the horizon above us. It blinked like a strobe light, and then went off every ten to twenty seconds. There was no sound. I got out of the tent and stood next to Randy, watching.

"Heat lightning," I said.

"There's not a cloud in the sky," said Randy, "and the birds are singing." Plus, he pointed out that the light seemed too near the ground to be lightning. "I thought it might be cop lights," whispered Randy, "but now I don't think so."

"Search lights?" I asked.

We thought about climbing the incline to the field above us, but the vegetation was so thick and it was so dark, we decided not to. We'd be covered with ticks and spider webs if we tried. Instead, we walked down a mown path to a fallen tree and took turns climbing up on its trunk. We told each other, yep, that's heat lightning and walked back down the path. Still, we stood by our tents and watched.

"There's a nuclear plant over there," I said. "I hope it's not blowing up or something."

"I think we would hear explosions," said Randy.

"There's one other possibility," I said.

"What's that?"

"Aliens."

Randy laughed nervously and described a television show that had footage of surgery done on an alien. I'd gotten an AM station a few nights earlier where the subject of a talk show was a group of scientists who had secretly studied aliens in the 1940s. I didn't get all of the details because of poor reception, but the interviewee, a child of one of the scientists, talked with calm conviction about conversations that he had overheard.

In his collection of folk stories about the supernatural, William Lynwood Montell has collected several tales about mysterious lights. There were two called "The Light on the Hill," and one of them was collected from a story-teller in Monroe County, the location of McMillan's Ferry.

After a while, the light was off more than on, and then it finally stopped.

We passed Hartsville Nuclear Plant the next day. Deer lurked in the woods just downriver of the fat cooling towers that dominated the horizon, their white lights blinking warnings to low-flying aircraft. The Hartsville plant was never finished, its construction abandoned in 1982. TVA was using the completed buildings for storage. According to some sources, there's a lot more going on at this plant than TVA wants you to know about. In July 2001, a Hartsville AM radio station, WJKM, had its power knocked out. According to station manager Ted Randall, there was a "flashing blue pulse" and not a cloud in the sky. There were other strange occurrences that day, such as sixty "fried" birds around the radio station. Some believe that the military is secretly testing "electromagnetic weapons" at the abandoned nuclear plant. There's quite a bit of detail about secret weapons and their effects on a few of these Web sites, one of them managed by Clyde Lewis, who was a talk-show host at WJKM. Lewis's site is called "ground zero," the article about the radio station titled, "Hartsvillefreakout." As his shortcut icon Lewis chose a little green alien head. He also reports a farmer who got run off the Hartsville site by a hovering Blackhawk helicopter, and Bigfoot sightings, among other phenomena most would call farfetched. Whether it was heat lightning or electromagnetic weapon testing that we'd seen the night before, Randy and I paddled past the abandoned plant with no apparent ill effects.

CHAPTER 15

OUTLAWS

Under the watchful eyes of Ranger Jane Polanski, we committed a sin of ignorance. Thinking we could go anywhere we liked in a canoe without inflicting significant damage, we blundered into the protected domain of giant carp, and for this we were reprimanded.

After only a few days on Old Hickory, Randy and I were united in our bad attitudes. Not since Harlan County had we seen so much trash, and Old Hickory lacked qualities that redeemed the often spectacular untidiness of the upper river, namely its current and shade. In short, Old Hickory stank. It stank mainly of dead fish, most of them carp, a species as ubiquitous as catfish but without the blue-collar glamour of the whiskered bottom dwellers. Carp are bony habitat hoggers, primordial beasts who can survive turbid, polluted streams that strangle everything else. In spite of their resilience, they often fall victim to Old Hickory's fluctuating water levels, stranding themselves and suffocating when the water drops, their stench filling the air and attracting flies, the kind that bite hard enough to draw blood. Although we'd seen deer on the banks of the river throughout the trip, these deer flies, which breed in low swampy areas, did not decide to attack us until Old Hickory. They seemed particularly attracted to my ankles, feet, and to areas of my back that I could not reach. They had no qualms about biting through my shirt. Have I mentioned ticks? Ticks also liked us; so far I'd pulled ten or twelve from areas that I'd just as soon keep free of trespass. I had chemicals to deter them, but the cure, to me, seemed worse than the pestilence.

At the mouth of Bledsoe Creek, we picked our way through a narrow shortcut past a pile of driftwood and trash as wide as a four-lane highway. In the waters of Old Hickory thus far, we'd seen unmoored buoys, two televisions, a doghouse, and several of the most common riverbound appliance, the refrigerator. I think Randy was growing tired of my fetish for settled campgrounds, though he didn't complain aloud when we started up Bledsoe Creek the estimated three miles to the state park. After the swampy site of two nights previous, where the strobe light haunted us, I was ready for the comfort of a shower, a picnic table, and the normality of bug zappers and screaming children. And I wasn't ashamed to paddle a few miles out of my way to get these things. That wouldn't stop me, of course, from complaining once we reached these havens of civilization.

I wish that I could live up to my own expectations of myself, to be a person of consistent convictions, but like Walt Whitman, I'm full of contradictions. I'm really not a people person, like my mother, a public librarian and state politician who helped start a community theater in Murray, Kentucky, where I grew up. I prefer the society of the woods, the water, and the mountains, but after a while I long for the proximity of humans, to observe their behavior, maybe to interact if I'm in the mood. In short, I like a little humanity mixed in with my nature, much as one likes a little tonic with the gin. Too much tonic, of course, ruins the gin. Small doses of humanity do me just fine. Not until the end of the trip did I realize the trials to which I was submitting Randy, gregarious people person, unaffected lover of birds and of campsites that he discovered himself.

Though we arrived on a Tuesday, all of Bledsoe's waterfront campsites were occupied. The nearest required that we tromp from the water through somebody else's site and across the road. Scouting on land, Randy found one that was fifty yards off the water but had a clear path to it through the woods. So we paddled the canoe farther up the creek to this landing. The water became so shallow that we had to "pole" with our paddles, pushing off the muddy bottom like the keelboatmen of the early nineteenth century. Our poling roused monstrous carp, fat two-foot-long daddies that rustled the weeds with their passing. Lolling about the surface giving us the google eye, they splashed like boorish aquahogs.

From the low snaky shoreline at the end of the path, we carried our gear to the site and left the canoe in the water, thinking it would be fine there. A ranger and a couple of workers were spreading mulch at the playground next to our site. The ranger stopped shoveling when I approached.

"Do you know of a Corps campsite downriver near the dam?" I asked, my gazetteer tucked under my arm, ready to show her.

"Where did you guys come from?" she asked.

"We came by canoe," I said and gave her a brief rundown on our project, expecting a grand welcome.

"You just paddled through a protected area," she said.

"Oh," I said. "Sorry. Is it marked?"

"Yes, it is," she said, pointing at the buoy that we had paddled fifty yards beyond. Though she wasn't rude or overly grim about it, she was terse and looked me in the eye as she confirmed our outlaw status.

"Can we just leave it there until the morning and paddle out from there?"

"If you do, I'll have to issue you a citation."

In order to avoid a ticket and further desecration of the protected area, we would have to carry the canoe and our gear about two hundred yards the next morning so that we could put in outside the area that the buoy marked. As canoeists, we thought that this buoy, like all the others, was intended for motorboats, a no-wake message telling them to slow down and travel at our speed. How could a buoy's message be intended for us?

Ranger Jane softened when I eagerly said we would comply, inwardly dreading not only the extra work but passing on the news to Randy. She said that people inadvertently violated the law quite often, especially paddlers.

"Don't worry about it," she said, when I kept apologizing.

I couldn't help it. Here I was, wearing a river cleanup T-shirt, having just violated a protected area with my plastic canoe and plastic paddle. Ranger Jane, having fulfilled her duty, was now up to small talk. She had lived near Knoxville, and she'd been to the Ijams Nature Center that was listed as a sponsor on my shirt. She told me what she knew about the campsites near Old Hickory Dam.

Randy was pouring water out of the bailer to clean our muddy ground tarp, which would get muddy again once we put it on the ground, where it belonged. I informed him of our status as violators of nature, ironic in light of all our recent bitching about Old Hickory's trash.

"What's being protected up there?" he asked.

"She didn't say. Maybe it's the carp."

"That's a dumb rule," said Randy loudly, his pitch elevated in irritation.

I shushed him. I didn't want to get kicked out, not after we'd exerted so much effort to get here. For a show of goodwill toward Ranger Jane and her directive, I persuaded Randy to help me carry the canoe to the camp site and prominently display it near the road so that she could see we wouldn't try to sneak out in the morning and crowd the carp.

The pendulum syndrome was kicking in, that swing of fate from good fortune to bad that kept us humble and pessimistic. The night before Bledsoe Creek, we had camped in a rockhouse that appeared to us when we needed it most, as a thunderstorm approached up the river. For a couple of miles we had searched in vain for a place to land the canoe, but one side was sheer solid rock, the other side, flat, swampy, and densely vegetated. The banks were so inaccessible that I thought we'd have to let the rain pelt us on the open water in our boat, hanging onto a branch somewhere. We'd paddled that day from the strobe light campsite at Beasley's Bend (Mile 288) to just downstream of Buzzard Island, almost a thirty-mile day. The cliffs on the right side were the beginnings of Seven Mile Bluff, which offered us little more than narrow rock shelves near the water with just enough room to stand on. The thunder grumbled louder as we searched the cliffside for a safe harbor.

We spotted it at the same time: a small opening in the sheer rock face opened up to a cove the size of a racquetball court with a dock two planks wide, perfect for landing a canoe. Sprinkles misted us as we picked our way up a path that weaved between boulders to the overhang that formed the rockhouse, about halfway up the face of the cliff, a five-minute climb fifty feet above the water. The room was about twenty feet long and fifteen feet deep, with a solid dirt floor. Horizontal strata lined the wall and roof, as if the rock layers had been stacked for artistic effect. Near the back wall sat a sturdy handmade wooden table, a wooden bed frame with bare box springs, two cane-bottomed chairs, and a latched chest full of cookware. No houses were visible, though a path led from the rockhouse diagonally across the cliff face to the top. Ordinarily we would avoid a place like this—frequented by someone who claimed squatter's rights if not downright ownership—but under the circumstances, with the thunder booming now and the spaces between the sprinkles diminishing, we decided to make this home for a night. It was my turn to cook, and I'd lucked upon a kitchen in the wilds.

As soon as we got our gear under the overhang and set up camp, the downpour started. Under the roof, we stood there and watched the rain hit the river. After supper, when the storm was over, I climbed up the path to the top of the bluff. There was a small road with no traffic and a farmhouse a quarter mile away. A green sign indicated the name of the road—River's Way—making me think that the land up here, with such a panoramic view of the river below, was on its way to being subdivided and populated with houses that looked alike and cost more than most could afford.

The next morning, starting out on a short twelve-mile run to Bledsoe Creek, we drifted into the current close beside the cliff. It was a quiet, calm morning, the sun insinuating its yellow glow through a light fog. Six-foot cedars leaned out from the cliffside as if poised for a dive, explosions of green against the tan rock. The one-hundred-foot-high bluff was not nearly as dramatic as Boone's Seven Sisters Bluff, but it created a dramatic contrast to the flat landscape on the other side of the river, and as we paddled beneath it, the rock shelves seemed to loom over the water, a commanding presence. Purple and yellow flowers bloomed in the crevices, and spiky green yucca grew on the shelves, interspersed with paler green ferns. The rock itself had created intricate patterns of horizontal outthrusts, crevices that snaked upward in tortuous paths, rocks that were jagged or rounded off, promising a hard but interesting climb to the top, where oaks and hickories towered, their green a lighter shade than the cedars growing out of the rock. Fish broke the surface of the water, shattering the silence of the morning and flashing silver in the gathering glow of the rising sun. I thought about what makes some landscapes more beautiful than others. Contrast and variety are the obvious answers, green against tan, the patterns of the rocks, the brash colors of the wildflowers. But there was more, the moment in time when you witness the landscape, the synchronicity of our unhurried pace, the quiet clarity of a morning after a storm, and the gratefulness we felt at the unlikely shelter of the previous night.

Five miles downstream on the left side of the river, we floated toward an opening in Indian Ladder Bluff. A great horned owl lifted itself from a dead tree above the mouth of the cave, flying over our heads upstream as we entered the shade of the bluff and the coolness of the cave's air blasted in our faces. We paddled into the cool darkness toward the back wall, the terminus not visible until our eyes adjusted themselves. Maneuvering through a tangle of floating logs, we paddled twenty feet to where the cave narrowed and a passageway led sharply to the right. Water drip-dripped from the roof, fifteen feet above us, and our voices echoed in the enclosed chamber. Faintly, from wherever the passageway led, a cascade of water fell. I expected bats to explode out of the opening at any moment. Randy climbed out of the bow to wade in the knee-deep water down the passageway. He stepped up on a shelf above the water and disappeared around a corner. All I could see was the flash of his camera.

"There's a little waterfall back here," he said.

"I heard it," I said. "Now let's get out of here."

●

Across from our site at Bledsoe Creek, two young men had an SUV with a canoe tied on top of it. We walked over and warned them about paddling into the protected area. Brothers, the two had just driven down from Mammoth Cave in Kentucky. They were touring the country before school started. Matt Gilchrist, with shaved head and goatee, was the oldest; his younger brother was fifteen, a high school student in Nashville. We soon found ourselves in the back seat of Matt's Jeep Cherokee on a wild ride to Gallatin to buy beer and other necessities. Matt's first order of business was to find a post office where he could mail a postcard to his girlfriend in Iowa. This involved a couple of U-turns and heavy use of the accelerator and brakes. After a while, I could smell the brakes. The brothers' dog, a black lab, was being slung back and forth in the small compartment behind the seat. The headliner drooped above our heads and shed foam from underneath. Matt's air conditioner wasn't on, probably because it didn't work, and we were all suffering in the heat, but no one wanted out of there as badly as the dog.

Upon finding out that he was in school at the University of Iowa, I asked Matt, on a pure whim, if he happened to be in the graduate writing program there, highly esteemed for well-known graduates such as Flannery O'Connor and John Irving. Indeed he was, he said, and in fact he had graduated from the University of Tennessee, where he had taken courses from one of my teachers, Allen Wier, who taught at the University of Alabama when I was there. We bought steaks, beer, and salad for our dinner, and the brothers bought beer. We were thankful for the ride into town and glad we had survived it. Judging from the condition of his vehicle, I could tell that Matt was well on his way to becoming a dedicated writer.

Bledsoe Creek was an active campground. All night people drove up and down the road, some making more than one trip. Two groups of campers arrived after 10 that night, setting up their camps in the beam of their headlights. Two women set up their campsite in record time—about fifteen minutes—and even had a fire going as if they had snapped their fingers. For us, these chores usually took quite a while, even in broad daylight. Ranger Jane, working horrendous hours, came by to check on late arrivals. I thought she might stop and chat with us, but she said hello to the brothers across the way and snubbed us, the outlaws. The next morning, soon after dawn, we were awakened by a diesel pickup with dual rear wheels cruising down the campsite road to the bathhouse. I couldn't help thinking it ironic that we had broken a law, paddling noiselessly, without emissions, while this clown was free to lawfully spew toxic fumes on a trip that would have taken him five minutes to walk. There appeared to be nothing wrong with his legs.

The closest put-in for the boat was maybe fifteen feet within the protected area, about a one-hundred-yard portage from the campsite. The next place, clearly legal, was another fifty yards up the shoreline. Randy flatly refused to carry the gear and boat any farther than the first put-in. I didn't argue. Hurrying, we put in at the sacred carp area and paddled past the warning buoy, examining it closely. You would have to paddle close enough to reach out and touch the buoy and squint hard in order to read the faint orange lettering. There was a reason that this protected area was so often violated.

Out of Bledsoe Creek we paddled toward the worst scenery of the trip, featuring Gallatin Steam Plant, Cedar Creek Campground, and a small, startled snake. We would regress from casual lawbreakers to pariahs.

CHAPTER 16

A LONG WAY FROM HARLAN

A LONG WAY FROM HARLAN

> People have changed. They've got no character. They've got no morals.
> They won't tell the truth. . . . They're not helping anybody; that help-
> ing business had done gone out.
>
> Ninety-nine-year-old Burkesville resident DR. W. F. OWSLEY
> from Lynwood Montell's *Don't Go Up Kettle Creek*

After coming away victorious at Defeated Creek, we thought we had the
Corps of Engineers reservation system solved. We figured we'd outfoxed the
managers and the authorities who didn't like us because we didn't fit into the
motorized culture of American camping and didn't know where we'd be
weeks in advance. Then we ran up against the camp manager at Cedar Creek
campground, the closest to a villain on a river that seemed amazingly short
of villainy so far.

Our plan was to camp at Cedar Creek, seventeen miles from Bledsoe, so
that we'd have a short paddle the next morning before locking through Old
Hickory Dam. Every couple of paddle strokes, I swatted at deer flies, who
scored multiple hits on my upper back and neck. At Gallatin Steam Plant we
paddled past several fishing boats; rockfish, crappie, bass, and catfish were
abundant in this area, attracted by the plant's discharge of warm water. Near
the plant's water intake lay a field of trash and driftwood so thick and vast

that night herons perched on it as they fed. The carp had gone there to die, and the flies had joined the party. On the iron railings near the intake, a group of buzzards waited their turn at the sea of trash. Power lines anchored on giant silver derricks crossed the river. Hundreds of feet above this spectacle the plant's twin stacks farted smoke into the atmosphere. Here, coal burned to produce steam that turns the turbines, creating electricity to power the steel guitars and neon lights of Music City, downstream. Many of the barges on this part of the river were carrying coal to fuel steam plants such as Gallatin, which had been operated by TVA since 1959.

We headed for a lunch spot on a pine-shady point below the steam plant, the shore lined with riprap. I had begun to perfect what I called parallel parking on the river, coming in at the shoreline and calculating wind, current, distance, and angle of land to get the boat to land sideways against the shore with a soft kiss of plastic against rock. Then Randy and I could each step over the side to the shore without getting our feet wet, curb service on the water. This landing below Gallatin Steam Plant was looking good, and I was feathering my paddle this way and that as we slid toward the riprap. Randy, poised in the bow to step out and moor us, started making this "Oh, oh, oh" sound— not loud, not shrill, nothing alarmed enough to spur me to action. I back-paddled gently, thinking we were headed for a rock but not wanting to ruin the aesthetics of the landing. Finally, Randy got out the word "snake." It lay on the rocks where I was propelling us. Randy managed to get his feet back into the boat, and the snake woke up and slithered away. From then on, before landing, he tapped his paddle around the rocks, as if knocking on Mr. Snake's door. We had lunch on the soft pine needles among the washed-up trash. Ticks fell on us from the pines. We found our first soccer ball of the trip, a harbinger of another shift in river culture.

Near the Highway 109 (Gallatin) Bridge, what appeared to be a ragged run of shantyboats lined the banks. This was Cherokee Boat Dock, near the town of Old Hickory, and it looked so ragtag because many of its slips, made of wood and tin, had been damaged in a recent storm. We stopped and chatted with the owner's son, Chris Cunningham, who, wearing a tool belt and holding a hammer, was perched on a crossbeam above a boat slip. He wore shorts and an old baseball cap that said Skil Saw on it. Vic Scoggin had told us that there was an excellent steakhouse here; Chris confirmed it, saying that he "kept waiting for them to slip up, but they never had." He said that maintaining the boat slips, especially the older wooden ones, was a continual job for him. In the early 1990s, a tornado had hit the dock hard. It came up the river toward the Gallatin Bridge, he said, then it broke up briefly before reassembling itself on the near side of the bridge, a great dark waterspout filling the sky.

"See that boat over there?" he said, pointing at a sixty-foot cabin cruiser. The twister, he said, picked up a boat that size and carried it off.

"Where'd it end up?" I asked.

"Kaboom," said Chris. "Disintegrated."

He looked at the sky and suggested it might be a good idea to ride out the coming storm under the boat slip of one Trippy Nix. "That's right," said Chris. "That's his real name."

We sat in our boat sipping canned Cokes next to Trippy's long-neglected cruiser as a curtain of darkness enveloped the bridge and overtook the boat slips, rain drumming so hard on the tin roof that I could hardly hear WSM at full volume. George Strait was asking me to tell him something bad about Tulsa.

When the rain slackened to a sprinkle, we paddled under the bridge, near Mile 238, where from the hazy distance emerged a fleet of boats such that we hadn't seen the entire trip: canoes! There were five aluminum crafts, noisy but sturdy, each one propelled by two boys of about twelve, campers at the vast Boy Scout compound called Camp Boxwell. Their leader, Jason Flannery, applauded when we told him where we'd come from and where we were going. We applauded him back for creating canoeists tough enough to continue through the light rain. We weren't setting a good example, our life jackets stashed away somewhere.

"They wanted to try to turn you over," he said. "I talked them out of it."

Vic Scoggin said he'd realized his love for the river at this very place, Camp Boxwell, where Cub Scoutmasters taught him woodland skills. One thing I regret about my boyhood is forsaking the Scouts at about twelve, before I really ever learned anything useful other than the fact that I hated wearing a uniform. After failing miserably at the Pinewood Derby—with a car that resembled badly chiseled firewood—I found other interests such as baseball and tennis to occupy my time. The time I spent outdoors was not camping, but fishing or exploring on my paternal grandfather's farm, a flat square of fertile land he'd inherited from his father. Jack had dug two fishing ponds and granted stays of execution to three separate squares of woods that survived his zeal to carve space for tobacco, corn, and soybeans. It was from my laconic, tobacco-chewing grandfather that I learned much about how to behave in the woods, stalking squirrels and rabbits and quail with him and curbing our communication to the occasional grunt or chuckle. Under his supervision I shot a .22 rifle bullet into a squirrel nest high in a hickory tree. To my relief, nothing descended from the nest but a few dry leaves. Instinctually under-standing my reluctance to kill warm-blooded animals—flying or creeping—my grandfather and father never asked me to quail hunt with them.

Downstream from the Boy Scout camp, Cedar Creek was another vast campground of mown green space on a gently sloping hillside. As always, we secured the boat at the shore and walked through the site to the manager's office. Hardly any of the sites were occupied, but almost all of them had a sign that said, "Reserved." Not until we got up to a circular drive, at least a half mile from the water, did we see five sites that were available. Each was tiny and treeless, like a cemetery plot. It would be about like camping in a parking lot. No one was inside the camp manager's booth, but a sign confirmed that the five sites we'd looked at were open. We circled the booth and eyed the mobile home next to it. The car parked outside it had Iowa plates. As if he'd been peeking out the window at us, a fat man opened the door and leaned out.

"What can I do for you?" he asked gruffly, wiping his mouth with the back of his hand.

"We'd like a campsite for the night," I said and started to explain our circumstances, arriving by a boat that we'd left untended a half mile away.

He interrupted. "Look at the numbers on the window. Those numbers on the window is what's available."

"We came by canoe," I said, "do you have anything . . . ?" I started to say "closer to the water," but he cut me off again.

Again he recited the numbers of the campsites on the circular drive. "I've got thirty-three people coming in the morning," he declared with finality.

Randy asked what time they were coming, and he dismissed us with a wave of the hand and shut the door of his trailer.

This was our Defeated Creek. We walked across the vast empty space of the campground and considered what was wrong with the system. There should be no reservations, said Randy. It should all be first come, first served.

"That's right," I said. "I bet half of those people don't show up."

What hurt the most was that the campsites could be reserved in such a way that they sat empty at night, waiting for arrivals in the morning. We could have camped anywhere on one of these sites and left, as was our habit, an hour after daybreak. Those who had "reserved," arriving sometime afterward, would never know. The national reservation system that the Corps uses holds reserved sites "until check-out time the day following your scheduled arrival date." The RV people, with a lot more control over their time of arrival than we had, could call the toll-free reservation number, give their credit card number to an operator somewhere in Texas, and for two days tie up a site that they weren't using. What made it even more difficult for us to take advantage of the system was the fact that the sites had to be reserved two days in advance. It was difficult enough for us to reach a destination that we planned one day ahead, much less two.

We paddled away from the site to a small island that plugged the middle of Cedar Creek's mouth, heavy with pleasure boat traffic. On the island was a clearing about the size of a hotel room littered with what we estimated were five hundred Bud Lite cans, along with large pieces of Styrofoam and an orange-striped road construction barrel hanging from a tree. Goose droppings littered the ground, and to the right, in the bushes, a duck sat on her nest. At the point of the island was a duck blind. It would have made a decent campsite had it not been so thoroughly trashed, apparently by the hunters who used it year after year.

We camped across the river at the edge of a mown field, within sight of a large old house on a hill about a half-mile away. From somewhere came the screams of peacocks. I called Vic to give him an update and to thank him again for the feasts upriver. He said we were camped at a farm that kept exotic animals. How is Randy doing? Vic asked.

Randy, I said, seemed to be doing fine, though now he's wrapping duct tape around an eight-foot-long stick, cutting it off, then re-wrapping. "To tell you the truth, Vic, I'm a bit worried about him."

Vic got angry when I told him about what happened at Bledsoe and Cedar Creeks. "They're just making up a bunch of rules so we can't use the river," he said. "The river should belong to the people. You should be able to camp anywhere on the banks."

By law, Vic said, the Corps owned a strip of the entire shoreline, so technically, we could camp in the yards of the finest houses on Old Hickory, completely within our rights on public land.

Vic said to look for Johnny Cash's house on the right bank the next day, though it would be out of our way, on a far-reaching outside bend away from our route to the dam. One of my biggest regrets is not seeking out the Man In Black while we were on the river; he died the year after our trip. His music, with its pounding rhythms, its downcast characters, and its rural settings, fit the tone of our trip. We never heard Cash's "Big River" on WSM during those weeks, but anything we heard—"Folsom Prison Blues," "Ring of Fire," "I Walk the Line"— carried a deep, soulful resonance that spoke directly to me and relieved the doldrums of paddling monotonous reservoirs. We didn't seek out the Cash house because we wanted to leave Old Hickory as soon as possible, and approaching a dam created an anxiety to arrive early in the day and get the lockage over with.

The peacock campsite didn't turn out so badly. Instead of having to carry our gear a quarter mile to the circular drive campsites at Cedar Creek, we tossed it from the boat to the hard-packed mud and exposed roots of the shoreline. A bright red cardinal tweeted loud and clear from a limb above us in the blaring light of the sunset. After dark, voices carried across the lake from the big houses set back in the trees. For a while we speculated the voices to be the sound of small kids playing, then we thought it was drunken teen-agers, and finally it sounded like a bitter argument between a man and a woman. Probably it was all three, friction among the privileged. Earlier that day, as we passed a monstrous antebellum mansion with a big lush green lawn and a carriage house, Randy commented, "We're a long way from Harlan."

An apt description. The little creek where we started out in Harlan seemed a continent away from this broad lake and its well-kept houses and monstrous marinas. Paddling the river revealed America as a land of the very wealthy, compelled to accumulate land and material, and the very poor, such that we'd seen above the trash pile the first day. The poor and working classes tended to live on the free-flowing sections of the river that could rise and drive them out of their homes, destroy their property, and even kill them. The best of them had developed an intimacy with the river and its history, and respected not only its destructive potential, but also what it offered in sustenance and pleasure. The weakest created trash heaps on the banks where they lived. Here on the reservoir the overall income level had risen. Wealthy and well-off people lived on a river that had been tranquillized, where they could build permanent structures near the water. The richest built houses big as cathedrals, docks as big as houses, lawns like football fields that leached fertilizer into the river. Conscious of appearances, highly visible to the law and to their neighbors, they bagged their garbage and had it hauled to a landfill. Among the reservoir culture, there were also those who loved the Cumberland, who resisted the urge to obliterate the trees on a lot for the sake of a clear view and to live quietly beside the stilled river without adding to its problems.

I'd grown up near the Tennessee River, what we called Kentucky Lake, and spent some of my happiest times on houses built on lots high above the reservoir, similar to the ones we passed now. My parents owned a small lake-house on Cypress Bay, in northwest Tennessee, and my sister owns a larger house in Kentucky, on the main channel facing the Land Between the Lakes. It's not as if I don't recognize the advantages of the lake culture from which I have benefited, growing up fishing and skiing and swimming there. At the same time, witnessing from canoe level the transformation of a river like the Cumberland, which had flowed so freely just weeks earlier in our journey, made me realize that the security, the predictability, and the economic stability of reservoir culture also represented a great loss.

During our short paddle that day, Randy kept taping and untaping a piece of hard black plastic to a stick about the thickness of my wrist and six feet long. This would be the boom for his video camera. When he finally finished, he asked me this: "So why did you choose me for this trip?"

The question took me by surprise, coming, as it did, two-thirds of the way through the trip, but I had a quick answer because I'd thought about it before I'd invited him along.

"I knew you were a tough little bastard, and I knew you had the mental stamina to finish a trip like this." I could have gone on and told him that no one that I could think of would want to go on a trip like this, with a moody, obsessed partner, and endure what he had endured, but I didn't think it appropriate to pile on too many compliments, especially since we had many miles to go.

What I said seemed to satisfy him, though I wondered why he asked me such a question at that point.

Two days ahead of us was the promise of sanctuary and rest at the home of Mack Prichard, the Tennessee State naturalist. Between us and sanctuary: Old Hickory Dam and a little town called Nashville.

CHAPTER 17

WELCOME TO NASHVILLE

WELCOME TO NASHVILLE

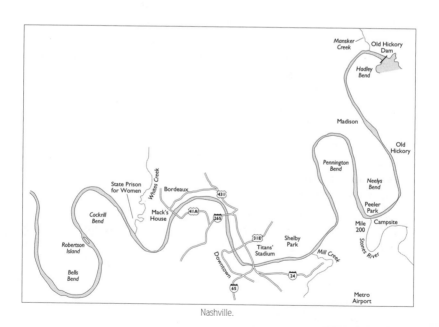

Nashville.

In the frigid winter of 1779–80, while the Revolutionary War raged in the eastern colonies, James Robertson led a group of men overland from East Tennessee through Kentucky to rendezvous with Colonel John Donelson and his fleet of flatboats at French Lick, the area that would become Nashville. Having scouted the land previously, Robertson and his men drove the livestock and built the first cabins, and Donelson brought the women and children later in the boats. On a bluff above the river, the settlers built Fort Nashboro.

The land they settled on was purchased through a private treaty drawn up in 1775 by land developer Richard Henderson at Sycamore Shoals in East Tennessee. For ten thousand British pounds and trade goods, the Cherokee, led by Attakullakulla (or Little Carpenter, one of seven Cherokee leaders who visited England with Sir Alexander Cuming in 1730), ceded much of Central Tennessee and Kentucky to Henderson's Transylvania Company. Attakullakulla's son, Dragging Canoe, refused to sign the treaty and at the proceedings told Daniel Boone in private that the settlement of the lands would lead to bloody conflict. For the next fifteen years the settlers defended themselves from attacks by the Chickamaugas, a tribe of Cherokee, Creeks, escaped slaves, and renegade whites led by Dragging Canoe.

At the Battle of the Bluffs in 1781, an estimated five hundred Indians ambushed Robertson and his men near Fort Nashboro. As the Indians were reloading their rifles, the women inside the fort set loose the dogs, who, accustomed to bear-baiting, mounted a fierce attack on the Indians, allowing many of Robertson's men to make it to the safety of the fort. The attacks ended in 1795 after Robertson's defeat of the Indians at Nickajack, a village on the Tennessee River.

Before that bloody time, long hunters such as Kasper Mansker, Timothy Demonbruen, and Thomas Sharpe Spencer trapped beaver, hunted bear and buffalo, and lived off the land around French Lick. The salt came from the residue of the sulphur springs in the area and attracted game from many miles around. Though the Indians grew uneasy about sharing this rich hunting ground, they did not trouble the hunters as much as they would the settlers in the late eighteenth century. Often loners, long hunters had no interest in building communities on what the Indians considered their land, and similar to the French voyageurs, the long hunters' lifestyle resembled the natives'. According to Arnow, Spencer, who settled in the area in 1776, was known as "the strongest man in all the west" (*Seedtime* 207), and lived in a hollowed-out sycamore tree.

Demonbruen, a Frenchman who hid from the Indians in a riverside cave that Randy and I would paddle past, was attracted to the area in 1766, to hunt the herd of buffalo that he discovered downriver near Sulphur Springs.

Frenchmen like Demonbruen had hunted their way down the Ohio River and gradually worked up the Cumberland in search of game, mainly buffalo. From Demonbruen's buffalo kills, writes Ted Franklin Belue, he cured the hides, salted the meat, made tallow for candles from their fat, and transported the goods by keelboat to sell in New Orleans. By the time Robertson and his settlers arrived in 1780, Demonbruen was settled in, living in a cabin, his kegs of tallow stacked outside ready for shipment.

Men like Demonbruen, the long hunters, and the early settlers were multi-talented in ways that we can hardly conceive. "When a man had to be a world within himself," he could, according to Arnow, "make a poem; sing a song; mend a gun; preach a sermon; shoot buffalo, Indians, British; make a moccasin or a boat; teach school; but always able to live in the woods if need be. The old west [between the Blue Ridge Mountains and the Mississippi] could not have been settled and won without such men" (*Seedtime* 171). To save a scalping victim, David Hood, James Robertson embarked upon a "medical" procedure that he had witnessed but never performed. With a shoemaker's awl, he drilled holes in the man's skull, allowing the oozings from the perforations to form a protective scab over his scalp. Hood survived for many years after this trauma, but like most survivors of scalpings, he was incapable of working or caring for himself.

Though an admirer of the long hunters' self-sufficiency, individualism, and toughness, Belue, who wrote *The Long Hunt: Death of the Buffalo East of the Mississippi*, also demythologizes romantic stereotypes that depicted them as soul mates of the Indians and enlightened trailblazers for white settlement: "Long Hunters broke treaties and laws to trespass and poach on Indian land. [They] despised their native peers as foes and competitors and were prone to shoot them on sight. Long Hunters did not care to 'civilize' the West. They headed west to make money in deer skins and fur" (85).

Herds of buffalo numbering as many as fifty to one hundred were common not only in Tennessee and Kentucky, Belue notes, but also in Illinois and south into Louisiana, Mississippi, Alabama, and western Florida. Hunting and destruction of their habitat—canebrakes and clover fields—led to their virtual disappearance east of the Mississippi by the early nineteenth century.

After locking through Old Hickory Dam on a hot, humid day, we paddled up shady Mansker's Creek, named after the long hunter, Kasper Mansker, who Harriet Arnow calls the "first actual settler of Middle Tennessee" (*Seedtime* 241). Mansker, of German descent, had a rifle named Betsy that killed much game and a few Indians. When the Robertson/Donelson party arrived, he was instrumental in helping them to adapt to the wild country, building a fort nearby called Mansker's Station.

Over two hundred years later, Randy and I sat in the canoe next to the creek's bare dirt bank and popped open cans of fruit for lunch. A railroad track ran above the bank opposite us, and upstream a busy highway bridge crossed the creek, but all around and above us grew thick green vegetation such that Mansker might have waded through in his moccasins and buckskins. Some waffle-soled footprints in the mud gave away signs of modern-day fishermen, who would have been easy to track, but the creek was ruled, on this hot afternoon, by a species in the same primordial mold as the snapping turtle and the paddlefish: the gar. Floating near the surface of the muddy water, their silhouettes long and sleek, their spotted tailfins slowly undulating, they waited until the bow of our canoe was within inches before darting away. Old-school predators, the lean muscled gar, some of them in the creek two feet long, use their sharp teeth to impale small fish and then swallow them whole. They had survived for millions of years in water too turbid for most fish. Despite their number and apparent accessibility, I had never heard of anyone trying to catch a gar or even snagging one by accident. Upstream, near Salt Creek Campground, gar had turned a patch of peaceful lily pads into a thrashing sea with their spawning, making the carp at Bledsoe Creek seem tame by comparison.

Like James Robertson and his fellow settlers, our reception in the land formerly known as French Lick was less than hospitable. After lunch, when we approached the mouth of Mansker's Creek to engage the Cumberland's heavy current, courtesy of Old Hickory Dam's discharge, a barge headed for the dam's lock pushed a load of sand and coal upriver, its prow coming within twenty yards of us. We waited for it to pass, then a few minutes after leaving the shelter of the creek, we met another one, its engines straining to push the load. Its exertions created a great turmoil of waters in its wake, a chaotic chop that bounced against the shoreline rocks in the narrow channel—only about thirty yards across here—and rocked us bow to stern, gunnel to gunnel like a toy boat in an unruly toddler's tub. There wasn't much we could do but keep paddling and hope we didn't meet another barge going upriver in such a narrow place.

Twenty miles from downtown Nashville (by water), we passed between the suburbs of Madison, on the right, and on the left, Old Hickory, named after Nashville's most prominent historical figure, Andrew Jackson, who earned the nickname for his toughness in the face of the hardships he endured during and after the War of 1812. Arnow, careful to withhold credit where it is not due, notes that Jackson, known for his Indian fighting, didn't arrive in Nashville until long after the Indian raids had ended, that he didn't even fight an Indian until 1813. Unlike earlier settlers, who fought the Indians in close quarters, often hand to hand, trading blows with enemies they knew by name, Jackson led whole armies against the Creeks farther south, at Horseshoe Bend, in Alabama, where numerical odds and firepower favored him and enabled him to decimate the tribe. Ironically, five hundred Cherokee warriors helped Jackson at Horseshoe Bend in 1812, the biggest Indian battle in the South. Jackson went on to become president, the first one to arise from a family of commoners, not aristocrats. It was his idea to "remove" what remained of the eastern tribes to reservations in Oklahoma. Jackson engineered the Trail of Tears march west, along which many froze or starved to death.

A tragic, regrettable legacy, to be sure, for the man who lived on a plantation called the Hermitage, outside Nashville, who not only owned slaves but traded them, a practice, Arnow notes, that he found "particularly wearisome" (*Flowering* 99). Still, regardless of his considerable flaws, and taking into account the influence of his times, Jackson is attractive as a figure with a refreshing lack of public relations skills, a bluntness and a temper that, in retrospect, seem endearing in light of the bland condescension and abstract doublespeak of modern politicians. He killed one man in a duel, skewered another with a sword, and shot or fought it out with many others who crossed him. Imagine Jackson's reaction to political commentators such as Rush Limbaugh. As Paul Threadgill noted, if Limbaugh had insulted Jackson, a Democrat, with the same invective that he used against Bill Clinton, Old Hickory would have thrashed him with a cane until he whimpered for mercy.

Arnow, noting that the conception of "normal" would not evolve on the frontier for many years, gives us an image of Jackson, in a drunken rage, charging down a banquet table in his boots. Certainly Jackson's long-suffering wife, Rachael, the daughter of Colonel John Donelson, did not approve of such table manners. Rachael died of heart failure in 1828, four weeks before Jackson's inauguration, her deteriorating health worsened by political opponents, who had dredged up scandal about her previous marriage. My favorite image of the general: weakened and thin from wounds suffered in a duel, he stood beside a cannon, poised to light the fuse that would maim and kill soldiers who threatened to desert him in his battles against the Creek Indians. Great compromiser he was not.

Arriving in Nashville, there were times when my temper rose as virulent as Jackson's, and it was a good thing we had no cannon in our boat. Hadley Bend and Neely's Bend made big zig-zagging loops that writhed through the city like a giant serpent held under a boot. Floating past a city park, we met our first Nashvillians: "Get out of that canoe!" said a young tough, who, strangely enough, made no effort to help us out of our boat or to give us a reason to disembark. We let the remark pass. A man standing at the end of an elevated pier near a water plant stared down at us mutely and broadly shook his head after we greeted him, a gesture that hinted at what was in store for us. Near the mouth of the Stones River, where Vic had recommended that we camp, we met a cabin cruiser towing a houseboat. The cruiser had locked through the dam with us two hours previous, where the lock operator had to tell the crew to put on their life jackets. Now, they were headed full throttle against the current, maybe twenty-five feet from us. Randy aimed the video camera. A bloated, hairy torso attached to a small head, arms, and legs held up a can of beer and said, "Welcome to Nashville!" An instant later, our hull slammed up and down in the troughs of the double wake. Water spilled over the bow and soaked Randy's camera gear, tent, and sleeping bag. The torso did not look back, nor did the pilot of the cruiser. We pitied the lock operator for having to deal with the drunken fools twice in a day. Encountering such uncouth heathens, Jackson would no doubt have lit his cannon's fuse. Having to paddle to meet the waves head on, we lacked the time for even a gesture of disapproval.

It was my intention to paddle up the Stones River to Clover Bottom, where Donelson first settled, though he moved to Kentucky a few months later, a desertion for which Arnow faults him. We paddled fifty yards up the Stones, then weary of the current, let it push us back to the confluence, where Vic had camped on his swim. We climbed thirty feet up a rocky path and set up camp in a vast green cow pasture on a bluff that commanded a view of both rivers. A line of trees along the edge of the bluff shaded our campsite and shielded us from the sight of those using the boat ramp across the river, a place at the end of Neely's Bend Road that Vic had called "party central." It was midafternoon, and we lay everything out to dry in the sunny, well-cropped pasture, the cow pies widely dispersed. Randy, who successfully dried out his camera gear, could not decide whether to put it away into dry storage when big boats approached or to hold up the video camera as a sort of weapon for those too ignorant to slow down. ("Behold, we are filming your bad behavior!")

After setting up camp, Randy and I took our first real swim in the river. Though we had splashed ourselves off in the cold water upriver, so far neither of us had fully submerged himself. Now, at the confluence of two rivers, what the Indians considered a sacred place, we dove under the surface and emerged reinvigorated, relatively clean, and ready to storm downtown Nashville, barges and cabin cruisers be damned. "Going to water" was a daily ritual that renewed the Cherokee, body and spirit. Usually preceded by a hot steam bath, the immersion served many purposes, from a pre-hunt ritual to a post-battle purification, from a treatment for ailments to a washing away of evil. Unlike the baptism that I underwent at age twelve, and never again, the river provided the Cherokee with continual sustenance, their mingling with it a part of everyday life in which nature was at the spiritual and physical core.

Some white men, instead of fighting the Indians, adopted their way of life, intermarrying into the tribe and becoming leaders. Martin Chartrier, a former carpenter in the LaSalle expedition down the Mississippi River, showed up in Maryland in 1692 with two hundred hungry Shawnee. He had deserted LaSalle in the area of the Cumberland, joined the tribe and married a Shawnee woman. Afterwards his status in the tribe and his European background enabled him to thrive as a trader.

In their book *Valley So Wild*, Alberta and Carson Brewer describe the eighteenth-century wanderings of Quaker botanist William Bartram, who traveled across the Blue Ridge Mountains to Cherokee villages and wrote of an idealized world of natural beauty and harmony. At the village of Cowee, he witnessed the bathing of Cherokee virgins in the Little Tennessee River, alongside a field of wild strawberries. In hiding with his trader guide, he witnessed the maidens "disclosing their beauties to the fluttering breeze . . . bathing their limbs in the cool fleeting streams . . . staining their lips and cheeks with the rich fruit" (46). Older women chaperoning the virgins discovered the white voyeurs and shooed them away, but not before giving them a basketful of strawberries. Bartram, unarmed, continued on his journey alone through Indian territory and was never harmed. Though he eventually returned to white civilization, he showed an enthusiasm and curiosity about Indian culture such that few white men possessed in those days.

After the swim, I hiked up the cow trail that ran above the river. We were only twenty miles north of the Nashville Metropolitan Airport, and by land less than twenty miles from downtown, yet this area was as secluded as any forest we'd seen in eastern Kentucky. Monstrous traffic whistled through the air above us, but as I walked down the deeply shaded path and turned away from the river, my feelings of calm isolation only increased, knowing I was so close to two major interstate highways and the stadium of an NFL franchise. On the other side of a barbed-wire fence, a bull broke out of a glade of trees and galloped through the field, almost bowling over some light brown, floppy-eared cows who had gotten in his way. I was afraid he might injure himself as a result of my sudden appearance, making me liable for the loss of a prized ejaculator. I'd forgotten about the red bandanna I'd tied around my neck for mosquito protection. An instant later, a tom turkey sprang from the ditch and trotted down the sunken path ahead of me. I turned back for camp when I saw a collapsing barn in the distance.

Vic said the Stones was "wild as the Amazon," though the wildness ended fifteen miles upriver at Percy Priest Dam, built in 1970. Across the Stones

River from our camp a small factory was hidden behind the riverside trees. Occasionally a low hum would signal something for the workers, and through the leaves a basketball goal was visible. I slept soundly in the pasture among the cow pies and purple blooming clover, big metal birds roaring low and loud in the night sky, loud talk and whoops from across the river at Party Central.

By noon the next day we were sitting under a canopy on the patio of Big River Brewing Company. Randy ate pizza, I a Cobb salad. We sipped micro-brewed beer. Nashville traffic roared just a few feet away, and more people passed us on the sidewalk in five minutes than we'd seen the whole river trip. Across the street was the Hard Rock Café. Down by the river park, where we'd hidden our boat, people waited in line for free handouts of food. We were feeling pretty cocky, under the influence of the beer and the morning's accomplishment: a ten-mile run into the guts of Nashville, barge terminals lining each bank, welder's sparks falling onto the water from a bridge under construction, fleets of cabin cruisers who ignored us, roaring upriver in a hurry to lock through Old Hickory Dam for a day on the lake. We waved broadly at the wait staff on the *General Jackson*, a steamboat replica docked below the Opryland complex. A north wind had blown away the humidity of the past two days, blasting the sky blue and filling up our Viking sail with favorable gusts that made the canoe leap forward as Randy held up the tarp with his maestro sticks.

So far it had been easy, the weather and current favorable. Though he and his men suffered from hunger and cold, James Robertson was also the recipient of good fortune when he arrived at Salt Lick, desiring to cross the river to the favored south bank. Afraid that the cattle would drown swimming the river, he was relieved to see that the frigid weather had turned it to ice that seemed thick enough to cross. According to Edward Albright's *Early History of Middle Tennessee*, when the men and cattle were about halfway across, the ice began breaking up, a screeching, cracking sound that must have horrified the men, who had traveled so far through hostile territory without a death. The ice was only settling, and everyone made it across safely.

Donelson, who would arrive a few months later by boat, was attacked by Chickamaugas in the area of present-day Chattanooga, on the Tennessee River, where several of his party were killed. Upon reaching the mouth of the Tennessee on March 20, he was faced with poling a few miles up the Ohio and then up the Cumberland almost two hundred miles. Why would these people undergo such hardship to settle in a relatively unknown territory, where they knew Indians would attack them?

Nashville historian Alfred Leland Crabb said it was because the river bottomland was rich for farming, trees for timber were plentiful, as were fish and game, salt for curing meat, and sulphur for healing "the ills of the flesh" (22).

Though modern Nashvillians treated the ills of the flesh and spirit with a larger variety of pharmaceuticals, and the buffalo and salt licks were long gone, apparently fish still survived, in spite of centuries of corruption and manipulation of the river.

The next morning a fisherman motored down the Stones River as we were loading the canoe. He struggled to idle in the strong current and commented that the river had risen a couple of feet overnight.

"Where you headed?" he asked.

"End of the river."

"Where'd you come from?"

"Harlan."

"Harlem?"

"Harlan."

"Ireland?"

"No, Harlan, Kentucky," I shouted.

He said if we were ever back in the area on land to visit Old Hickory Steak House, which he owned. Then he motored up the Cumberland. After we were afloat, he came back.

"There's a barge coming downriver," he said. "Though you might want to know."

That we did. We were at the bottom of Neely's Bend where the river made an elbow almost ninety degrees to the north. In order to make these kinds of turns pushing a load of barges five long, more than two hundred yards of tonnage, the towboats had to make considerable use of the outside of bends. This happened to be where we were paddling. Prudently, we hung onto some branches and waited for the barge to pass. The empties rode high out of the water, a complication for pilots on windy days like this one, when the surface area acted like sails, adding another variable, with the current and the bend, with which the pilot had to contend. This man, piloting the *Charlie Everhardt*, used reverse and forward and alternate thrusts from his two massive engines to ease his long load around the bend.

After lunch at the restaurant, we tried to prepare ourselves for the last few miles to Mack Prichard's house, the takeout just beyond the Martin Luther King Highway Bridge. As we walked to the boat past the line of homeless waiting for free meals, one guy came up to Randy and said, with some concern, "You doing okay?" We had just spent more on one meal than he probably lived on for a week, though I guess we might have looked a little haggard after a few weeks under the open skies.

We had already passed one gauntlet of barge fleeting areas, where we felt insecure because there was no clear bank to escape to. Ahead was Ingram Materials Fleeting, its barges moored three deep on each riverbank. As we entered the Ingram gauntlet, the friendly wind turned against us, blasting twenty-five miles an hour and kicking up one-foot waves against the current. Even worse, we met a barge and a houseboat, no big deal under normal circumstances, but in this case the wind and the moored barges created a little maelstrom under the bright sunshine. Each large craft's wake bounced off the metal barge hulls and came back at us with nearly the same strength. Past Lower Nashville Island, we were home free.

Mack's small cove did not come into view until after we'd crossed under the bridge. Randy whistled loudly, as Mack had instructed, and in minutes a stout goateed man, shirtless and in shorts, greeted us atop a sheer fifteen-foot bank of hard-packed (but slick) mud. Buena Vista Falls poured from a rock shelf ten feet away, and a naked drain pipe protruded obscenely to our left. As soon as we got out of the boat, I slipped and fell in the mud. Randy laughed, then slipped himself. We were a mess by the time we got the boat unloaded, our hands, elbows, and knees black with muck. Mack helped us carry our gear up the wooded, bushy path to his house, then with surprising strength, he grabbed the bow of the canoe, which Randy and I had slid to the top of the bank, and dragged it upward as if it were made of balsa wood.

Mack kept apologizing for the state of his basement, where we were staying, and we kept assuring him that it was the best place we'd camped the entire trip. It was probably the most interesting room outside of museums that I'd ever set foot in. While there, we would benefit greatly not only from his hot showers, solid roof, and soft beds, but also from the wisdom and enthusiasm that he passed on to us.

CHAPTER 18

REFUGE
REFUGE

"I keep waiting for some woman to flash us," said Randy, as we sat in Mack Prichard's basement sipping rum.

"I got news for you, buddy," said Mack, longtime river rat, naturalist, and observer of nature, human and otherwise. "You need to be in a much bigger boat to get flashed."

In Mack's basement, three floor-to-ceiling bookcases sagged with the weight of his library, many of them rare editions that could not be found in libraries or bookstores. "Most of my books are upstairs," he said apologetically as I scanned the shelves, making a long mental list of the ones I needed to read.

On the wall was a clock that struck each hour with the call of a different bird. There were plaques and awards Mack had been given for his services as an educator and conservationist. An Indian chief in full headdress, carved from a log, glared from one wall. In a framed photograph a pretty dark-haired girl snuggled up to a baby raccoon; in another, the raccoon snoozed alone on the couch where Randy would sleep. Black baseball caps on a shelf announced in bold lettering: "Hard of Hearing and Nearsighted—Please Flirt Aggressively" and "Bad Women and Good Whisky Will Cure Anything." In his bathroom was a framed photo of a place called "Ghost River," where a wolf howled in the fog.

Besides the rum, which his uncle used to manufacture, Mack offered champagne, wine, and beer. He broke open potato chips and mixed nuts.

"Don't fill up on this," he said through a mouthful. "We're going out to eat in a little while."

Mack's ex-wife Tonya joined us, and we rode together to a restaurant in Germantown to meet Bill Griswold, co-inventor of the Blue Hole canoe, and Marshall Spencer, the president of the Tennessee Scenic Rivers Association. It was strange to be riding in a car, zipping around Nashville, going over and beside the river, but barely able to glimpse it from bridges and roads.

In the restaurant, we sat at a big table across from Bill and Marshall. Two women not with our party sat on one end, and another three at the opposite end of the table. The waitress brought platters and bowls of food that we passed around family style: catfish, chicken, cornbread, Jell-O salad, casseroles, green beans, corn on the cob, and so on. Mack poured me wine from a paper bag, and Randy beer, from a different bag. As I chatted with Marshall and Bill, I half-listened to Randy's conversation with the three women at the end of the table. At first they seemed wary of such an animated white boy.

Did I know the low brace? asked Marshall, a slim bearded man.

I did not, I admitted.

It was a stroke I needed to know, said Marshall, if my canoe were about to capsize. You hold your paddle out flat, parallel to the water's surface, he said, then you bring it straight down and through the water toward you, and that should keep you upright.

Randy was leaning toward the women, eyebrows raised, his food untouched. The women were holding their hands over their mouths, giggling at something he'd said.

"It's a last resort," said Bill Griswold, who, Mack told us, had been able to negotiate treacherous rapids barely getting his paddle wet. He knew how to shift his weight in rough water to help with steering, where others had to paddle like windmills to stay afloat. His design of the Blue Hole canoe, said Mack, was a work of art—beauty and grace combined with practicality.

Marshall said he wanted Randy and me to speak to TSRA members after our trip. I glanced at Randy, who was still mugging with the women. They were laughing out loud and glancing at him sideways. The nearest leaned toward him and told him something in a low voice. He roared with laughter.

I told Marshall that we'd love to speak to TSRA.

After dinner we sat outside—Marshall and his wife, Bill, Mack, Tonya, Randy, and me—and listened to Bill tell snake tales.

Though he worked as an aeronautics engineer, Bill apparently had a passion for herpetology that went all the way back to his childhood, when he collected snakes on visits to his grandparents' house near the Gulf of Mexico in

Mississippi. On one bus trip back home to Tennessee, Bill carried three snakes—including a coral snake and a hog snake—in a two-layered bag, the first burlap, the outer one innocuous brown paper. He put the sack under his seat. After the bus was under way, he checked the bag and saw a good-sized hole in it. He said he could picture the snake creating chaos in the bus, causing the driver to lose control and run off the road. Young Bill sweated as he slowly opened the bag. A pretty young woman sitting across from him noticed his discomfort.

"What have you got in that bag that's so interesting?" she asked.

Bill said he was so scared that he went ahead and told her: "Snakes," he whispered, relieved to see that none had escaped through the hole.

She held a finger to her lips. "I won't tell," she said. "I'm a high school biology teacher."

Bill made it home with the snakes intact, though it was a long, nerve-wracking bus ride.

He told us that for a long time after the coral snake was discovered, people didn't know that the beautiful orange, blue, and yellow serpent with the mild disposition was poisonous. Women used to carry the live snakes in their purses as decorative accessories, he said. Not until a mailman carrying one of the snakes accidentally pinched its head a certain way and was bitten did people realize their bite could be lethal. The mailman died.

Mack hadn't talked much that night, allowing Bill and Marshall to hold court. The next morning, he let loose a torrent of information that was dizzying to keep up with. He recited from memory wise words about man's threat to the natural world. America's first conservationist president, Teddy Roosevelt, said this of the Grand Canyon, which he made into a national park: "The ages have been at work at it, and mankind will only mar it." Havelock Ellis, a British physician and writer, said, "Civilization began when the first tree was cut down and will end when the last tree is cut down." Peacemaker Gandhi said, "Nature provides for our need but not our greed."

Mack's love of books was only exceeded by his fondness for animals. A crunchy layer of sunflower seeds carpeted his backyard and porch, leftovers of squirrel and bird feasts. He had named some of the animals who frequented his property.

"Was that fried-egg possum?" asked Tonya as we pulled onto Mack's street the night before.

"I think it was," he said, explaining that he had fed a near-frozen possum a fried egg last winter and revived it. In a cottonwood tree down by the Buena

Vista Falls, he had counted forty-two raccoons one night. Mack fed them, too. Now, he said, they were getting too uppity, moving in under his porch.

We lingered in the basement most of that morning, talking, listening, and eating an omelet that Mack prepared. As we headed down to the canoe with our gear, Mack pointed across the river to an industrial park, Metro Center, where workers toiled on a bare wasteland of dust, stirred up by earth-moving machinery. Mack said he regretted telling the developers that the river would wash such a place away. In response, they had constructed a levee of riprap at least three miles long, the trees along the bank pushed over and hauled away. "Nothing can live over there now," he said.

Every day, Mack said, the wakes of big boats crash against his shoreline, causing more and more of it to fall into the river. The game and fish people, he said, aren't interested in enforcing laws against excessive wakes. Most skippers pretty much ignore safety and environmental impact when they feel like revving the powerful motors of their cabin cruisers, said Mack. "Their arrogance is unreal."

Mack's not the only one who gets upset about the effects of boat wakes. During a 2003 Bassmaster tournament in Louisiana, Dale J. Silbernagel, an owner of a camp on a narrow canal in the bayou, fired a shotgun blast over the head of professional bass fisherman Gary Klein, who had just gunned his motor in a no-wake zone. Unfortunately for Silbernagel, Klein was accompanied by an ESPN cameraman, who filmed the warning shot. The local was charged with aggravated assault. Klein finished second in the tournament, winning fifty thousand dollars.

Frustration about the damage that wakes cause has often fueled violence. Not only do big wakes wash away the banks of rivers and lakes, they can destroy property such as docks and endanger those who happen to be standing on the docks. In the muddy water created by wakes, fish cannot see, smell, or breathe properly; aquatic plants are smothered, and birds can't spot their prey in the water. No-wake zones help, though most of the river is an "Okay Wake Zone," where disintegrating banks are gradually filling up the waterways. Water safety manuals often mention dangers that wakes create, but rarely do they emphasize that boaters are legally responsible for the damage of their wakes. Farther downriver, on Cheatham Lake, we passed one lakeside home with a sign that read, "Please flatten your wake!" Underscoring the words, an image of a cannon and a stack of cannon balls.

Our bellies once again full, Randy and I departed Mack's sanctuary, less than two hundred miles from the end of our journey. Ahead of us was another day of navigating the affluent waters around Nashville, where commerce and recreation created an insistent chop that unsettled the omelet in my stomach.

CHAPTER 19

ONE MULE AND A JACKASS

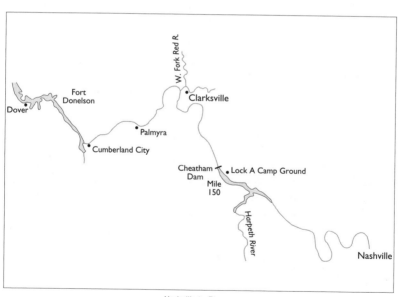

Nashville to Dover.

"Hey, throw me a beer!" barked Randy at an anchored cabin cruiser to starboard, two couples grilling meat on the rear deck. I was startled and chagrined at his impromptu panhandling. We'd been cursing big boats all day, and it seemed hypocritical to turn around and beg one of them for beer. In an attempt to darken his tan, Randy hadn't worn his hat all day, and I wondered if he'd sunburned the sector of the brain that prevented us from saying everything that popped into our heads. At best, I expected the boaters to ignore us, at worst to holler back an insult, like "Get a job" or "Buy a motor."

After Randy's command, the youngster standing next to the smoking grill had glanced up, a bit surprised, and recovered quickly. "Come on over here, then," he said, deciding that we were good-natured eccentrics and not marauding pirates.

We pulled hard across the current toward the back of the boat, where the women in their skimpy swimsuits smiled down at us. As the current began to push us away, Randy accepted not two but four ice-cold bottled beers, then a hot dog. The cook threw the second hot dog underhand, a toss that led Randy perfectly as we receded with the current.

"Thanks!" we said.

"You guys deserve it for what you're doing," said the cook.

Busy catching food and saying thanks, we hadn't really the time to tell the boaters what we were doing. Perhaps because we had become so grizzled and in need of fumigation, it was obvious that we were canoeing the entire river. Even Mack's showers could not wash off the scent of the river and that desperate haggard look that comes from battling wakes and storms and biting flies for almost five hundred miles. Even so, I'm not sure we deserved free food and drink, or what exactly we did deserve, but the charity toward us along the entire river more than made up for those who lacked proper navigational etiquette.

After leaving Mack's, we had paddled up Whites Creek toward the state prison for women, which was landmarked in the *Tennessee Gazetteer*. I thought it an odd location to note, especially if the map was designed for normal tourists, but it worked for us. The creek's current offered scant resistance as we paddled upstream for a scenic view of the prison, curious if cell windows allowed inmates a view of moving water and the solace that it would provide. A mile or so up the creek, while examining the ruins of a washed-up fishing boat with Ohio registration, a powerful stench enveloped us. It briefly occurred to me that the stench might be coming from the Ohioan who owned the boat and still inhabited it underwater, though the smell had a more generalized presence, not concentrated around the boat. As if that weren't bad enough, a large rat swam across the river *toward* us, ducking under a log and showing off his long ratty tail. Out of Whites Creek we paddled without a view of the women's pen; Mack later said that the smell came from a sewage plant on land, not from the creek itself, which Marshall's TSRA outfit cleans up every spring.

Under Briley Parkway we passed for the second time. Ford Glass, where Vic worked, was to port, a wrecked compact car to starboard, half of it submerged in the water next to the concrete bridge pier. Up above us, on the bridge, Mack leaned over and shot photos of us, waving howdy-doody style as we floated out of camera range. Farther down was the pop-pop-pop of small arms fire. Though it sounded like a Civil War reenactment, the shooting came from a firing range. A crowded firing range.

That night, we trespassed more brazenly than we had thus far, on the mown grass of a house under construction, opposite Gower Island, where we were unable to find a decent campsite or landing. Three cabin cruisers were anchored downstream, at the point of the island. On the farthest one raged a raucous party, where a male stripper gyrated on the deck for a crew of women, who hooted and squealed and cringed away from the boogie boy. We wondered if he was a professional or an acquaintance who'd been inspired to dance under the influence of liquor and flattery. We were too far away to tell and too tired to walk down the bank for a full investigation. The whoops ended early, and a suggestive silence ensued.

At three in the morning, a barge passing on the far side of Gower Island awakened me. Fading in and out of sleep, hearing the drone of the engines, I thought it was taking the pilot a long time to pass. At daybreak, the whole rig was still there, idling at the point of the island. Just as we passed it in the canoe, the pilot of the tow, the *David K. Wilson*, revved his engines and headed upstream into the rising orange sun. Downstream a bank of fog blocked the river like a solid gray wall. As we entered it, the border distinct, like a threshold, the air turned cool, and the world silenced itself. Visibility was only a few yards. We paddled close to shore so that fishermen wouldn't run over us. Hung from a small tree was a spider web big as a bed sheet, its intricate pattern glistening with moisture in the sun that was rising above the bluff behind it.

Randy had been craving bacon and eggs the entire trip, so we stopped upriver from the Highway 49 Bridge at a lakeside restaurant. We were starting to figure out that setting up tangible rewards for ourselves downriver made us paddle harder and that time passed faster. Now that we were in West Tennessee, during late June, the weather was warming, and our energy diminished with the miles. The restaurant advertised itself with a billboard-sized sign that featured a giant catfish, napkin tucked under his "chin," as if prepared to dine on his fellow mud suckers. The doors would not open until ten o'clock, one hour hence, and there would be no breakfast served, we learned. I bought a local newspaper, which I discovered to be three days old, and strolled around the area with it under my arm. Next to the restaurant was a boat ramp, under repair, and above that a small RV court. Somebody had settled there long enough to plant a garden. In the newspaper were reports of the usual car wrecks and local sports achievements, but also a poetry section and a homespun movie review questioning the prevalence of action movies. Across the river was a county fair, its Ferris wheel idle in the gathering haze.

The waitress let us inside fifteen minutes early, and we watched as she and the cook set up the salad bar and buffet. The cook, whose gait was heavy enough to shake the building and set the lake to rippling, dumped the metal containers into the buffet bays with a rattling, clattering flourish each time he galloped out of the kitchen. We ate our salads and considered the incoming clientele. One woman in her forties was painfully thin, as if suffering from a serious illness. A man larger than the cook came in and stood near the kitchen, ignoring the salad bar and waiting for the cook to bring out the rest of the buffet chow. Another couple arrived by boat, neat and preppy, worthy of a marina brochure. On the wall beside the salad bar were two black-and-white photographs. In one a boy in dark bulky clothing rode a bicycle across the snow. Behind him was a bridge. The waitress told me that the photo was taken in the 1940s, when the river froze over solid. The boy was riding his bike across the river.

As we neared the mouth of the Harpeth River, boat traffic increased, and soon the water was transformed from the fog-shrouded ghost river of the morning to another clamorous reservoir filled with pontoons, fishing boats, jet skis, and runabouts. It was not always so easily navigated. Before the era of the gasoline-powered engine and before the construction of Cheatham Dam, steamboats struggled to make the passage here at what was known as Harpeth Shoals, where shallow swift water blocked the way to Nashville. In 1818, the original *General Jackson* (not the Opryland replica) was the first to attempt the trip up the Cumberland to Nashville. That time it failed to get past Harpeth Shoals, but the following March, in high water, it chugged over the shoals and made it to Nashville. In 1821, the shoals wreaked revenge on the General, baring its teeth and sinking the steamboat. The wreck was salvaged and sold at public auction.

In 1822, a light steamboat called *The Leopard* got past the shoals but not without a mighty struggle. According to Leland Johnson in his history of the Nashville District Corps of Engineers, dramatist Noah Ludlow was onboard, trying to get back to Nashville from New Orleans. Having transferred from a grander Mississippi River steamboat at Smithland, he called *The Leopard* "the most miserable apology for a steamboat that could have been started anywhere . . . The main shaft of this boat was made of *wood*, with four or five buckets on each end about the dimensions of a laundress's washboard; and her power . . . must have been *one mule* and a *jackass*'" (28).

Below Harpeth Shoals, *The Leopard* stopped to cut wood for its boilers to power through the swift water. Ludlow retired to his cabin and fell asleep to the sound of the steamboat chugging upriver, burning the fuel that had been cut. The next morning, when he came up on deck and looked about, the surroundings seemed familiar. In fact, the scenery was the same. *The Leopard*, having burned all its fuel on the shoals crossing, had drifted back to where it had started the night before. After another attempt, the captain hired a team of oxen to pull the boat through the shoals.

By 1832, the Corps of Engineers, under the supervision of Captain Henry Shreve and Captain William McKnight, worked to make the river more consistently navigable for steamboats. They removed snags and trees and deepened the channel by dynamiting and removing rocks at places like Harpeth Shoals and Smith Shoals, near Burnside. They also constructed wing dams, built out from the shore, to direct the water through a narrower channel, increasing its depth. In the early twentieth century, the Corps constructed several low dams with locks along the river to aid navigation, though these were blown up after the Flood Control Act of 1938 authorized the Corps to begin building high dams such as Wolf Creek that formed the reservoirs that we now traversed.

It was near the site of old Lock A where we headed that midafternoon to camp before locking through Cheatham Dam, a few miles downriver, the next morning. As we approached the riprap wall to land at Lock A Campground, Randy, poised to disembark, started singing the "Oh, oh, oh" snake song. This time he fell backward into the boat to avoid the sunbathing serpent. We tried another landing, and this time he tapped his paddle on the rocks before climbing up to the green lawn of the campground. Taking the cue from the know-it-all marina cashier at Defeated Creek, I had planned ahead, calling to reserve a place at the campground, not using the national reservation system but the number of the campground itself. I'd talked to the wife of the campground manager, who gave us a site on the water, next to a little boat dock inside a tiny inlet, only about thirty feet from our campsite, which was situated out on a point of land and shaded by an immense walnut tree. It was the most convenient official site so far, and only one campsite bordered ours.

Past the line of RVs waiting to empty their waste we strolled to the swimming area, a patch of sand the size of a basketball court, which on this hot Sunday had not enough empty space for a behind-the-back dribble. Crowded together were partially clothed people of all races; much tattooed flesh; hard-lived faces aged beyond actual years; babies crying, laughing, gurgling; fat bulging out of too-tight clothing; cigarettes afire in the heat; many aluminum receptacles glinting in the sun as they were raised to dry lips. We lay our towels in the shade next to a group of Mexicans wearing long pants and T-shirts.

Fort Campbell, a military base, and Clarksville, a medium-sized city, were not far away by road. The water was still cold, the influence of Lake Cumberland's dark depths still evident this far downriver, this deep into the summer. The swimming area, partitioned by a floating plastic fence on which bathers sat or stood, was so crowded that no one could lay flat out and swim even one stroke. This was a long way from the Cherokees' "going to water." On our walk back to the campsite, a shirtless young man staggered under the burden of an inflatable raft/couch, a cigarette burning in his downturned mouth, his feet bare on the hot pavement. He looked like an advertisement for a resort in hell.

When we returned to our campsite, we had company. Two guys had a boom box blaring top-40 music at the site next to us. They had two tents, each of which could have housed both of ours, a portable refrigerator, and an industrial-sized propane stove bigger than Vic's. One of them was tall, with a shaven head, the other short and stocky, wearing baggy cargo shorts and sandals. I turned up my tiny radio as loud as it would go to WSM, and we exchanged glares. When they turned off their boom box, I snapped off the transistor, and the buzzing of motorboats, their wakes slapping the shoreline rocks, became our campsite ambience. A few hours later, I offered to share with the neighbors the stack of wood that had been left at our site. In exchange, the guy with the shaved head brought us pieces of grilled salmon, chicken, potatoes, and then grilled pineapple for dessert.

"I hope this isn't just enough to piss you off," he said apologetically.

It was just enough to get me out of cooking that night. We were getting to the point that we expected charity, especially after we went to the trouble of telling someone what we were doing and answering all their questions. We were becoming jaded by kindness. A soldier who had camped before us on our site had left behind the stack of logs. The campground manager had told us to go ahead and burn the wood, that the guy expected the next camper to do so. Our fires glared long into the night on the point above the dark river. Randy snored so loudly that I didn't get to sleep until long after midnight. I dreamed that our tents were floating on the water and that we were without a paddle. In my sleep, I asked Randy, "Are we floating?" and awoke both of us.

Cheatham Dam, the next morning, would be our second to last, Barkley Dam 120 miles farther downriver. As we entered the lock, the portly, bearded lock operator leaned over the wall above us and said, "You made it just in time. There's a barge waiting on the other side. Would have been a three-hour wait. . . . tie up where you want to."

In about fifteen minutes, Cheatham had dropped us twenty-six feet. It is a run-of-the-river-type dam, meaning that it does not store water for flood control purposes and maintains the stream flow of the river itself to power its generators.

When the lower gates began to separate from the middle, the opening was filled with the front end of a load three barges wide. We had a ten-foot gap on the left side between the barge and the fully opened gate. A young deckhand—William Jewel, he told us—stood on the edge of the front left barge with a heavy line as thick as my forearm.

As we paddled out the narrow threshold, the lock operator shouted, "Don't hit it as you go out."

The tow pilot didn't waste any time. As soon as we'd cleared the gates, he revved his engines and eased his load forward into the lock, William Jewel poised to loop his line around the forward mooring bitt.

I was getting used to the professionalism of the lock operators and the barge crews. They operated the big boats with such precision that the possibility of a mishap seemed remote. The job wasn't always so easy. In the spring of 2001, during a high-water period, a tow pushing a load of sand and concrete locked through Cheatham Dam going downstream. As the barges emerged from the lower gate, the elevated current grabbed them, torqued them sideways, and snapped the cables holding them together. One barge sank and two others listed dangerously, threatening the structure of the dam. It took quite a rescue effort to haul the barges away from the dam before they sank or did any more damage. No one was hurt. The lockmaster said he knew trouble was coming when he heard the captain over the radio call his deckhands off the barges and up to the tow.

Below Cheatham, the landscape flattened out even more than it had between Burnside and Celina. There would be no more Seven Sisters looming above us. Now, above a twenty-foot mud bank grew corn and more corn, vast fields that started at the dam and continued, it seemed, without interruption on the left bank, well past Clarksville. As we entered this flatland at midmorning, the sun bore down harder, and we felt as if we were frying in a vat of grease, except that the predominant smell was of wet mud. We were coming down off Tennessee's Western Highland Rim going north and descending in elevation toward the Ohio River Valley of western Kentucky. This was the part of the river that Vic Scoggin said was the weirdest and scariest of his trip. To me, it was home, the landscape that formed most of my memories, the weirdness with which I was most familiar. Approaching it by river, in a canoe, after such a long trip, I was anxious to monitor my own impressions and to see how Randy viewed the land of the abnormal, my old Kentucky home.

CHAPTER 20

BUSH FEVER
BUSH FEVER

"He was obeyed, yet he inspired neither love nor fear, nor even
respect. He inspired uneasiness."

CONRAD
Heart of Darkness

I'm not sure with whom I had the most in common: Gulliver, Captain Ahab,
or the officious Central Station manager in Conrad's dark tale about a steamboat trip up the Congo. The heat, the length of the trip, and the flat land and
water of West Tennessee were fueling conflict and irritability in our little green
boat. Part of my Chronic Cranky Disorder (CCD) also came from the foolish feeling of paddling a tea cup at a snail's crawl among so many who zoomed
past in small sexy craft or big boats that bespoke their prosperity. What had
we done wrong to be sweating and panting when so many others were
screaming with pleasure all around us? Never mind that neither of us was
poor, that we could have afforded a motorboat for this trip if we really wanted
it. Never mind that we'd agreed on *paddling* this seven-hundred-mile river,
that we scorned even considering any vessel propelled by more than muscle.

Despite our stubborn resolve and the Big Ideas behind our trip, one fact
remained: we looked dumb and ugly in the middle of such speed and glamour. This alienation and resentment intensified the closer we got to each

dam, where recreational boating thrived. I began to think along the same lines as Gulliver, who after being thrown off the ship he captained, landed on Jonathan Swift's fictional island of the Houyhnhnms (talking horses) and confronted the Yahoos. Tree dwellers covered with body hair, these primitive humanlike creatures snarled and threw feces at Gulliver, who fled to the company of the genteel horses who ruled the island. By the time he returned home to England, he was so repulsed by humans that he couldn't stand the smell of his own family and sulked in the stables instead.

Like Gulliver, I was surrounded by screaming savage humans with back hair, emanating the foul smell of suntan lotion and cologne. Instead of tossing turds like Swift's Yahoos, they lined up at "pumping stations" to unload; the exhaust of their boats lingered far longer than their digestive exhaust. They were fiercely attached to their picture boxes and sound machines, just as the Yahoos coveted their shiny useless stones. Like Gulliver, I began to doubt that my species' redeeming qualities—for example, the generosity from which we had repeatedly benefited—outweighed their irrational behavior and the sad fact that there were so damn many of them.

Below Cheatham Dam, we did not experience the same "reborn we're on a river again" feeling that we had on previous dams. The twenty-six-foot drop in the lock and the fact that Cheatham was a run-of-the-river dam meant that the reservoir did not dramatically transform itself from a flat-water expanse to a narrow, winding river below the dam. The current, though strong, did not assert itself with enough force to uplift our spirits. In a smelly creek next to a herd of lackadaisical cows, we ate lunch and listened to Johnny Cash sing "Folsom Prison Blues." Downstream, after lunch, an affable fisherman with his feet propped on his gunnels, cocked back at such an angle that his boat listed dangerously, told us that we might see some eagles. Randy, the bird man, perked up at this.

Though Randy and I still worked together well and made good decisions concerning logistics and navigation, we began to disagree on just about everything else. I couldn't believe that he considered the country singer Faith Hill sexy. Beautiful, yes, but not sexy, I argued, as if such designations mattered, and then we argued about the relative merits of beautiful, sexy, and cute, scoffing at each other's celebrity examples. I hooted at the notion of paying to see the country group, Alabama, which Randy loved. In short, I was being a snob to my faithful, hard-working crew, cause enough for mutiny.

Randy, for his part, began to argue with everything I said about the river. I guess he was getting tired of me spouting off information, but his habit of disagreeing became particularly irritating when he would ask me a question and then invariably contest the answer. These issues were of high importance, of course. For example, we planned on celebrating at the Mile 100 marker, but the Corps had not been accommodating enough to post a marker that said exactly 100 on it. Instead it said 100.1. So we argued about how far short to stop of the mile marker, instead of being happy we'd made it that far. There was also an ongoing contest about being the first to identify the animals who crossed our path, and when one of us guessed wrong, the other would over-correct: "There's an eagle!" I might say, pointing at a faraway bird in my zeal to be the first identifier. "That's not an eagle," Randy would scoff. "That's a freaking buzzard."

Back at Celina I'd given Randy the *Tennessee Gazetteer* to help him fight the monotony of the voyage. I kept the Corps' charts. We argued when the maps contradicted each other or when one contained information that the other didn't. Randy's singing was killing me, and when he wasn't singing or arguing with me, he made these strange clicking noises with his tongue against his teeth. At this point, within 150 miles of the end, we were begin-ning to feel the effects of sharing a small boat for such a long period each day. Even the most compatible personalities, two easygoing guys with a common goal and similar politics, would clash under such circumstances. Though our good humor was deteriorating, neither of us seemed to hold a grudge and neither, so far, seemed inclined to violence. We took each other's CCD in stride. In short, we recognized the Yahoo, and it was us.

While the nadir of the voyage for Randy came below Wolf Creek Dam on the night of the Long Rain, I sank lowest in the haze of Clarksville, Ten-nessee, where we wandered about on the sidewalk next to a busy four-lane looking for a grocery, a liquor store, an interesting person, a conflict, anything to break the monotony. I'd wanted to camp above Clarksville and invade it the next morning, early, when it was cool and we could find a good place for breakfast, replenish our food supply, and purchase another bottle of whiskey. It should be noted at this point that it was your mad captain, me, who con-sumed most of the whiskey, while Randy drank beer when he could get it, and after his small cooler ran out of ice, he'd drink it warm with almost equal relish.

In these days of guilt and finger wagging, I was ready to justify my whiskey ration to anyone who challenged me. Lewis and Clark gave out daily rations of brown liquor to their men on their little trip out west. Even Harriet Arnow notes that on the eastern frontier, whiskey was used to cure just about any-thing: "Whiskey was to the pioneer what tranquilizers, stimulants, disinfec-tants, vitamins, rubbing alcohol, and anesthetics are to us today" (*Flowering*

277). I had ibuprofen tablets, coffee, Aspercream, calamine lotion, Pepto Bis-mol, and Tums, all of which I used in moderation, but combined, these reme-dies did not replace the soothing effect of an ounce or two of whiskey in the evening. Who was I harming with my ration, which seemed minuscule com-pared to a relative of Arnow's, who drank a "fog-lifter" as he got out of bed, a pick-me-up at noon, an appetite inducer in the evening, and a nightcap before bed, amounting to an average of more than a pint a day? He was never drunk, she claimed, was "a most respectable farmer and businessman" (278), and lived to ninety-two.

We had already paddled twenty-eight miles from Lock A Campground that day, unable to find an acceptable campsite above Clarksville. Once at the city's riverfront park, we could not find a decent landing and had to tie our boat around a large rock that was part of the riprap-lined bank, too high and steep to pull our canoe up and over onto the mown grass without unloading it. Glancing warily back at our fully loaded boat, unsheltered from the con-siderable barge and big boat traffic, we trudged up the hill to an O'Charley's restaurant, where a waitress and a cook were having a cigarette break.

"Can you tell me how far it is to the nearest grocery?" I asked.

"You want to find a grocery store?" said the young waitress.

I looked at the cook as if this should have been obvious by my question. He grinned back. The waitress picked up on my condescension. The sun had bleached out all semblance of civility from my soul.

Despite my rudeness, she started to give me directions. The route seemed overly complicated, the destination too distant.

I interrupted her before she finished. "Is there anything closer? We're on foot."

Now it was her turn to play smartass. "I can see that," she said, looking us up and down, not a pretty sight. "It's only a couple of miles."

I sighed. "Where's the nearest liquor store?"

Cook and waitress eyed us. We hadn't told them about the canoe parked below or anything about our quest. For all they knew we were common vagrants, unshaven, carrying backpacks, spending most of our money on booze, while they were about to sweat for a night's wages. Our next question, they were thinking, would be whether they could give us a ride and lend us some money. But the waitress went ahead and gave us directions to the liquor store, which sounded even farther away than the grocery. Randy, who wasn't about to walk two miles in ninety-degree heat for a bottle of whiskey, bought some junk food and beer at a convenience store and waited for me at the boat. I walked a half mile, stopped next to a cemetery, and pondered my situation, my quest. Surely I could survive without whiskey. I seemed a pathetic figure, walking so far in this heat to replenish something so expensive, so unnecessary, and in spite of having guzzled two bottled waters, I was dehydrated and heat sapped.

I returned to the boat, and we ate at a sandwich shop, and then paddled a mile past the mouth of the Red River to camp on a shelf below a cornfield, where chemicals seeped in orange rivulets down the mud bank into the river. Randy decided to swim. I told him to go ahead, sure, but that I wouldn't be swimming in this water, just downstream from a small city, that orange stuff contaminating it. Coming out of the water, toweling off, Randy made a big show about how great the swim had made him feel. There were many ooohhs and aaahhhs. Then he opened a beer and drank deeply, saying "AAAAHHHH, that's good," and smacking his lips. He continued to gloat over his swim and his beer, while I stewed in my own heat, sipping the last two inches of my whiskey among the swarming mosquitoes.

A few feet from our tents stood a yellow "private property" sign, but we were too tired to care. The next day, we saw that the signs were posted along the bank every one hundred yards or so, prohibiting trespassing for hunting, fishing, trapping, and threatening prosecution "under the law." They were posted by the whimsically named Corn Silk Farms. That night something big rustled through the corn leaves, deer I assumed, not only trespassing but robbing the farmer. Later a towboat's powerful searchlight swept the shore where we camped. Then the barges themselves came forward, their prows brushing against the limbs that leaned out from our campsite, water sloshing against the bank. The closer the towboat got, the louder the engine noise, a constant whirring that increased to a roar, gradually swallowing up everything else that cried out into the night. By this time of the trip, the roar of a tow seemed almost natural, something that belonged, and after it passed, the animals filled the silence with their song and dance: tree frogs, crickets, night birds, and the moving deer.

At midmorning the next day, the hottest of the trip, we came upon a group of kids lounging in the shade next to the river. Nearby a frayed rope hung from a tree limb.

"Is this Palmyra?" I said. We floated at the outside of a bend in an eddy where the current was slack.

"Yeah," said the oldest boy sullenly. He looked to be about thirteen.

"What are y'all doing?" I asked.

"Just got up," said the boy.

"Why don't you jump in?" said a little girl behind him.

He ignored her. "Where y'all coming from?"

"Harlan."

"No f*&#g way," said the kid in amazement. "How long you been at it?"

"This is Day Thirty-one," said Randy.

"Holy s*#t," said the kid, waking up now, his voice getting louder to display his off-color vocabulary.

"How far you going?" asked the little girl.

"Smithland."

Silence. No reaction. Then, from the boy, solemn advice, free of profanity. "You got a lot of days ahead of you, buddy."

"Watch out for them currents," the little girl called out as we floated downstream.

At midday we pulled in next to the ferry ramp and walked up to Cumberland City. Whoever lived there, if anyone did, was holed up indoors. Everything was closed on this, a Tuesday: the bank, an antique shop, a service station. We returned to the ramp, where the ferry was waiting for its next passenger. Randy asked the woman gatekeeper how far it was to buy beer. Without hesitation, C.J. volunteered to desert her ferryboat post and give us a ride. She took us to the Busy Bee convenience store, where the rest of Cumberland City had gone to stand in line. Everyone, without exception, was buying at least a six-pack of beer. The workers at the four-stacked steam plant had just changed shifts, and they had worked up a thirst. Back at the landing, C.J. told us about the ferry to the right of the ramp, which had sunk while moored. Part of it rested on the bottom, though the rails peeked above the surface. C.J. thought a cabin cruiser's wake had sunk it. We sat in our boat under the scant shade of some bushes next to the wreck as the working ferry—the *Lucille II* was the tow—took on two pickup trucks pulling trailers piled high with wheels of hay. C.J. had to leave the gate ajar to accommodate this long load.

"I ain't gonna roll off," said one of the farmers, his front bumper inches from watery oblivion.

Though this was a spectacle, watching all that grass cross the river, we could not recapture the magic of McMillan's Ferry. C.J. and the pilot had not heard of the other ferry on the Cumberland. They thought they were the last one working on the river.

That evening we camped on an unnamed island in the shadow of the steam plant. The river had flooded the island completely at some point because it was covered with driftwood and trash along its quarter-mile length. I tiptoed across the one-hundred-yard-wide island toward the steam plant. In grass up to my knees I surprised a baby deer speckled with white across its light brown coat. It stared at me a couple of seconds and stumbled away unhurriedly over the driftwood. Across a narrow channel, the steam plant hummed, its four red and white striped stacks puffing faint smoke that blended with the haze.

Back at camp, on the other side of the island, we burned driftwood and listened to WSM's live broadcast from the Grand Ole Opry. Porter Waggoner, the skinny guy with the blonde bouffant and embroidered rhinestone suits, came on first. Most famous for having discovered Dolly Parton, a regular on his 1960s TV show, and perhaps elsewhere in his life, Porter's music was on the sappy side, with songs like "The Green, Green Grass of Home," about a prisoner on death row who has a vivid dream about a return to his family and sweetheart. "If you like what you hear tonight," Porter crowed to the audience, "tell folks about it. If you don't, then just don't say anything." Dolly, whose hair had been just as puffy and blonde as Porter's, sued her mentor over contractual problems in 1979. She went on to major stardom in music, movies, and amusement parks, while Porter's star faded. Having watched his TV show with my family, I was glad that he was still alive and performing.

The next night, after a fifteen-mile paddle, we camped at the mouth of Hickman Creek, just below Fort Donelson, where General Grant's forces won a victory over the poorly organized and outnumbered Confederates. Randy said he thought the mounds near our swampy, mosquito-infested campsite were Confederate rifle mounts. I thought Union but was too tired to debate it. Both of us were wrong. According to Shelby Foote, who wrote the definitive three-volume history of the Civil War, Grant's forces approached by land from Fort Henry, on the Tennessee River, and by water, coming upriver on the Cumberland and stopping short of Hickman's mouth to fire shells at the fort. None of the Rebs were down here swatting skeeters and sweating in the heat. They were across the creek, up on the bluff with the gun batteries and behind rifle pits, shivering in the cold and poised to fire at Union Admiral Foote's fleet of gunboats.

Grant's land forces spent a bad night that February 13, when the weather turned cold and the skies spit sleet, then snow. Many of the young soldiers had thrown away their blankets and overcoats on the sunny march from Fort Henry, which they had captured, and they were camped so close to Confederate lines that campfires were forbidden. On Valentine's Day 1862, Admiral Foote's five gunboats arrived downstream of the fort, probably not far from our campsite. As they bombarded Fort Donelson, many of their shells whistling over the heads of the Rebel gunners or falling short, the Confederate water battery scored two hits, disabling two gunboats, killing one pilot and ten others, and wounding Foote himself. They cheered from the bluffs as the gunboats retreated. The next day the Rebels attacked the right of Grant's line and broke through in an attempt to escape from the fort. Grant arrived on the scene and restored order, while the Confederates, who hesitated in their escape, were pushed back by gray-mustachioed Union General C. F. Smith. The Rebs, led by General Simon Bolivar Buckner, a classmate of Grant's at West Point, surrendered on February 16.

Buckner's superiors, after much hand-wringing, escaped the fort, as did General Nathan Bedford Forrest, with fifteen hundred men on horseback. After sending a courier with a letter asking for terms of capitulation from Grant, to whom he had loaned money before the war, Buckner received this terse reply: "No terms except unconditional and immediate surrender can be accepted" (Foote 2:212). It was a comment for which Grant became famous, creating his reputation as a hard, uncompromising fighter, though he was also a deeply sensitive and intelligent man, prone to drinking binges. After capturing Fort Donelson, Grant was promoted from brigadier to major general, and because of his victory there and control of the lower Cumberland, Nashville fell to the Union a few weeks later. His next major battle would be at Shiloh, on the Tennessee, a much bloodier affair, with results that were less favorable.

Randy and I, traveling in reverse from Grant's rise from failed farmer and binge drinker to military hero, attacked Dover coming downriver, landing at the Surrender House, where Grant arrived that morning of February 16. There he found his old classmate Buckner sharing a breakfast of cornbread and coffee with Union General Lew Wallace, who would later write the novel *Ben Hur: A Tale of the Christ*, which became famous as a film that starred Charlton Heston. On the grassy slope outside the Surrender House, a sign told us, thirteen thousand "dejected" Confederates waited for transport by steamboats to prisons in the North. Now, inside the house that was once known as the Dover Hotel sat a lone park ranger, a young man working over the summer. When we started firing questions at him, he suggested we watch a video of the surrender in the dark, air-conditioned parlor. The actors' pendulous whiskers seemed hastily glued to their faces, dangling in the heat, as they recited their lines on a dimly lit set.

Having determined that Dover proper was two miles from the Surrender House, we paddled under the Highway 79 Bridge, where we approached a bass boat containing one man and two women in swimsuits, each of them casting top-water lures. Through the binoculars, we had seen them earlier and remarked on the good fortune of the fisherman. Alas, the young fisherman's circumstances were much different from what we had hoped and imagined in our puerile fantasies. The older woman was his mother-in-law, Jean, the younger his wife, Rhonda. Just as we approached David, the fisherman, he pulled a keeper out of the water.

"Can we take a picture of you and the fish?" asked Randy.

"Hell," he said, tossing the largemouth bass back into the water. "You don't want a picture of this. Show 'em what you caught," he said to Rhonda.

From the live well, she pulled an eight-pound largemouth, a trophy fish that she would take to the taxidermist that afternoon. As Randy snapped photos of her, Rhonda rubbed her chin across the bass's upper lip and said, "Brings you luck."

As we held onto the gunnel of their gleaming bass boat, Rhonda told us a rural myth I had heard many times, growing up about fifty miles north of Dover: the nest of snakes story. In Rhonda's, a man jumped off the Dover Bridge, a risky prospect in itself, and when he emerged, he was covered with snakes. When they pulled him from the water, he was dead. The versions I'd heard always involved a fallen water-skier. When I asked Maryville College biologist Drew Crain about it, he laughed and asked me if I'd ever talked directly to the survivor of such trauma. He doubted that cottonmouths would behave in such a way. Biologist Ben Cash, also a colleague at Maryville College, said that water moccasins or cottonmouths do not nest in the water, nor do nonpoisonous water snakes. As a reptile specialist, he said he'd heard many myths about snakes that made him ponder their origins; he'd heard tales about aquatic snake nests and noted that the TV movie *Lonesome Dove*, an otherwise entertaining movie, featured an episode in which an unfortunate cowboy fell from his horse into a river, where dozens of moccasins attacked him. Ben theorized that the nest of snakes myth might originate from the fact that water snakes do like to gather around artificial structures in lakes, such as underneath docks, but that these are not nests.

Rhonda handed down two cold soft drinks to Randy and me. David had another snake tale that his mother had told him. This had happened in the "old days," he said. A woman thought she had swallowed a bug one day, and subsequently, in spite of having a healthy appetite, she began to lose weight. Months passed, nine months to be exact. She went to the hospital where X-rays showed that she had swallowed a baby snake, and that it was feeding off the contents of her stomach.

We kidded David about his wife's outfishing him.

"Just gives me more motivation to fish," he said, clearly proud of her.

After the trip, I learned that Rhonda had begun to participate in a professional fishing league associated with Wal-Mart. The day we met her, she told me, was the most memorable, the start of her "fishing career."

After walking into Dover for a hamburger, Randy and I invaded Fort Donelson by water, tying off to a ruin of concrete below a descending iron stairway that had been broken off at shoulder level. We lifted ourselves onto the stairway, avoiding the poison ivy that snaked around the rusty broken handrail. After a steep, unsteady climb up broken steps, we emerged onto the rolling grassy hills of Fort Donelson National Battlefield. Up the paved road we marched, examining tiny reconstructed cabins where the Confederates had been lodged, the different caliber cannon, and the overlook where the Union gunboats had been defeated on Valentine's Day. A few tourists drove their cars to the overlook, which commanded a two- or three-mile stretch downriver. The Confederate gunners began firing their biggest guns when Foote's fleet was within a mile and a half. The boats did not fire back until they were within a mile. Though Foote could see dirt and sandbags flying from the Confederate battery, their guns kept firing and inflicting damage upon his boats. The Rebels' biggest gun, the 128-pounder rifle at the top of the bluff, had malfunctioned and was out of action, but as the gunboats got closer, the battery scored more hits with their smaller guns, culminating in the strike on Foote's flagship, the *St. Louis*. Now the boats were within a few hundred yards and the inexperienced Rebel gunners gained confidence. "Now boys," said one gunner, "see me take a chimney!" (Foote 2:204). He took aim and down went a gunboat stack. The Union had fifty-four wounded, eleven dead, while the Confederates had no casualties in that first day of battle.

Tourists from Nebraska had their pictures taken next to the 128-pounder, a sinister black barrel ten feet long, sandbags stacked neatly around it. One of the men told his wife that the Confederates might have won had the Union not used the concrete highway bridge downriver for reinforcements.

"I assume he was kidding," said Randy.

THOUGHTS OF DOOM

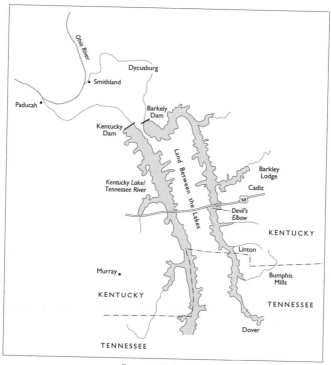

Dover to Smithland.

Hysterical ospreys ruled the river borderlands between Tennessee and Kentucky. Their nests of sticks and twigs, big as shopping carts, sat atop the Corps' wooden poles that marked the boundaries of navigational channels. When we approached these poles by boat, one of the big gawky birds would lift itself from the depths of the nest and fly in crazy, diving circles above us. Circling, she chirped in rapid-fire alarm—one note rising to a glass-breaking pitch, held a few seconds, the next one lower pitched and full of threat. This kept up until we were fifty yards downriver from the nest. Ospreys had none of the grouchy charm of the great blue heron. They seemed unduly alarmed at us, panicky in their overprotectiveness.

Even more disconcerting than the osprey was the buzzard roost near Saline Creek. On a power line derrick, hundreds of the big black scavengers roosted in nests slightly smaller than the osprey's. They had pickets posted upriver, who flew ahead to warn the others of our approach. I had never seen so many buzzards together in one place and didn't like the way that they eyed us.

The humans of West Tennessee resembled the unhappy animals. While we camped in the littered swamp at the mouth of Hickman Creek, three fishermen arrived at the riprap across the way, on the periphery of Fort Donelson battlefield. We could just see parts of them through small openings in the trees and bushes that hid us, but what we heard told us that these were not happy fishermen. From what we could understand of the shouting and cursing, one of them, a teenager in a basketball jersey and baggy shorts, had, upon arrival, dropped the minnow bucket and lost the bait in the snaky gaps between the rocks.

The older man had a belly of exceptional breadth that strained the fabric of his shirt. What glimpses we got of him always featured the belly. He seemed oblivious to the crisis, his tone calm and childlike. "Those bass are going to start running soon," he said after the teenager had been silent a few seconds.

The bait dropper kept cursing himself. "I can't believe I dropped the f*%&#$g minnows. That's just great! What a dumbass thing to do."

"Well, if we had them minnows we'd really be catching them now," said the older man, unwittingly adding to the boy's misery. "There's two dead minnows right there," he said, presumably pointing down at the rocks.

"Well, take 'em goddammit," said the angry boy. "Take 'em. I don't want them."

No reply.

"Hell, we might as well just leave. I can't believe . . ." And so on it went, among a clattering of plastic tackle boxes and the heavy cracking sound of rocks rolling down the riprap. Finally, they quieted down and began to fish, the angry boy croaking residual curses every few minutes, the fat man's optimism silenced.

Just before dark, a cabin cruiser crept up to the mouth of Hickman Creek, a man calling out numbers to the pilot: "six feet, five feet, three feet, three point five feet," a human depth finder. "What's the draft of this boat anyway?" he asked at one point. More cursing in reply, and the big boat backed away from the creek.

The next day, one man in the bow of a small boat yelled orders to another who operated the outboard motor.

"Reverse," he said, loud enough for us to hear all the way across the lake, at least a quarter of a mile. "I said 'reverse,' back it up!"

On the local radio news later that afternoon, we learned that a western Kentuckian had fired his shotgun in the air seventy-five times near his residence at Sunshine Trailer Court. The sheriff's department deduced that he had "personal problems" (as opposed to the impersonal kind). We also heard the last part of a story in which a body had been found "folded up" in a wheeled suitcase. Also of note, the antisodomy laws in Texas were ruled unconstitutional, and in the following days conservative talk-show hosts began to squawk about it through our happy yellow transistor. They reminded me of the osprey.

At the Hickman Creek campsite, even the birds sounded angry, loud caws and twitters and cooing such that we had not heard, of such a variety that I suspected a confederation of species preparing to launch an aerial assault on our tents. Mosquitoes attacked our flanks so viciously that we retreated early to our hot tents, silently sweating through the evening as curses filled the air. I fell asleep hoping for battlefield nightmares, but the dead soldiers stayed in their graves, across the creek and up the bluff. Early the next morning, we beat a hasty retreat downriver from the angry Stewart Countians, their grouchy birds, and the pinpoint artillery of their mosquitoes.

We would cross the Kentucky border that day, back to the land of the abnormal, according to Vic Scoggin, who, accompanied by his wife, Julee, was accosted by three drunks on this last stretch. The tattooed drunks, who were "the roughest-looking guys I'd ever seen," said Vic, threatened Julee and started throwing dead fish at the couple. At Julee's urging, Vic restrained himself, got into their small boat, and motored away from the fearsome trio, who got hung on a gravel bar in pursuit. Unable to raise law enforcement on their radio, Vic and Julee watched the marauders ram a pontoon with a family onboard. Like me returning to my home turf, where I had spent the first twenty years of my life, Vic said he'd had his guard down in western Kentucky, so close to finishing his swim. We were within a half-hour drive of Calloway County, where I grew up.

It is difficult to judge the strangeness of one's own home. Whatever happens in the land from which I originate, I feel partially responsible for, and I either laugh about it or feel compelled to explain it. There's plenty to crow about in Calloway County: a decent college of ten thousand students that claims status as "Kentucky's Public Ivy University"; a safe, quiet, and for the most part affluent town, which, oddly enough, prohibited the sale of alcohol until the twenty-first century; little heavy industry polluting the water and air; spectacular and fertile farmland; quick proximity to the waters that we now paddled. Indeed, Murray was once voted by Rand McNally as one of the top retirement destinations in America. The town, like most, holds a darker side, spawned, I think, from the boredom of stability and the panic that accompanies the scrutiny of small-town life. Notoriety arises from prominent aberrations, such as the teenage vampire killers of the 1990s and a deliberately set dormitory fire that resulted in the death of a student. It is a quiet, beautiful place that I love to visit, and it haunts me because I can't escape it. All roads, all rivers, it seems, lead me to Murray.

Having passed through the Western Highland Rim of Tennessee, which forms part of the border around the Central (Nashville) Basin, we were now reentering Kentucky's Pennyrile Region, at its far western edge. Just a few miles to the west, at the Tennessee River, was the Jackson Purchase, part of a larger geologic region called the Mississippi Embayment, low lying plain with river bottoms and sloughs. Though steep slopes still rose above the river, this borderland would soon turn into the flattest land of our journey and some of the most fertile. For the first time, the shoreline turned to fine brown gravel, ancient sediment made up of unconsolidated sandstone.

The Land Between the Lakes (LBL), an undeveloped strip of land between the Tennessee and Cumberland rivers, was on our left, to the west. Created by John F. Kennedy in the 1960s, LBL was a retreat for camping, hunting, and fishing that prohibited commercial development such as marinas, restaurants, convenience stores, and the like. The residents of the small settlements there were forced to leave, and some of them were still bitter about it. Communities such as Golden Pond were known for the manufacture of moonshine, exporting it as far away as Chicago during prohibition. TVA managed LBL until the late 1990s; now the U.S. Forest Service was in charge.

I wanted to camp that night on LBL, which meant much to me growing up, one of the places where my father took me to fish, from the banks of man-made Hematite Lake, where we cast our lines below the spillway, and further down Long Creek, where the trees hung over the muddy water, cool respite on summer days. At LBL I'd learned a little about nature and a bit about girls at a summer camp. Continuing the educational legacy, I'd force-marched my nephews Sam and John, barely beyond their toddler years, around Hematite Lake, their first hike. Even into early adulthood, my friends and I would, during wintertime college vacations, climb the silo overlook to spot eagles, hawks, and geese flying over the blue water in bright winter sun.

Randy and I scanned the shorelines for landing places, but it was all deep bays and swampy peninsulas, the shorelines blocked with impenetrable aquatic shrubs, guarded by squadrons of biting, stinging insects. As the wind quickened, promising rain, I overcame my obsession about recovering childhood memories and took Randy's suggestion that we cross to the other side of the river to look for a campsite.

Near the end of the journey, passing familiar landscape, I could not fend off an impending sense of doom. Ahead of schedule, we had only six short paddling days to go. We were traveling at a civilized rate such that normal people on vacation might deem acceptable: six to twelve miles a day, quitting in early afternoon to make camp before the heat descended or taking more time to explore bays or other stops along the way. Despite our bickering and the small annoyances such as mosquitoes, ticks, and humidity, things were going smoothly. *Too smoothly,* I thought, *for too long,* unlike the pendulum-swing of fortunes on the first two-thirds of the trip. The pendulum was hung somewhere in the good fortune arc, and we were due for something bad to happen, which could be disastrous so close to the end, when at our relaxed pace we were so vulnerable.

The same thing had happened near the end of my Tennessee River trip, when I stopped at my sister's lakehouse for a two-day rest. By the time I roused myself from the comforts of indoor living long enough to resume the journey, the weather blasted in a front that raised chilly October gusts of thirty miles an hour and whipped up three-foot waves. I didn't suspect the Cumberland of more weather mischief, having seen everything short of a tornado, but my guard was up, even though I didn't know what to look out for.

There had been evidence of the kind of hostile clannishness we'd feared in eastern Kentucky, but which hadn't played out. At the Hickman Creek campsite, when I had inquired by phone about a campground near Bumphis Hills Marina, a woman told me it had been shut down because of "water problems." I asked her if she knew of any other places nearby to camp, and she said she sure didn't, none at all. I thanked her and began to conclude the call when she interrupted me and said, "You best not camp in anybody's yard. You're likely to get shot if you do."

Not shot *at*, but *shot.*

"Well, thank you for that information," I said, a bit of an uneasy laugh in my voice.

She did not laugh or kid back, nor did she elaborate in a way that would assure me she had our welfare in mind. She hung up with the poison of her warning hanging in the swampy air. The next day, just short of the Kentucky border, we stopped at a boat ramp near Tobaccoport, just downstream of Bumphis Mills. I walked up to the town, which consisted of a Baptist church and three houses. In these little towns, less than an hour from where I grew up, apparently some folks would shoot you for laying your head on a few feet of remote and undeveloped acreage for which they possessed a deed. It occurred to me that the owner of the marina probably owned land and a house on the lake, and that it was she who had the shotgun, and us, the trespassers, who were her potential targets. She was right. We were repeat offenders, trespassers of much land, where in most cases getting permission had been impractical.

I wondered if we deserved more concrete hostility directed toward us, something besides negligent boaters and incompetent campground managers. Wasn't it time for at least a spoken threat, a jeer, perhaps a mild beating? I just wanted to get it over with. There had to be folks around who would accommodate us. But not in Tobaccoport, where the only soul was a woman on a riding mower who waved big and friendly when she looked up and saw me standing there in the road in a floppy khaki hat and sweaty shirt. She didn't shoot, just kept on mowing.

A couple of years before our trip, Kira Salak had kayaked alone six hundred miles down the Niger River to Timbuktu and written an article for *National Geographic Adventure* magazine. In the villages along the way, she was often greeted with jeering and threats, unable to get food or water or any kind of help from the natives. The men wanted to rape her, and the women silently scorned her. Like many of us who undertake such trips, Salak was fueled by her misfortune, and she seemed, at least in recounting the journey, to welcome bad things as a self-flagellating rite of passage:

> I often wonder what I seek when I embark on these trips. There is the pat answer I tell the people I don't know—that I'm interested in seeing a place, learning about its people. But then the trip begins, and the hardship comes, and hardship is more honest: It tells me that I'm here because I don't have enough patience yet, or humility, or gratitude. So I've told the world that it can do what it wants with me if only, by the end of the trip, I have learned something. A bargain, then. The journey, my teacher. (78)

I guess this was part of what drove me, overcoming obstacles that would teach me lessons. Because I expected something to happen, I almost wished for it, thinking that I deserved it, though Randy—out here taking pictures, singing along to bad country music, talking to the birds, oblivious to my strange, secret longings—certainly did not.

At our next campsite, near Linton, Kentucky, a bit of reckless curiosity almost resulted in the crisis that I'd been expecting. We settled on a fifty-yard-long forested flat below a steep bluff. As on most of our lower river campsites, high water had washed driftwood and trash over the entire area, but we were able to land on a gravel beach and find a clear flat spot near the water to pitch our tents. There were small trees in the flat, larger ones towering above us on the bluff, but none of the heavy brush and claustrophobic feel of Hickman Creek. Using driftwood and his tarp Randy constructed his most elaborate canopy, with a bench for sitting and a platform for cooking. He called it the kitchen and made a sign that said, "Smithland or Bust," wedging it between two poles. As the approaching storm stalled, I climbed the bluff. Above an exposed section of limestone, the land angled steeply upward through oaks and hickories, dead leaves ankle deep. At the top of the ridge I found a gravel road, power lines, a Realtor's sign, and a no-trespassing sign. Down the road a ways, a vacant new cabin.

I wondered how many places remained where you could climb up from the river and not find a road, a house, power lines, a railroad track, or some other mark of human development. Even on the remote riverine sections of the Cumberland there were fences, cattle, and four-wheeler tracks. In the Daniel Boone National Forest we were never far from a road. Here in the eastern United States, we had multiplied to the extent that we could no longer escape ourselves. We weren't pushing back frontiers but obliterating vestiges of the land that had entranced Boone and Mansker, Dragging Canoe and Hanging Maw, John Donelson and James Robertson, men who loved the land so much they would kill and die to keep it. Now, our numbers multiplied and our ability to maim wild land greatly increased, we blithely developed, without much thought about what had happened here before, what we were destroying, what we could not reconstruct, no matter how sophisticated our technology, no matter how much we might want to.

I stood at the peak of the rocky bluff and surveyed our campsite far below, a blot of order in the chaotic flatland of plastic bottles, lighters, toys, shoes (never a pair), and objects that surprised even Randy and me, veterans of river trash who had, earlier in the day, seen an entire portable toilet (Port-a-John) washed up in Barkley Wildlife Management Area near Saline Creek. We had also seen a toilet seat and lid hanging from a tree, ornament-like, and a two-gallon plastic jug of Roundup weed killer that I hope was empty. The type of garbage that disgusted me the most was not the most damaging to the environment, nor even the ugliest, but it seemed emblematic of so many things that had gone wrong: soiled plastic diapers. The tossing of diapers into the river, onto the shore, no doubt witnessed by children, influenced a new generation to behave like the Yahoos, throwing their waste where it didn't belong.

Aside from diapers and the usual detritus of bottles and cans, the trashy banks still fascinated me as a kind of anthropological laboratory. As Randy and I explored the trash heaps around the Linton campsite, we would be rewarded with a rare specimen of American desire. When he found it, Randy let out a small cry of surprise similar to his snake-sighting vocalizations. He stumbled over the driftwood and broken glass toward me with a big grin across his face.

"This is what I have to take back," he said proudly.

In his hand he held up a key chain, but this was no ordinary key chain. There was a metal ring onto which one could slide one's keys, but attached to it was, let us say, a novelty of the sexual variety. And quite an anatomically correct novelty it was, flesh and rose colored. As Randy quickly discovered, the "part" was squeezable. What happened when you squeezed the thing I will leave to the reader's imagination. We named her Millie because Randy had found her abandoned near a mile marker. He put her away somewhere and resumed his scavenging. He came upon a piece of foam padding about the dimensions of a king-sized bed. When he lifted it off the ground, he caught a glimpse of a snake and laid it back down again. Then he called me over for a look at the poor creature, who thought he'd found a private place to doze. I stood ten feet away with my microcassette recorder and narrated in the calm monotone of the old Mutual of Omaha *Wild Kingdoms* I used to watch on TV.

"All right, we're going to toy with this snake that's under this black plastic thing. Randy's lifting the pad. . . ."

When I saw what was underneath my narrative voice escalated into pure panic. "Oh s*&t, it's a f#&*ing rattler!" Sure enough, not a rattler but a copperhead was coiled and ready to strike at Randy, about three feet away from it. He dropped the pad and jumped back, the snake still exposed and hissing mad. When I realized it was a copperhead, my excitement and dread was no less intense. While not as lethal as the timber rattlers who frequent the area, copperheads are poisonous enough to make you quite ill. We left him alone in his little kingdom of perverted trash. If the copperhead had bitten Randy, it would have taken at least a few hours for me to get help. No boats were out, and the little gravel road at the top of the bluff had been empty since we arrived. That he wasn't bitten I considered more good fortune for which we had to compensate.

Randy's canopy and bench served us well when the storm finally arrived, a mild one by the Cumberland's standards that spring. The rain fell straight down and thunder rumbled in the distance, north of us. After an hour, the sun dropped through a solid lid of clouds covering the upper sky and blasted an orange shaft of light across the surface of the wide lake right up to the shoreline where the canoe was beached. As night fell, thousands of lightning bugs illuminated the dark, flat trash field as if celebrating the passing of the storm.

Next morning, as we paddled slowly in the shade of the sloping forested bluffs of the lower Cumberland, a pontoon approached us. This was the Coast Guard Auxiliary, led by Jerry Turley, a retiree from Chicago. He and his friends, also retirees from the Midwest, patrolled the waters in their pontoon on weekends, helping people in trouble and reporting serious problems or wrongdoing to the regular officers. Upon learning what we were doing, Jerry said he would call reporter Sam Burrage, who did feature stories for the Paducah TV news (Channel 6) to come see us at Devil's Elbow campground, where we were bound. When I was a teenager, I watched Sam, an effusive man with a giant Afro, and I looked forward to meeting him in person and to see if the years had diminished his cheerful energy. Sam never showed, but Jerry dropped by with a plastic bag filled with ice and cold beverages.

Devil's Elbow Campground, named after the tortuous path of the channel in the middle of the lake, was a typical Corps of Engineers plot, deeply shaded, our site a few yards from the water, well mown and clear of trash. Having arrived there by early afternoon, we hiked about a mile to Canton on Highway 68, where we had lunch at the Canton One-Stop, a gas station/convenience store/diner, where locals had gathered at the five or six tables. In this case, the locals were, like Jerry Turley and his crew, retirees from elsewhere, who were blending in pretty well, it seemed. Our waitress, pretty in the prime of her late teens, had not yet been dragged down by work or isolation. Later, as we were leaving, we'd see her cheerfully heaving rotten watermelons into the dumpster outside the store. Across the room, a fat man wearing a straw cowboy hat and tennis shoes, who from his accent and manner was obviously a longtime local, stood and talked with a table of four: a woman who weighed close to three hundred pounds; her husband, not quite as large, who wore a T-shirt dominated by a leaping bass; and an Asian couple. The big woman, from Florida, and the local, known as Doc, did most of the talking, though the Asian couple seemed to know as much as they did about the comings and goings and renovations of the retirees in the area.

Before he left, Doc referred to the Asian man as the "only Oriental redneck in Trigg County." They all laughed heartily at this. I wondered if the name of the town—Canton—had attracted the Asian couple.

We walked up the road to a fruit stand—Gil's Produce. There were peaches, apples, tomatoes, cucumbers, onions, a few watermelons, but no Gil. Beside the apples was a coffee can for payment. In Gil's yard behind the fruit stand were five vehicles, including an RV, four lawnmowers, and two boats. Apparently Canton had a low crime rate and a high level of trust.

Back at camp, Randy, ever industrious, took advantage of the low humidity after the storm and went fishing in the canoe. He guaranteed that he would catch a fish. Randy was welcome to my lures, but the paltry collection had grown even scanter after my inept attempts at fishing, and Randy took to recycling lures he found on the shoreline. With a salvaged white plastic grub worm he caught two bass. He paddled back to camp, showed them to me, and gently returned them to the water.

As a boy of ten or so I fished this bay with my father on a foggy morning in the 1960s before the campground was built and not long after Barkley Dam was completed. On the pre-dawn drive from Murray, I was intoxicated by the name of the destination—Devil's Elbow. At the deserted put-in, my father backed the trailer down a gravel ramp. The aluminum utility boat clanged and boomed as it slid off the trailer into the water. I sat on a red painted bench near the bow, casting live bait toward the shore, my father in the back casting a lure and minding a pole that was held in place by a holder he'd designed. With a small wooden paddle he scooted us parallel to the bank with occasional one-armed strokes. We floated past a grove of pine trees, where the needles had fallen to coat the ground, a cushiony foundation for a campsite. Without talking, we cast toward the brush beside the bank but caught no fish. Though I don't remember much else about that morning other than the sinister name of the place and the seclusion and quiet of the fog, it remains one of my most vivid images of the lakes area.

The days of easy seclusion had passed, with the official campground established; the boat ramp crowded with gleaming pickup trucks, tires and bumpers swollen as if on steroids; the hilltops sprouting dream homes of cedar, brick, and glass.

That night we were to be picked up by my mother, Margaret, and my wife, Julie, who operates an antique shop once a month not far from Murray, where she also grew up, about a half-hour drive from the campsite. Randy and I, having already eaten hamburgers at the diner, were feeling guilty about such easy access to restaurant food, but not so guilty to turn down an offer. I waited for Julie and Margaret's arrival above our campsite near the bathhouse because it was near dark and our site was fifty yards from the campground road. After thirty minutes, I didn't worry. After an hour, past dark, I began to pace. I called my in-law's, where Julie's sister Sharon was staying. She told me that they had called her to report their status: lost. I described again where we were, emphasizing that we were in the back of the campground behind the bathrooms.

"Oh, that sounds nice," said Sharon. "I bet it smells good."

"You can't really smell it," I said, and then started to explain that proximity to a bathhouse was a good thing for two guys on a long canoe trip, who considered running water and porcelain accessories luxuries, but I lacked the energy. I also chose not to mention that the drinking water at the campground had apparently given Randy and me a mild case of the runs.

"I'll take the Four Seasons any day," she said.

Three hours later, at ten, Julie called. They had turned at a sign that said Devil's Elbow in the Land Between the Lakes (LBL) before the Highway 68 Bridge over the Cumberland/Lake Barkley. They wandered the dirt roads of LBL for an hour, Julie getting out of the car and yelling out our names into the dark, empty landscape. Our campsite, across the river from LBL, also claimed the colorful name, "Devil's Elbow," because the elbow itself was on neither shore, but in the middle of the lake.

Randy did not complain as I threw together a mélange of dehydrated food products and produced a meal that was best consumed in the dark by hungry campers used to such primitive fare. I vowed to make it up to Randy, who was still craving breakfast, so I arranged for us to meet my mother and Aunt Robbie at Barkley Lodge the next morning, a five-mile paddle to the mouth of the Little River, then "a little ways up the river to the lodge," as I assured Randy. A little ways, indeed. We would pay dearly for this breakfast, but not in cash.

CHAPTER 22

SEA OF WAKES

"Just a little farther," I kept telling Randy, after we turned into the mouth of the Little River, a half-mile-wide bay where fleets of pleasure boats raced past us toward the main lake. In the hour that we paddled up the river toward the buffet breakfast with my mother and Aunt Robbie, not one minute passed without a wake to ride. They came in all directions, in all sizes.

Though I had never approached Barkley Lodge by water, I knew it should be rising like a monument from a hillside, a giant A-frame built of dark wood and glass. We dug in hard to make it there before they put away the breakfast buffet. Hot, thirsty, and winded, we tied off at the dock's cleats and hoped that our boat would not be rocked so hard in the traffic that it would be overturned. Past the pool we sauntered into the hotel buffet. It was 10:35, fifteen minutes after breakfast had officially shut down. My mother had talked the waitress into leaving the food out for us, and Randy and I scooped up what was left of the eggs, sausage, hash browns, gravy, biscuits, bacon, and pancakes. Randy was a big hit with my mother and aunt, and no wonder. He was the one who looked like he had actually reaped benefits from the voyage. His clothes were relatively clean, his face was shaven and evenly tanned, and his labor in the bow had further defined the muscles in his already lean upper body. By contrast, I looked like a castaway—dazed and shadowy and sloppy enough to frighten small children in the air-conditioned cave of glass and wood.

Outside, in the parking lot, my mother handed over the supplies that Julie had bought—two canisters of propane and a blank video tape for Randy's machine. Like Vic, my mother was concerned about our contracting scurvy. She gave us a grocery bag filled with apples, bananas, oranges, peaches, and blueberries, enough for a fruit basket centerpiece.

I told her I hadn't had any dreams about Ben, my father.

"That's because he approves of this trip since you have Randy along," she said.

Exiting the Little River was more of a rockinghorse ride than entering had been because now, near noon, all of the big boat captains had awakened, gathered their gear, filled their coolers, thrown off their numerous lines, run the blowers, started their engines, gassed up, and raced toward the open waters to compete for tiny corridors of space where they could run full out, as if at sea. Traffic was the worst on Barkley, the widest, longest reservoir on the Cumberland, and also the nearest to three other major rivers: the Ohio, Mississippi, and Tennessee. We paddled steadily in a sort of stupor after the big meal, letting wakes hit us from all sides, not bothering to turn the bow. Sometimes we'd get pounded so hard that a paddle stroke would miss the water, striking only air.

The most frightening part came when we exited the mouth of the Little River and gazed out at the vast blue lake. I wanted to camp at LBL in Cravens Bay, on the west side of the lake. Unfortunately, we were on the east side, about three miles away from the opposite shore. Crossing all that open water in such a small boat was intimidating in itself, but more so because we had to sprint across the navigational channel. Marked by red buoys on the left, green on the right, the channel was about a hundred yards wide. In this corridor, the biggest boats, including the barges, had to navigate to ensure adequate depth for their hulls' draft. On this Saturday of low humidity and bright sunshine, the channel resembled a busy six-lane expressway, with traffic that ignored the lanes. To cross, we would have to jaywalk like staggering vagrants into the whizzing stream of fiberglass, hoping that the big guys saw us and veered a safe distance away. In thirty minutes we were in the open water on the far side of the channel, our breakfast worked off with panicked muscles. My breath came in ragged gasps.

Though I was still troubled by a vague sense of impending doom, our time within the karmic noose was narrowing. We had three days and forty miles to go. We didn't expect to be treated like celebrities, and we didn't tell people what we were doing unless they asked, but we thought we deserved the occasional open-mouthed amazement when we answered the question about where we'd come from in the little green canoe. Aside from Jerry Turley, the Coast Guard helper, the reactions of western Kentuckians ranged from puzzlement to apathy. A cabin cruiser captain off the coast of Barkley Lodge idled over to us and asked where we had started out. When we proudly told him Harlan, he nodded and a vacant look came over his face. Without another comment, he motored away. Clearly, he did not know of Harlan, as many did not, though some had the guts at least to ask, as did the campground manager at Devil's Elbow. The manager's reply, however, was of a type that was beginning to annoy us, the "I can top that" retort.

His was seeing a fleet of jet skiers who had come to the Elbow down the Ohio from Pittsburgh, on the way to New Orleans. Quite a trip, to be sure, and mileage that dwarfed ours, but they were on jet skis, with the luxury to detour deep into bays and to backtrack with little consequence in terms of energy and time, to make one hundred miles or more a day if they had plenty of sunscreen and cash for gas. The next campground manager at Cravens Bay, after learning of our voyage, said he had once rented a campsite to three old men who were boating the Cumberland from Paducah to Nashville. *In a johnboat. With a motor.* The oldest of the men, in his late seventies, was a writer. The campsite manager gave them a ride to the nearest town for groceries.

"That's really something," I might have said, had I acted out my inner Gulliver. "Did the old guys get windburn going so fast? Did they take turns at the throttle to avoid carpal tunnel syndrome?"

At least people were talking to us. We wanted to hear what they had to say, and we were polite, good listeners. We flinched but did not protest when the Cravens Bay managers charged us an extra seven dollars because we had two tents instead of one. There was also a sign in the bathroom that said you would be "prosecuted" for using the electrical outlets, so we couldn't charge our phones there. Despite the official policies, the couple that managed Cravens Bay were affable and informative, and later on they let me charge my phone at the outlet next to their RV. The woman said she'd lived in LBL before Barkley Dam was built at a place called Calhoun Settlement. She extended her arm toward the bay and said there were stores, a bank, a post office, and houses out there before the "big flood." She wasn't bitter about it, just matter of fact. The couple said that the Forest Service's management of LBL was an improvement over TVA. Forest Service workers actually enforce laws against littering and illegal homesteading, said the manager. The TVA employees never knew how long they would have jobs under the organization's budget constraints, so they tended not to do their jobs as thoroughly.

We set up camp across a drainage ditch from a small camper. On the other side of us, about thirty yards away, two teenage couples had quite a setup: two large tents, two hammocks strung bunk-bed style under shade trees, and big rubber floats on the water. The kids were eerily quiet and industrious that afternoon and through the night. One of them lay in the hammock reading most of the afternoon. Another started a fire in the evening and kept it going most of the night. In the camper across the ditch from us an old couple sat at a table. They had to be roasting inside the un–air-conditioned metal shell, and it seemed to me, glancing at the cloudy windows, that they were glaring at us. Later on, the old couple left and the man, named Sullivan, came over. An ironworker who lived in St. Louis, Sullivan grew up in nearby Paducah, and the old folks were his parents. He was here to fish, and he was alone because his St. Louis girlfriend hated camping. As a child he'd lived on a farm near Paducah and caught catfish from Clarks River, a tributary of the Tennessee. His brother worked on a towboat until his arm was crushed between two barges; now he farmed the family acreage. Sullivan, who wore a "God Bless America" T-shirt, said he would not trade places with his brother, though he was worried about his job at the steel mill in the depressed economy.

Randy launched the canoe to fish with his scavenged lures, and I walked down the road a couple of miles, anxious to reconnect with familiar land. In the deep shade of the narrow paved road lay a small clearing and a cemetery. The graves were marked with plastic flowers, small white crosses made of PVC pipe, and concrete blocks. No names or dates. A local historical society maintained the cemetery, populated by settlers who had lived and died from "illness, injuries, or other dire circumstances," said the green sign at the entrance. They had named it Sillian Cemetery, after a family that had lived in the area, though none of the remains, which were dated before the 1870s, could be identified. Between the Rivers Preservation Organization, through their "Rescue Our Cemeteries" project, had rediscovered this plot in 1997 after consulting old TVA maps. In all, they had documented 164 cemeteries in LBL. They were all that TVA had left behind when it exercised eminent domain in what was then known as the Land Between the Rivers. All the people were forced to move, their homes and outbuildings burned. For former residents like the campground manager, a cemetery might be the only link to their childhood home.

Most of the 164 LBL cemeteries contain ten plots or less, family graveyards where, as one volunteer said, a mother could look out the window of her house and watch over her dead child. Many died in childbirth, as evidenced by the plots with mother and child next to each other. Records show deaths from every war since the Revolutionary War, and also from whooping cough, diarrhea, and lightning strikes. Among the white settlers' graves, the organization also found slaves and Chinese immigrants who worked in LBL's iron furnaces. Volunteers for such a project worked on discovering, document-ing, and maintaining these sites in the winter months, when ticks and snakes weren't a problem. For these people, the past was important and alive, not something to be forgotten, taken over by weeds and honeysuckle.

Walking down the empty road in the heat of that late afternoon, I felt, for the first time, the influence of home. The woods were deep and lush, as I remembered them, and toward the bay was a swampy field of reeds, where a few deer grazed. Birds sang energetically through the heat. The Forest Service had planted a corn crop, and even that seemed to fit in. I hadn't lived here, as the campground manager had, but I'd spent so much time here that it felt like home. Although the educational attractions, such as the iron furnace, the nature center, the buffalo herd, and the pioneer village taught me much about the past, I liked most of all just being there, without a plan or itinerary. I never had to be doing anything in particular to get that sense of relaxed familiarity. Part of that attraction came from the fact that LBL had generally been left alone for forty years. Aside from roads and some habitat encourage-ment such as mowing and a couple of small artificial lakes, the natural life on LBL had been allowed to thrive. That nobody lived here and hadn't for a long time made it different from any other place on the river, including the national forest upstream, where people can live. There were no lawns, no lawn mowers, leaf blowers, marinas, convenience stores, or billboards, and there hadn't been for almost fifty years. If you wanted a snack or to get gas, you had to leave LBL. The campers at Cravens Bay fit in with the quiet, unobtrusive landscape. There were no monster RVs, and the bay was too shallow for big boats. Our neighbor, Sullivan, had pulled his bass boat up the ditch a ways and moored it to a tree. Up the hill, two campsites had kayaks. I walked past two women catfishing from the bank with chicken livers. Though I kept waiting for a loud outburst of music or yelling from the teenagers, the only noises they made the whole time were with small charges of gunpowder that they threw on the ground to ignite a tiny pop, like the breaking of a brittle twig.

Julie braved the dark back roads of LBL to visit that night. The kids across the way—sitting around their roaring fire—were so quiet I felt guilty about our loud laughter until midnight. After Julie left, I had another float-ing tent nightmare.

"Randy," I said, waking myself up, "Are we floating?"

"No," he said wearily.

Later a couple of coons as big as Jasper, my German shepherd mix, invaded camp, waking me with the clink of cans. In the glare of my flashlight one of them reared up on his hind legs with one of our stewed tomato cans between his paws. His eyes glowed red. After I scolded them, they slinked off in search of better quality garbage.

The next day, getting closer to the dam, Randy and I fought the increasing wakes like stoics, without complaint. We stopped for lunch on a bare dirt bank scarred and dwindling from the constant pounding of boat traffic. We ate quickly as deer flies attacked and waves crashed broadside against the canoe. The stench of death—strong though no animal corpses were visible—made our breaths shallow. We faced a crossing from the west to the east side of the river, where our next campsite, Eureka, would be.

Randy wanted to cut straight across to make our time on the open water as short as possible. I wanted to make more of an angled cut across and down-river, which would mean we'd be in the channel longer but make better use of our energy. Besides, I pointed out, if we cut straight across to the Money Cliff, we would have to paddle down the part of the channel that ran flush against the sheer cliff. No place for us to escape in case of an emergency. Randy yielded, but he was worried, and weary of the big water.

"This will be one of our last big tests," he said.

"I doubt it," I said.

After we'd almost made it to the other side, the biggest pleasure boat of the trip, a seventy-footer, sent big swells at us from a quarter mile away. Randy called it the "million-dollar boat."

We had passed the Castle on the Cumberland, the Kentucky State Prison at Eddyville. From across the river, its pale gray limestone façade and green roof resembled some kind of retro resort. There was a house in front of it beside the lake, and a water tower with KSP painted white on it. I wondered if inmates could look out the windows and see the blue lake with people motoring up and down it in their boats, going where they wanted as fast as they pleased, the breeze in their hair, women baring their tanned, oiled flesh. Bill Cunningham, novelist and local historian, wrote *Castle: A Kentucky Prison,* a dramatic account of the prison's history. Completed in 1886 by Italian stonemasons, the prison was nicknamed "the castle" because of its medieval demeanor. Soon after completion, a sign was placed over the front entrance with a quotation from Dante's *Inferno*: "Abandon hope, all ye who enter here." One hundred and sixty two men had been executed at the state prison between 1911 and 1962.

Before the prisons in this area, back in the time when the rivers ran free and the keelboat ruled the waters, brutal and murderous desperadoes roamed the lower Ohio and Cumberland. According to R. E. Banta, the early nineteenth century's most notorious were the Harpe Brothers, Micahjah and Wiley, who robbed, raped, and murdered their way across Tennessee and Kentucky, concentrating on the area between the Ohio and the Tennessee rivers. The Harpes, who traveled with two women, were known for their brutality. One killed his own baby just after it was born. The brothers' idea of a prank was to push a hostage tied on horseback off a cliff above their partners in crime, camped below on the river, terrifying the fellow robbers as man and horse screamed in the fall into the bonfire below. The Harpes' allies were a renegade band of Cherokee who accompanied them on some raids.

Micahjah was shot in the spine by pursuers. As he lay paralyzed, he told his captors that his murders had been divinely inspired, though he regretted killing his own child. As they beheaded him, he was still ornery enough to criticize the way that his executioner used the knife against his throat. Micahjah's head was attached to a tree near a road in Nashville as a warning to other evildoers.

Colonel Plug, an Ohio Valley desperado, developed an elaborate subterfuge for robbing keelboats. Pretending he was stranded and in distress, he would wave down a passing boat from shore. Onboard, he would collapse on the deck and pick away the caulk between the planks until the boat sank, and his partners, one of whom was named "nine eyes," would paddle out and collect the goods. Plug's demise was fitting. He drowned below decks of a boat that he sank.

Before the Harpes, in the eighteenth century, Simon Girty, known as the "white savage," was one of the most feared villains in the Ohio Valley. In an article that critically examines the myth of Girty as a sort of white devil, historian Daniel P. Barr not only recounts Girty's exploits but also attempts to explain them. Girty was reared by the Seneca Indians, who during the French and Indian War had captured his entire family in Pennsylvania. Girty watched as his stepfather was burned at the stake. Having grown up with the Indians and fluent in native languages, he became valuable to whites as a scout and interpreter. First, he worked for the Americans as a spy against the British. Then, after becoming disgusted with Americans during the "Squaw Campaign," in which he witnessed the murdering of Indian women and children under Colonel Edward Hand, Girty defected to the British side and led Indians on raids against Americans on the Ohio and Kentucky frontier during the Revolutionary War.

The most famous scene of his cruelty against whites occurred in 1782 when he was in the company of the Delaware Indians, who had defeated the force of Colonel William Crawford, a militiaman who was a friend of George Washington's. Crawford had been tied to a stake, beaten with clubs for hours, his body burned with lit twigs and repeated firings of powder at point-blank range. His ears had been cut off. And he didn't so much as even cry out until, after hours of such torture, he beseeched Girty, whom he knew: "Girty! Girty! For God's sake, Girty, shoot me through the heart!" Girty replied, "I cannot, for as you can see, I have no gun." Then he is reported to have "belched forth a sinister giggle." Girty became mythologized much as Daniel Boone had, though he represented the flip side of frontier nobility, seen by some as the white man corrupted by amoral savages, but by others as an evil influence on natives intent on impressing him with their cruelty.

In view of the prison that housed some of our modern-day desperadoes, Randy and I saw the first bald eagle of the trip. As it soared east toward LBL, we paddled into a cove in sluggish pursuit. Bald eagles frequented western Kentucky and West Tennessee thanks in part to the help of TVA, the U.S. Fish and Wildlife Service, and the state of Kentucky. In 1980, when reintro-duction of bald eagles was begun in LBL, nesting eagles hadn't been seen in the area since the 1930s. Illegal hunting and habitat loss had placed them on the endangered species list. Between 1980 and 1988, forty-four bald eaglets were raised and turned loose in LBL. By 1999, fourteen bald eagle nests were counted in LBL. As we would find out during the next few days, they thrived beyond their refuge in the narrow peninsula.

Eureka, within sight of Barkley Dam, would be our last Corps camp-ground. We landed our canoe on the beach of the swimming area and secured a site about fifty yards away. The campground was nearly full on this, a Sun-day. Kids rode their bikes up and down the campground road, and from multigenerational sites such as the one next to us drifted fragrant smoke from grills and deep fryers. Bug zappers popped. Mothers scolded. Kids whooped. Fathers grumbled. Next to us, a family had hung multicolored lights that they left on all night. Two little girls came by on bikes and asked if they could turn around in the little parking place at our campsite. The camper on the other side of us had prohibited their U-turns in his parking place. Since we had no vehicle, they had plenty of room to make the turnabout safely. Each time they came by they smiled sweetly at us. I strolled the circular campground road while waiting for Julie to arrive and take us to a Grand Rivers restaurant. Randy had a phone message from his parents and girlfriend saying that they had arrived and were camped downriver on the Ohio, near Smithland. The tribes were gathering. I gave them all an estimated arrival time of two o'clock on Tuesday.

Randy and I had become experts on esoterica such as wakes, wind, swim-ming holes, and Corps of Engineers' campgrounds. Though Eureka had the shady, well-kept, orderly character of almost all Corps sites, its showers were substandard, quite scummy with inadequate water pressure. The best bathhouse (and shower) was the first site, at Waitsboro, though Lock A, above Cheatham Dam, was a close second. When she arrived that evening, Julie was impressed by our multilevel site—parking place above, tent area with fire ring below, iron hanging hook at the corner, water spigot and power outlet on the middle level, all of it sprinkled with fine limestone gravel. She much preferred the order of the Corps site to the primitive campsite at Cravens Bay, though Randy and I valued the laid-back seclusion of the LBL site.

We had made much fun of the RV people and felt alienated from their culture, particularly when they brought multiple refrigerators, microwaves, and burned multicolored lights all night, but the more I considered them, the less I felt the need to criticize. I was glad that people still felt the urge to spend time outdoors, even if they did have to carry a house and kitchen with them. So what? It took a lot of trouble to move all that stuff. You had to be motivated to spend time with kids and grandkids near the water, under the trees. It would be far easier to set them in front of a television or a computer in a darkened, air-conditioned living room each weekend, tranquilizing them with advertisements so they could grow up and be good consumers.

The closer we got to the end of the journey, the more fastidious Randy became. We hadn't had access to a laundry since way back at Lock A, but his clothes seemed amazingly free of blemish. Though I know he had no more than three shirts, he always had a fresh one to put on once we set up camp. Mine I usually peeled off like a damp epidermis and hung somewhere to air out and stiffen for next day's use. My clothes were soiled and smudged while Randy's remained immaculate. I finally figured out that besides my overall sloppiness, I was consistently carrying out a chore that got me dirty: folding the ground tarp, inevitably caked with mud, sand, or worse. When Randy helped me fold the nine-by-twelve-foot sheet, neither of us got dirty. But I was always impatient to leave in the mornings and usually did it myself as he was brushing sand off his tent or cleaning his shoes. Randy even acted as custodian of the wilderness. When we pulled in at Eureka at the swimming area, a dead carp lay nearby. I stepped over the fish and took a load up to camp. When I returned, the fish was gone.

"Did you move that fish?" I asked Randy, who stood there holding a forked stick.

He smiled and said that he had.

This was something I never would have considered, though it made me happy, and a little amused, that I had someone along who would go to the trouble of eliminating unpleasantness whenever possible.

That night we ate obscenely thick pork chops in Grand Rivers and drank good red wine that Julie brought. The waitresses wore bonnets and long fluffy dresses in the style of the nineteenth century. Alas, we were attended by a waiter, who didn't wear a dress. We had an awkward moment when, as we gave him two clumps of money for each part of the bill, he kept it all without giving us our change. This would have amounted to a 30 percent tip. He was good, but not that good, and besides he wasn't wearing one of the fluffy dresses. Lacking the finer points of civilized discourse, Randy and I bestowed upon Julie the chore of lowering the waiter's self-worth a few notches with the news that we were giving him the conventional 15 percent. Julie accepted our humble thanks for navigating the treacherous waters of waiter/diner discourse.

Next morning, a man came up to us as we were loading the canoe.

"I know what you guys are doing," he said.

That's good, I felt like saying, would you tell us so we'll know?

"I think it's great," he said. In chatting with him, a native of southern Illinois, I learned that he was one of the few downriver folks who seemed to know the geography of the entire Cumberland. A vagabond himself, he had sold his house and was living in an RV. He had driven to Eureka for a family reunion. Though he didn't say he envied us, as several men had, he stood there and gazed after us as we paddled across our last lake toward Barkley Dam, the busiest and largest dam of the trip. Finally, we'd met someone in western Kentucky who seemed to understand our quest, though by this time my brain was so clouded by the heat, exertion, and camping fatigue that I needed to be reminded that a canoe voyage was a noble enterprise, the best way to truly know a river in its entirety. I looked forward to locking through Barkley Dam and floating on moving water once more, the matrix that fired my imagination, that soothed and calmed me and restored my energy. Ironic that rivers below dams, where they resembled their natural state, seemed to discourage development, boaters, campers, and the general tourist horde. Did they know what they were missing?

CHAPTER 23

HELL BROKEN LOOSE

HELL BROKEN LOOSE

"Going up that river was like traveling back to the earliest beginnings
of the world, when vegetation rioted on the earth and the big trees
were kings. An empty stream, a great silence, an impenetrable forest.
The air was warm, thick, heavy, sluggish. There was no joy in the
brilliance of the sunshine."

CONRAD
Heart of Darkness

"Violent crime is unusual in Livingston County," said the newscaster perkily
from my yellow radio as we floated into Livingston County. "But two murders in one weekend is unheard of." A Grand Rivers man, she told us, had
repeatedly shot a Smithland man with a .22 rifle and then finished him off
by beating him with the rifle until it broke apart. The accused man, named
Doom, had turned himself in. Later, he would testify that the victim had sex-
ually assaulted him moments before the murder. A place called Doom's Landing was marked on the charts, a few miles downriver from us. The other murder, in Ledbetter, was the result of "multiple blunt force trauma" with a claw
hammer. The victim worked for a transport company that shuttled towboat
crews from Paducah to boats across the country. With large amounts of cash
on hand, he had loaned money to the employees he transported. The man

who turned himself in for the murder had once borrowed money from the victim.

Rush Limbaugh followed up the news to rage against the overturning of the antisodomy law in Texas. The landscape took on a hellish, desperate demeanor, not unlike the African jungle that enveloped Conrad's pilot, Marlowe, who descended deeper and deeper into darkness within and without. We had been descending as well, and now we were at the lowest altitude on the river. Heat gathered and hung in the air, the sky a white glare, the sun a remote yellow smudge.

People think that these are strange and violent times, and I agree that they are, but during 1811–12, this area was the scene of events—natural and unnatural—that were as dark and cataclysmic as an Edgar Allan Poe story. Just a few miles north of Smithland, our ultimate destination, were the farms of the Lewis brothers, nephews of Thomas Jefferson, whose tragic exploits have been chronicled by Boynton Merrill Jr. Prone to drink and depression, Lilburne Lewis became enraged that George, his slave, had broken a water pitcher that had been a favorite of his recently deceased wife. He hacked the slave to death with an axe and ordered his other slaves to cut up George's body and burn it in the kitchen fireplace. That night, the first of a series of powerful earthquakes hit, collapsing the chimney. The next day, after a neighbor saw Lilburne's dog, Nero, carrying George's head, Lilburne and his brother, Isham, an accomplice, were arrested and charged with killing the slave, which was considered murder at that time in Kentucky. Incredibly, if Lilburne had publicly claimed he was beating George and "accidentally" killed him, he would not have been arrested; concealing the body, however, suggested forethought.

Some considered the earthquake a divine intervention that uncovered the brothers' crime. Indeed, even those in the region who didn't know about the murder considered the earthquakes as God's punishment of a frontier society known for its killing, robbing, gambling, fighting, drinking, whoring, and inability to enforce law and order. The Indians also considered the quakes cosmic punishment, brought on, they thought, because white men in the Rocky Mountains had murdered an Indian who was under "special protection of the Great Spirit" (Merrill 254).

The earthquakes, whose epicenter was in New Madrid, Missouri, seventy-five miles southwest of the Lewises' farms, warped nature in ways that nobody had witnessed before and we North Americans haven't seen since. During the quakes, which started in December 1811, a thunderous noise rumbled in the Earth's bowels, audible as far away as the Atlantic coast. Tremors jarred people from Canada to the Gulf of Mexico. In Kentucky, the tortured earth roared, hissed, and whistled like some enraged dying animal. Between shocks, a dark, rank-smelling fog or smoke arose, reminding inhabitants of hell's smoldering brimstone. At night the sky was illuminated as if a distant city glowed over the horizon. Near western Kentucky, on the Mississippi, the river's bottom buckled and rose during the strongest quakes, at one point forming a six-foot waterfall all the way across. Waves rose thirty feet above the normal level, and the river boiled and ran backwards, forming Reelfoot Lake in West Tennessee. Only because the area was so sparsely populated was there no great loss of life, though people on the rivers, especially on the Mississippi, were in the gravest danger.

Other strange and portentous events of that year—known as Annus Mirabilis—led up to the quakes. The Ohio River flooded in the spring of 1811; a great comet glowed from April to October; there were tornadoes, hurricanes, drought, and intense heat. Animals such as squirrels and pigeons fled the region in massive migrations. There was a total eclipse of the sun in September. In August, the Shawnee chief Tecumseh and twenty warriors floated past Smithland in their canoes on the way to attempt a unification of tribes to fight against white settlement. After Tecumseh met with reluctance from the southern tribes, he warned them that "when he returned to Detroit he would stamp his foot, and the earth would tremble and their houses would fall to the ground" (248).

The first steamboat to appear on the Ohio passed Smithland that year, alarming many. Some, who had never heard the sound of a steamboat engine, thought that the "devil incarnate" (253) had arrived. When the boat reached Owensboro, Kentucky, up the Ohio from Smithland, the first earthquake struck.

The river pushed Randy and me to the center of this ominous setting, so troubled by great historical forces that coalesced near the gathering of four powerful rivers: the Mississippi, the Ohio, the Tennessee, and the Cumberland. We had one more night to spend on the river, and it would be an uneasy one. Having left settled and populated Lake Barkley, we had once again embarked on the free-flowing river, relatively uncharted for camping; likely we would have to trespass one last time. With the moving water that I loved so much came the inconveniences of isolation and the confrontation of the unknown, which though uncomfortable, restored our sense of adventure.

Our last lockage had been a social occasion. Randy's parents and nephew, Ryan, had persuaded security to let them through the heavily guarded gates at the dam to watch us descend one last time. When we got to the guide wall on the upstream side, we heard clanging from inside the lock and guessed a barge was locking through. Over the loudspeaker, the lock operator told us to paddle around to the side, near the riprap where the dam joined the northern shoreline.

It was there that we craned our necks upward to converse with Randy's family thirty feet above. We chatted for an hour as the barge locked through.

The Corps, having been informed of our arrival, gave us the star treatment at Barkley Dam. Inside the lock, we were joined by a workboat, a steel platform with an outboard motor and scaffolding. A public affairs officer stood on the scaffolding and shot video and stills of us tethered to the mooring bitt. Randy shot back. For fifteen minutes, the officer ordered the boat's pilot back and forth for favorable angles. The inside of the lock heated up like a barbeque pit as we waited to descend.

"Okay, let me get this straight" said the officer, upon finishing his series of shots. "It's Curly on the left and Moe on the right."

"No," said Randy, "it's the Skipper and Gilligan."

"Next time, bring Mary Ann," countered the officer, a scholar of landmark sit-coms.

He looked up at a man standing above us on the wall. "How much are you discharging?" he shouted.

I couldn't hear the reply, but the officer told us we'd have a five- or six-mile-an-hour current below the dam. For some reason, we thanked him.

"Y'all have smooth sailing," he said. Before departing through the upstream gate, he ordered, "You see a towboat, get up on the bank."

Easier said than done. We didn't see any barges on the final stretch, at least not while we shared the water with them, but we did meet *Miss Debbie* coming upriver near the bend at Iuka, where the river had narrowed to thirty yards or so between steep, muddy banks impossible to "get up on." *Miss Debbie* was a cabin cruiser that we estimated at sixty-five feet, and she was coming at us about half throttle. Behind her, five-foot wakes crashed against the bare banks, silting up the channel and clouding the water deep brown. Randy took aim with the video camera. We both gestured with thumbs-down signals. I drew my finger slowly across my throat. Two boys lounged on the deck, a pair of middle-aged men at the helm above them. In this narrow channel only the most callous captain would look the other way and maintain his speed. Just when it mattered most, about fifteen yards upstream from us, *Miss Debbie*'s captain pulled back on the throttle to let us jump her large but manageable wakes. We waved and thanked them, though Randy and I wondered if the captain would have slowed for less demonstrative canoeists, without a video camera. From Newburg, Indiana, they had come from the big waters of the Ohio, where it was unlikely they'd seen a canoe.

Around midafternoon we stopped at a boat ramp in Dycusburg and considered its campsite potential. There were three houses and a narrow road, paved and potholed. A man with a shaven head, smoking a cigarette in his backyard, looked up at us wandering around above the ramp. I worked up enough energy to state the obvious: "We're just doing a little canoeing."

A deranged grin spread across his face. "Boilin' hot, ain't it? Cain't even stand it in the car with all the windows down."

We had entered another realm, a somnolent atmosphere, latently hostile, that held us like flies in amber. Geologic eons from the eastern Kentucky coalfield, we had descended to this steamy soup of humidity and heat, where the border between river and sky was no longer distinct, both variations of a brownish gray matrix. According to the ancient Mayas, people traveled by canoe on rivers to get to the next world. They called it the Watery Path, an inversion of earth and sky. Archeologist David Freidel explained it to writer Christopher Shaw thus: "At night the cosmos inverts itself, so that what was below is raised above. To reach the sky, like First Father, or the Hero Twins of the *Popul Vuh*, who played the ball game with the Lords of Death in the Otherworld and defeated them, you had to get on the 'escalator down,' which is the Watery Path. The Watery Path would carry you directly into the sky" (131–32).

We continued to escalate downward. Two bald eagles stared at us from a dead tree. Catfish bigger than beer kegs swirled to the surface and gulped, startling Randy in the bow. Like the "poisonous snakes nest" myth that Rhonda retold at Dover, the "catfish as big as a man" myth flourished on southern reservoirs, usually near dams, where the big ones gather. Often in these stories, a frightened diver would surface to describe the oversized cat, comparing it to a car or a boat in size. Sometimes, the teller would say that the fish was big enough to swallow a man, though I'd never heard a myth in which a man is actually consumed by the fish. Though it's not uncommon to see photos in newspapers of people posing with catfish over a hundred pounds, I've never heard a firsthand, reliable account of one as "big as a man," unless that man were quite small. Transcending southern myth, catfish in the Mekong River in Southeast Asia actually grow up to nine feet long, though their existence is threatened by flood control projects that may obliterate the deep pools where they live.

In *Jefferson's Nephews*, his book on the Lewis brothers, Merrill notes the great variety of animals in western Kentucky during the early nineteenth century. Of particular note because of their number and their exotic nature were Carolina Paroquets, solid green birds the size of a hawk, with a scarlet and yellow neck. Flocks and flocks of them flew over the lowlands, squawking constantly in flight. They are no more. Even more numerous were passenger pigeons, whose flocks were so vast it took two days for them to pass going at a mile a minute. They blotted out the sky like a cloud, their groupings were so dense. Men killed them with sticks and ate them until they were nearly extinct.

Wolves, bears, and panthers ruled the woods and canebrakes. One pack of wolves killed and ate a slave in 1813. In nearby Muhlenburg County, hunters killed a panther eleven feet long.

Other than the eagles and the catfish, the Cumberland seemed deserted. Except for the boiling-hot bald man at Dycusburg, we had seen no humans on land. *Miss Debbie* was the only boat we passed. Distant thunder rolled, a signal that we needed to find a campsite high off the water, someplace where we wouldn't be lightning bait. From the right bank jutted shelves of tan rock just a few feet wide, where we would be exposed to the weather. The left bank was consistently steep and muddy, preventing us from landing, unloading, and climbing to a flat field above. When I spotted the sand bar partially hidden in the trees, I knew it would be our last good spot. It was a hard-packed sandy slope with a terrace fifteen feet above the water, hidden in a grove of small trees. Above us was an uncultivated field. Somewhere downriver a tractor prowled. Across the river sat a small cabin, a horse trailer, an empty corral, and a tattered American flag. We were somewhere between Dycusburg and Pickneyville, about eighteen miles from Smithland.

Randy set up a canopy, and we waited out the last rain of the trip, a gentle shower that lasted about half an hour. Around the bend came a tow, the *T. H. Kelly*, with a covered load three wide and three long. Close behind was another towboat pushing just one barge. The lead barge threw his engines in reverse and idled on the right side of the river as the lighter barge passed it, quite a maneuver on the narrow river. Knowing it was our last night on the river, I just sat there most of the evening and watched it flow past. *It is for this I have come*, I thought, echoing Least Heat-Moon's words. Watching the river flow emptied my mind, restored me, and I could have sat there like that for days had my back not begun to ache. I was dirty, grouchy, and despite my reverence for the restored river, a part of me was ready to sleep under a roof, in a bed, with my wife.

With the end of the trip immanent, melancholy and regret hung over the campsite. Had we missed something the river had offered us? Would we, with time away from it, lose what we had received? We tried to work ourselves into a mood to celebrate the last night but just fell back into our old habits, me idly meditating on the river, Randy busy with organizing and cleaning. He danced around under the heavy foliage of our campsite in an attempt to get a clear signal on his cell phone so he could talk to Lara. I stood, squatted, and sat, trying to ease my back.

Fish broke the surface of the moving water every twenty seconds or so, rousing me from my self-absorption to pick up the rod and reel. Determined to catch at least one fish before the end of the trip, I tied on my last Rooster Tail and began casting furiously up the river as darkness came on. Deer flies feasted so savagely on my feet that I hopped back and forth on the sandy bank while casting and reeling, a strange sight, I'm sure, for the fishermen in the small boat below the bluff on the opposite side. I did catch a sauger about six inches long and showed it to Randy. He nodded, preoccupied with his phone call. Hoping for a strike from one of the giant cats, I continued to fish until flat dark when the flies formed an alliance with the mosquitoes to torment me. I ran to the tent and shut myself inside, sweating, my legs and arms sticky with insect repellant. On the radio I found a New Orleans talk show. People from different parts of the city were calling in with news of flooding. Somebody informed the host that the power at his (the host's) home had gone off, and he argued that he didn't think so. A woman told a long tale about her cats, and after she hung up, the host made fun of her. "We need content that's a little more broad-based," he said. With the next caller, he discussed how oil refineries dredging the bays had contributed to the decline of the marshlands, which along with the Corps of Engineers' other attempts to control the Mississippi, made the floods worse. At night, on the river, in a tent, I loved listening to random thoughts from radio shows, something I would never do on land. There was something about the voices coming from far away that added to the solitude of our situation, and on the best shows, which were about nothing in particular, someone would always bring up a subject that seemed synchronous, like the discussion of the Mississippi.

After a dreamless night of shallow sleep, I awoke early, determined to beat the forecasted storm activity. By now, we worked with machinelike efficiency at breaking camp and loading the canoe, each of us repeating the same tasks and helping the other one with his tasks if one of us got ahead. A half hour or so after waking up, we were on the river, floating on strong current in the cool of the early morning. The back of the canoe, where I sat, was a mess of sand and mud, the wrapper of a granola bar crackling beneath my sandals, which had a half-inch layer of wet sand/mud glued to the soles. Randy was leaning over in the bow dipping his sandals in the water and rubbing them together to clean off the sand. As he dipped, the boat lurched left; when he rubbed, we lurched right. The more he dipped and rubbed, lurched left and right, the more sudden came the shifts, requiring me to counter his weight with a shift of my own in the rear. I knew that cleanliness was important to Randy, that he didn't want to shuffle around in the grit for the next eighteen miles and that he didn't want to arrive in Smithland slogging up the boat ramp in mud-clogged sandals, so I took it for as long as I could—about five minutes.

"Dammit!" I said. "Are you about finished cleaning your shoes?"

With a nervous chuckle, he put them on and started to paddle. I didn't bother apologizing.

After their arrest for the murder of the slave, Isham and Lilburne Lewis were released on bail. Lilburne, in despair, planned a double suicide with his brother. They met at the family cemetery on Rocky Hill, where Lilburne's wife was buried, and prepared to shoot each other. What followed was so bizarre it would have been comic had the circumstances that brought the brothers to the hill not been so tragic, so emblematic of problems relating to privilege, bigotry, brutality, and guilt that would haunt America for many years to come. Because Isham was worried about one of the rifles misfiring, Lilburne agreed to demonstrate to his brother how to kill himself in case his shot went astray. As he held the rifle to his chest in the macabre demonstration, it fired, delivering a mortal wound. Merrill speculates that Isham was so shocked at watching his brother die that he could not kill himself. After testifying in court about his part in the suicide, Isham escaped from the Salem jail and was never heard from again.

During this volatile time, Boone, nearly eighty, had just finished his last epic journey, a trapping expedition with old friends to the upper Missouri River, as far as Yellowstone. Not much is known about the trip except that he returned with a load of beaver skins and intended to sell them in St. Louis. A resident of Missouri, near the Osage River, Boone probably endured the freakish catastrophes of 1811–12 with stoicism and cool practicality. He lived eight more years.

I like to think that he died happy, but I doubt it. By American standards, he was a grand failure, despite the myths that he generated, the way we insist on thinking of Boone—heroic civilizer, brave defender of the American right to develop the wilderness—regardless of the facts and his ambivalence about the development he helped make possible. Assured Ben Franklin set the standard for success in this country—self-reliance, resourcefulness, frugality, and material wealth. Boone failed miserably at the last two. While Franklin was no doubt a great man, his example of success and how to achieve it never inspired me as much as Boone's failures. Biographer Elliott, summing up the worth of Boone's life, put it well: "He had seen the land when it was new, and it had gladdened him as riches never could" (202). For Randy and me, it was too late to witness Boone's virgin wilderness, but we were coming as close as we were able, submitting ourselves to the length of a river in a small boat without a motor, trying to connect with what remained of Boone's wilderness.

CHAPTER 24

RIVER'S END
RIVER'S END

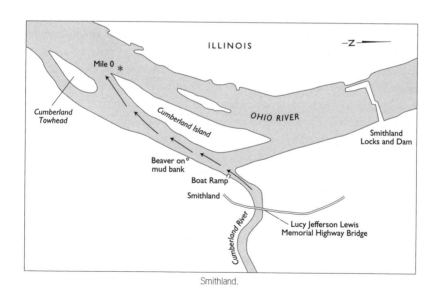

Smithland.

In penance for my outburst about Randy's shoe cleaning, I agreed to chase eagles back and forth across the river so that he could shoot photos of them. One of them, flying out from Claylick Creek, showed a mantle of white on the backs of his wings, a startling contrast to the darker feathers. After Randy pointed out the fourth eagle that day, perched in a tree on the shore opposite us, the novelty had worn off.

"Enough already," I said.

"It's our last day on the river," he said, his voice rising.

Our CCD was rising to its highest level at the worst possible moment. For two companions in a small boat, in relative isolation for over a month, this was not unusual. Eric Sevareid, in *Canoeing with the Cree* (1968), recounts a twenty-five-hundred-mile voyage he and a friend, Walter C. Port, took from Minneapolis up through Canada to York Factory, the beginnings of Hudson Bay. At a point in the voyage where the scenery and routine became monotonously oppressive, the two boys, each eighteen, came to blows. "Something in our minds snapped, our moral strength broke down. We leaped at each other. Hitting and twisting violently as though we were fighting for our lives, we rolled over and over until we struck a tree trunk" (166). Sevareid didn't remember what "trifling incident" ignited the violence, but both canoeists stopped fighting when they realized they couldn't survive alone. Still, they didn't speak for a couple of days.

I didn't think Randy and I would fight, but something about the pressure of ending the voyage, the weight of the days behind us, and the increasing heat of the final day frayed our patience with each other's oddities. No longer were those annoying idiosyncrasies in each other so amusing.

With the heat came power generation, which produced strong current below Barkley Dam. We floated six miles an hour that morning, on a course to arrive before noon, two hours before our rendezvous party. Near the end, from Mile Three on, barge fleeting areas lined both sides, and on the right was Martin Marietta Materials, where mountains of limestone were being ground up and carted around in dump trucks. *This*, I thought, *was the source for much of the riprap that lined miles of the river's shoreline.* In the distance appeared the Lucy Jefferson Lewis Memorial Bridge, named after Thomas Jefferson's sister, who was Lilburne and Isham's mother, mercifully deceased before the time of her sons' tragedy. She was buried high on a bluff overlooking the Ohio River, which we were fast approaching.

"There's my dad," said Randy matter of factly, pointing at the bridge. Sure enough, in the time it took us to float a half mile, the white van crossed the bridge four times. The reception had begun. At a half-mile from the boat ramp at Smithland, we pulled over to the riprap to look through our binoculars and see who had arrived at the ramp two hours earlier than we had announced. Randy's parents and Lara were there, Randy's dad looking back at us through binoculars. My family tended not to arrive places ahead of schedule. I called Julie and told her we were within sight of the end, earlier than we had planned.

"You better wait until we get there," she said. "The mayor is coming down there, too."

"The mayor of what?"

"Smithland!"

Randy and I lay back on the riprap under the clouds and dozed while my side of the reception party drove from Murray, over an hour away. The last time I did something like this, on the Tennessee, I arrived in Paducah over four hours after my family, which might offer additional reason for their not arriving early this time. That last day on the Tennessee had been brutal, sixteen hours of paddling, locking through Kentucky Dam, feeling my way through the busy Paducah waterfront after dark. Arriving at Broadway Wharf, exhausted and delirious, I felt a great sense of relief at having finished an ordeal.

Getting to Smithland ahead of schedule and waiting across the river seemed absurd and staged, like some kind of reality show, where we paddle up to the ramp and proclaim victory over the river. Still, we had to be considerate of loved ones, who wanted to witness the drama of our canoe voyage ending safely.

When I awoke from my drowse and raised my head from my pillow—a flat rock—the ramp crowd had grown to over ten people. Not likely had Smithland seen such activity since the days before the railroads, when everybody used the rivers for travel. As incredible as it seemed to an Ohio Valley native like me, people from the Deep South used to travel to Smithland's riverfront hotels for relief from the heat. Smithland was a kind of resort in the early to mid-nineteenth century. Among visitors to the Gower House hotel during Smithland's heyday were prominent figures such as the Marquis de Lafayette, the Frenchman who helped Americans win the Revolutionary War; Aaron Burr, the hotheaded Kentuckian who shot and killed Alexander Hamilton in a duel; Henry Clay, the great compromiser; Presidents James K. Polk and Zachary Taylor; Charles Dickens; Clara Barton, the nurse who founded the Red Cross; and General Lew Wallace, who fought with Grant at Fort Donelson. As of 1990, the population of Smithland was 384, and from the looks of the landing across the river, we were the main attraction.

When my wife and mother-in-law arrived with dogs Jasper and Brushy, we decided to make the grand crossing. Ahead of us, the mouth of the Cumberland expanded into a great bay to meet the Ohio. The confluence was a welcome sight but fell short in the scenery department, the land around us flat and featureless, the air hazy, the water gray under the clouds. Still, it was good to feel the final concrete ramp under our feet and to throw our gear out of the boat for the last time. A reporter from my hometown newspaper was there, as was the mayor, who congratulated us. It was a low-key but warm welcome.

We had one more chore to make it official: the final two-mile run to the end of Cumberland Island, the true Mile Zero, and back to the ramp against the current. Randy took his camera gear and we took on a passenger, panting Jasper, veteran of the Tennessee River, along for the honorary final two miles. Drizzle commenced. Expecting a hard rain, I put on my nylon jacket without a shirt under it. Jasper whined and rocked the boat as we crossed the wide water toward the shoreline of the island, which separated the mouth of the Cumberland from the main channel of the Ohio. Without our stabilizing load, the canoe handled differently, and Jasper, as was his habit, only became more excited and mobile as we approached the island. Though Jasper was a great companion on the Tennessee River, his agenda had been quite different from mine. He constantly wanted to get up on the shore and do what dogs do: make water, sniff, and if he was lucky, find something rotten to wallow in. To complicate matters, he had gained fifteen pounds since the 1998 trip, so his shifts from side to side rivaled Randy's morning shoe cleaning. Though Randy did not protest Jasper's honorary ride, I think he was remembering that the last time the three of us got together, on the Little River, we tipped over in ice-cold waist-deep water. Tipping over now would be even less fun.

We didn't linger at the official Mile Zero to celebrate because the current was pushing us farther and farther away from the boat ramp, and we had to turn and paddle before it pushed us all the way down to New Orleans. We stayed close to the island for a while, unable to pause in our frenzied strokes because any hesitation would cause us to lose ground. The rain had stopped, and my nylon jacket clung to me like a snakeskin. Randy wanted to keep paddling alongside the island, but I convinced him that if we slanted across to the Smithland shoreline, we might find some slack water. Out here, the island was dividing the strong currents of both the Ohio and the Cumberland. So we crossed, returning to the ramp on a different route than our outward trek. As we veered away from land, Jasper protested, shifting from side to side with greater frequency. When we were twenty yards from the Smithland shore, maybe a half-mile upriver from the boat ramp, a cabin cruiser came up behind us, heading into the mouth of the Cumberland. Randy wanted to go to shore immediately before the wakes reached us, and I wanted to turn the bow and ride it out, as we had done hundreds of times. I suspect that Randy feared Jasper as a jinx, and that he was frightened that the river was going to use this one last chance to extract its measure of payment for all the good luck that had been lavished on us.

I told him that I did not want to go to the bank, which was a low wall of bare mud, no rocks—not the place to properly land the boat. I argued that going to the bank would cost us energy. Randy countered that he did not want to ruin his equipment on the last day of the trip. I conceded. At the shore, he jumped out of the bow and immediately pulled the front end of the boat as far up the bank as he could. I guess he was thinking about protecting his cameras, but now I sat in the stern, unable to move, the boat inclined at an angle that put the water line only an inch or so from the gunnel at my side. Jasper, still in the boat, was whining crazily now, not only wanting to get out on the bank to explore, but to greet the large beaver that sat up not ten feet away, staring mildly at the three of us.

"I can't do anything here," I said to Randy, trying to keep my voice calm. "You've got to get us parallel for me to get out. We'll get swamped for sure like this."

He pushed the boat back out and turned it sideways to the bank. I hopped out, sloshed onto the muddy slope, stumbled, and squatted, holding onto the gunnel as the big wakes rolled toward us. I convinced Jasper to stay in the boat and not to make acquaintance with the beaver. The waves hit us broadside for about a minute and splashed over the side, leaving a couple of inches of water in the bottom.

Randy got back into the bow as I held the boat steady. I got one foot in, and then lost the other one to the mud, sinking up past my left knee trying to push off. I did not think I could pull my leg out of the sucking mud. As I wriggled back and forth to extract myself from the bank, I felt sure I would lose a sandal. But it all came clear, and we were in the boat paddling the last quarter mile.

The beaver sat on the bank in the full sunshine cleaning its paws. "Is that a cat or a beaver?" asked Randy, trying to make a joke.

"A beaver," I said, dreading an animal identification debate.

"Thanks for pulling onto shore," said Randy, knowing I was flustered and exhausted in my sweaty long-sleeved nylon jacket after my war with the mud.

By the time we got back, the crowd had grown. My mother, sister, and two nieces Mady and Libby, were there. Jasper jumped out and romped up the ramp. A guy in a red and white van was putting in his johnboat to go fishing.

"What did y'all do?" he asked.

"We canoed the Cumberland River," I said.

Two beats passed. "From Harlan," I added.

"Where in the *hell* are you from?" he asked.

I had to laugh. This was the strongest reaction we'd gotten in western Kentucky. I told him I was from around here, and he invited us to ride in his johnboat sometime. "Look me up," he said. "I'm the only Quigley in Ballard County."

●

On my second night off the river, my first night at home in East Tennessee, I had another river hallucination between waking and sleep.

"There's a couch in here!" I said sometime after midnight.

Looking out over the room from the bed—our "boat"—I thought that Julie and I were coming in for a landing at the back of some narrow bay and somebody had discarded a couch—our white slip-covered couch—into the river. Everything in the room appeared as it usually did, except that the hardwood floor had turned to water. Jasper and Brushy floated on their pillows in the drink.

"Is the canoe floating?" I asked. That's when I woke Julie up, and she replied in such a way that brought me fully awake.

I had arrived home physically, but my spirit still dwelled on the dark water, which had flooded its banks to invade my everyday life. The river embraced the furniture of our most intimate room—where we slept—just as I had slept by its side for over a month. It was not quite ready to let me go, and there was nothing I could do about its incursions except to let them pass, to observe myself as if on a screen. I enjoyed the hallucinations and regretted their fading from my subconscious after a few months off the river. Submitting to hallucination is one thing; asking for it is quite another, testament to the river's power over me.

I concede that the trip itself was, in part, an escape, an attempt to flee work and responsibility to reach a place of peace far away from the slideshow of anxiety and banality that has become modern life. And maybe that is what, at bottom, I intended, to pursue on the river an existence from another era, where I could play-act at living on a more elemental level, as some do when they pursue adventure travel or rough it for extended periods in remote regions. The river herself cooperated with this fantasy, hosting storms and fog and steamy doldrums for us to endure, nurturing the flickering flames of our fears about the unknown. Returning us safe and whole and undamaged.

Still, by the end of the journey I didn't feel like I was returning from the past, or that the river had offered me a sort of experiential nature course from which I would return refreshed and renewed. It felt less an escape than a voyage of confrontation, as much against external forces as internal demons. On the river, I grew irritable just as I did on land. I became frightened, often about foolish potentialities. I argued—with myself and others. Sometimes I felt at peace; other times I worried, often needlessly. On such a voyage, one can only hope that between periods of drudgery, terror, and annoyance, there are moments of transcendence, which come only through hardship, exertion, and a bit of danger, actual or perceived.

Boone's life, so full of suffering and disappointment, was full of such high moments. One in particular struck me. At sixty, pained by rheumatism, plagued more than ever by debt, he took his youngest son, Nathan, thirteen, on a hunting trip near the Kanawha River in West Virginia. One evening Boone heard the chopping of wood from other side of the river. Realizing their camp had been discovered by Indians, who were constructing a raft to pursue them, Boone told the boy to lie flat in the canoe while he pushed off into the dense fog. Bending low from the stern, he drifted downriver away from the ghostly outline of the Indian raft coming toward their abandoned camp.

We had our moments of transcendence: the first comfortable camp, on the beach above Cumberland Falls, in view of the flashing rapids; the morning of wispy fog tornadoes on Lake Cumberland; the grass waving on the river bottom below Wolf Creek Dam; going to water at the confluence of the Stones and the Cumberland; laying back and ruddering as the wind filled the Viking sail and carried us through downtown Nashville, skyscrapers towering above us; sitting under Randy's canopies through rains; watching the river flow past camp on the last night. In the end, this was a voyage of confirmation: of friendship, of completion, of knowing that as absurd as such a voyage may seem to most, it was somehow right for Randy and me.

The trip taught me that the Cumberland was not something I could easily define with words or that Randy could encapsulate with photos. It could transform itself from bucolic stream to violent sea in a moment, and no matter how long we experienced the river or studied it, its inhabitants—human, plant, animal—surprised us with gifts and mischief when least expected. I came away still thinking of the Cumberland as the dark sister of the Tennessee, the isolated, mysterious one, hauntingly attractive. Even though it was an eastern river, far less wild and isolated than rivers west of the Mississippi, and even though, to advanced paddlers, it was pedestrian compared to other eastern rivers such as the Chattooga and the Gauley, I still got the sense that much about the Cumberland had remained unchanged after the last three centuries, its history accessible, near the moving surface, dancing in the fog, sighing on the breeze. At the same time, we could see that its wildness and its mystery were threatened. Population increase, misguided conceptions of progress, and an unquestioning belief in the virtue of economic growth threaten to turn our rivers into the culture of sameness, monotony, and false security that so often characterizes our cities, towns, and disappearing countryside.

My strongest feelings about the Cumberland—attraction to its mystery, sadness at the dams and abuse, joy at its changing moods—came from my own perspective, of course, not from the river itself. And though I tried to woo her back into my dreams, I discovered that she demanded fidelity, prolonged commitment, that only through sustained hardship and discomfort would she reenter my subconscious. Returning to it, even for a short trip, I thought, might restore the magic that it worked on my spirit and create that place where I could travel between sleeping and waking.

EPILOGUE

Chest deep in cold, muddy Judio Creek, Sidney Matthews struggled to extract his feet from the gluey mud bottom that gripped them. His friend, Don, sitting in the canoe that Sid had so unwisely stepped out of, offered soothing advice. After slipping a couple of times and bemoaning his fate, Sid dug his fingers into the muddy bank and with great effort extricated himself from what could have become a dire predicament. He scrambled to the top of the bank, where he slipped and fell again. Loud and long, Sid cursed whoever had painted the SOCM (Save Our Cumberland Mountains) sign on the sheet of tin, marking the takeout point of our three-day relay down the Cumberland from Wolf Creek Dam. Don looked at me with a wide, trembling grin. It was all we could do to hold in our laughter. No matter the anguish of the sufferer, there's always some slapstick humor to be found in mud slips.

It was July 2004, over a year after Randy and I had been through here. Sid, Don, Boomer Winfrey, Rachael Johns, and I were part of a relay team canoeing and boating four hundred miles of the Cumberland to protest the practice of blowing off the tops of mountains to harvest coal. We had picked up Bobby Clark at Wolf Creek Dam, where he had brought a glass jug of water from a creek off the Big South Fork of the Cumberland. It looked worse than dishwater, clouded and contaminated by debris from a mountaintop coal mine in Campbell County, Tennessee. Two weeks later Bobby would give the jug to a Tennessee state official in Nashville.

Here at the mouth of Judio Creek, dark and shady, we waited for Boomer to return from a reconnaissance downstream, to make sure that this was indeed the takeout, where we would hand over the jug (and Bobby, who was going the whole way) to another SOCM team. The takeout was far from ideal, the steep bank too slick for even the most light-footed and nimble of us. Sid's boldness had exceeded his agility.

After Boomer returned from his reconnaissance, we paddled farther up the creek and found a muddy ramp someone had cut into the bank, just as slick as where Sid had fallen, but the slope less steep. It led to a threshold of daylight where someone had bush-hogged a rough path through a field. This was the farm of Johnny Brewington, a friend of a SOCM member who had

agreed to let us use his riverside farm as a takeout and to let the incoming
relay crew camp in his field. Boomer and I walked across the sweltering field
the half-mile to Johnny's sawmill, where he met us in a Toyota pickup that
bounced crazily along on the rough path.

"You must be the canoeists," he said. "Would y'all like something cold
to drink?"

●

The river itself had been less hospitable than Johnny during our three-day
journey from Wolf Creek Dam. Early Monday we scooted along on strong
current from water that the dam was releasing. Bobby soloed in his aluminum
Ouchita, and I stayed with him, alone in my plastic Old Town, missing Randy
in the bow. Boomer paddled in the stern of his fiberglass Blue Hole, with
Rachael in the bow, and Don guided a green Mohawk with Sid sitting point.
As always, the frigid Cumberland exhaled a cool misty fog that swathed us
from the neck down. Everybody seemed happy, floating along and paddling
at leisure. I watched them closely, feeling like a guy introducing a girl he likes
to his best friends, hoping desperately that they approved. The Cumberland,
a difficult friend, was showing her best face.

Then came the fishing hook incident. Bobby, on the bank, grabbed a
bush for balance, and a treble hook bit into his thumb. He extracted it himself with little loss of blood and gave it to Sid, who tied it onto the end of his
fishing line, replacing a rooster tail that was scaring the fish away. Beyond the
rockhouse, where we stopped for lunch, what we thought would be a mild
summer storm came upriver. Mild it was not. First came the wind that swept
the fog into a ball that enveloped us in blank whiteness; then just as suddenly
it blasted the air clear just before the rain blew in. The water darkened like
strong cider under the boiling sky. It only lasted about half an hour, but we
emerged shivering and soggy from our bankside eddies, where we'd cringed
in our boats from the thunder and lightning. That's just her, I wanted to say
with a shrug, she can turn on you at a moment's notice. We paddled hard
through the chilly fog to try to get warm.

This group of paddlers was nothing like what I had expected. Sid and
Don were large, powerful men who brought prodigious quantities of food:
dozens of eggs, pork chops, hamburger, a ten-pound bag of potatoes, and
twenty-four small water bottles. Sid, a truck driver from Crossville, wore a
leather fedora with a John Kerry button. He liked to talk and to smoke. On
his left arm was a butterfly tattoo. "My girlfriend's on my back," he said, and

I assumed it was her name. It turned out to be a naked woman, faded but still clearly visible from the waist up, her lips and nipples tinted red.

"What's your wife say about that?" I asked.

"Mostly she says, 'Put your shirt back on,'" he said.

Don, a transplant from Michigan, was a construction contractor with a quiet, patient manner. He was quick to help others, whatever the task or problem at hand. Both men prayed before each meal. Since I was the first to arrive at Kendall Campground on Sunday afternoon, I drove to the other side of the dam to pick up Bobby Clark, who had arrived by johnboat from Burnside with a young volunteer named Christopher. Bobby was even quieter than Don, a short, spare man with a heavy gray beard, bushy gray hair, and a slightly humped back. When I first saw him, I thought "prospector," like the forty-niners who stampeded California in the nineteenth century. Remarkably, I found out later, he was, indeed, a gold prospector, having learned the craft from reading and from visiting a place in North Carolina where you could pan a stream for a fee. But there was much more to Bobby, who lived on a small farm near Chattanooga "off the grid," as he said, on solar power, propane, and a generator, who sold the vegetables he grew and the roosters that he bred. Bobby was, as Boomer put it, "grizzled." When he paddled his canoe, leaned back, with his feet up, I strained to catch the sound of the slightest splash or movement. Not once did he hit the side of his boat.

Boomer was a veteran canoeist, our leader, who was full of stories from his years on rivers. As always, no canoe trip is complete without at least a passing reference to *Deliverance*. Boomer knew a stunt man who worked on the movie. Now the head of well-known river guiding service in North Carolina, the guy earned seventy-five thousand dollars for his services, quite a bit of money in the 1970s. For one stunt, they handed him a broken paddle to use in the bow, while the actor Jon Voight, a novice canoeist, floundered through a rapid in the stern. For another stunt, the filmmaker sawed a canoe crosswise until just a bit of the gunnels held it together. He asked the stuntman to navigate this canoe over a waterfall, where of course, it broke apart.

Boomer had helped plan and organize the SOCM trip, the media relations and publicity his sole responsibility. He was a big man, though nimble for his size and a strong paddler. In his younger days, he had taken a little solo canoe trip across the Southeast, covering two thousand miles. Rachael was an athletic, blonde eighteen-year-old interning with Save Our Cumberland Mountains. Though she suffered in the cold after the storm and got bored with all the paddling and the man-talk, I heard not one complaint from her, and Boomer repeated often that she was wearing him out with her strong, steady paddling.

I had helped Boomer plan the route for the entire trip as well as this leg of it. The first campsite would be somewhere around Howard's Bottom, the second at Gar Whicker's Traces on the Cumberland. I dreaded landing at the soggy pasture of the long rain, where Randy and I had holed up for fifteen hours, but that was the only decent spot we could find that first day. We had paddled twenty-seven miles from the dam, a long day even with the strong current. All night lightning flashed in the distance, but the rain held off. Sid snored so loud the whole camp kidded him the next day.

We paddled seventeen miles to Gar's place and lounged in the shade all afternoon, working up the courage to baptize ourselves in the frigid river at the boat ramp. Sid invented a sort of backward sitting-down dunk that seemed the least painful and kindest to the heart, the shock of the cold water taking your breath no matter how tough you were. Don said the heck with it and dove in a few times.

That evening, Sid and I prepared a supper of chili con carne with all the food that we had to eat before it spoiled. Bobby, a vegetarian, declined to eat the chili even before we added the two pounds of hamburger, saying his digestive system couldn't take it. He cooked a skillet of popcorn for his supper. I made fun of Boomer for pegging down his tent on Gar's mown lot. I'd left my ground tarp in the canoe and was sipping whiskey in anticipation of a long, lazy evening of tale-telling under a clear cowboy sky. There was a smear of wispy clouds to the west. Just for kicks I turned on the weather radio. "Brrrrrinnngggg, Brrrinnngggg, Brrrinnngggg!" went the alarm. Severe thunderstorm warnings in the counties west of us, a big-ass storm with high winds and dangerous lightning coming our way from the northwest. Sid and I sat on coolers discussing the darkening sky to the west when suddenly the wind rose and it was upon us.

I hammered my stakes in with a half-empty propane canister, and Don tied the boats to a stake on the riverside. Bobby and I stepped inside our tents and hunkered down, while Rachael moved her tent under one of Gar's boat storage units, and Sid and Don did the same. Boomer's tent almost folded up, its 1970s aluminum frame bending in the high winds that roared for over an hour. On a Nashville radio station, announcers told folks to stay off the roads and get in their basements. Trees were falling, power was failing. Gar's security light flickered off and on. We were in tents near a compound of large metal buildings, and I envisioned flying sheets with sharp edges. It could have been much worse. We could have pushed onward and camped in some cow pasture where no one would know where we were and the storm would menace us without remorse. Here at least we had Gar's flickering security light and the shelter of the buildings for those with fragile tents. My tent held dry and steady in winds that sucked one side, then the other, like a beast inhaling and exhaling. The earth trembled under the thundering skies. The trees along Gar's bankside leaned hard toward the river, their roots straining to hold the ground. After it was over, Don and I walked to the river. The boats were fine, and the river had risen, but not from the rain, which was sparse in the storm. The dam was generating, business as usual.

Next morning at sunrise, the sky darkened once again and threw down a heavy rain for an hour or so. Gar, who visited before our departure, said he'd never seen anything like the big storm at daybreak.

Sid cooked the rest of his eggs, sausage, and potatoes, and we feasted before the last river day, all but Rachael, who ate a granola bar, and to Sid's consternation, shunned his breakfasts. All the same, she helped with the dishes.

The storm had swept the skies clear of humidity, and we started out the last day in bright sun, the air crisp and cool. The current had slackened and we all worked harder, Bobby and me falling behind. Bobby liked to get up close to the bank and explore, and he wanted to paddle up creeks, but our schedule demanded expediency. The day before Bobby had lingered on the bank, gathering the bark of river birches to start a fire that evening. "They burn just like you poured kerosene on them," he said. During the afternoon at Gar's, Bobby paddled his canoe upriver, parked in the shade, and took a nap. When he came back, he'd collected strange little fossils called crinoids, which resembled hollowed-out screws. Crinoids constituted the stem of a water-lily that lived 350 million years ago. Bobby and Boomer, who was educated as a geologist, also collected geodes, round rocks that, when cracked open, reveal a shiny crystallized interior.

Sid was the only one fishing, and he hadn't had a bite. On the first day he asked every fisherman he saw if they were catching any, and no matter what their answer, he would reply, "I haven't even gotten a bite!" He commiserated with Gar, who returned from guiding a couple of clients with just one brown trout. "This is the worst day fishing I have ever had on this river," said Gar.

By the last day, we talked less. Most activities extraneous to getting down the river had tapered off. Sid cast his line occasionally and Bobby lagged back in the shadows of the bank, but generally we were all ready to get back to life on land. I tried to fight the boredom that long-range paddling inevitably brings. Even Bobby admitted that the white water of the Big South Fork was more fun. Rachael looked bored in the bow of Boomer's boat, but she kept paddling without complaint. The last day had its moments of grandeur. A tailwind gave me a chance to hold up my tarp as a spinnaker, giving me a few moments of free locomotion. Up above, the trees on the bluffs nodded and swayed in the wind, showing the pale undersides of their leaves. I wondered what we looked like from the top, what the world above was like. Down here in this river, at the bottom of the gorge, we were in a world that few frequented. We saw only one other boat, a smartass kid who motored his johnboat at top speed right between our group of canoes. "That was cute," said Boomer.

Johnny Brewington, dressed in spotless ironed jeans and a light blue polo shirt, towed our canoes up the muddy bank to the field with his Toyota, accompanied in the cab by his Chihuahua, Ginger. He had an acre or two of tobacco, a cash crop that would soon be extinct in Kentucky, where allotments for growing it had been limited by the government. Lumberjacking and sawmilling were about the only way to make a living around here, said Johnny. You couldn't make it farming, he said, with equipment costs rising and the payoffs for crops diminishing. His son and son-in-law worked under the hazy sun on a machine that grabbed logs and cut them. Dogs of various breeds wandered around the area. Bobby examined the sawmill, and Boomer asked him if he were going to crank it up.

"I might have to study it some longer," said Bobby.

"Ever run one before?" asked Boomer.

"I own one," he said.

When our ride arrived with a canoe trailer, we left Bobby all our spare supplies and food and said good-bye. I told him to go up Kettle Creek, just a few miles downstream, to look for Boone's Seven Sisters Bluff and the cave near Indian Ladder Cliff on Old Hickory. Riding in the van back to the dam, I thought of a hundred other landmarks that would fascinate him.

Everybody seemed glad they'd made the trip, despite the hardships. We'd had a little adventure, a lot of good food, and generally good current with cool breezes and ghostly fog. The worst damage was sore parts and wet gear. Boomer, a sampler of many rivers, said he wouldn't mind canoeing this stretch again, maybe in the fall when the leaves were changing.

Two weeks later, on July 24, Bobby stood on the concrete steps below the Tennessee Titans football stadium and presented the jug of dirty water to Karen Stachowski, deputy commissioner of the Tennessee Department of Environment and Conservation. Bobby had led a flotilla of fifty-seven canoes and kayaks two miles from Shelby Park, under the interstate and a couple of other highway bridges, past Nashville's waterfront, Bicentennial Park. From there, we made a big semicircle across the river to the stadium.

When I had arrived at the ramp at Shelby Park, our put-in, Boomer handed me an orange mesh vest and told me I was a team leader. It was my job to lead the "white team," the folks who were wearing white signs that bore the name of a Tennessee stream or mountain threatened with contamination from coal mines. Mine said "Rich Mountain." Others wore signs with names like Hell's Point, Butcher Hollow, Zeb Mountain, and so on. Vic Scoggin, a late arrival, paddled up beside me in his Old Town Canoe, onto which he had duct taped a big blue banner that said, "SAVE THE CUMBERLAND." He was still fighting against a monstrous marina planned for Mill Creek, a few miles upstream. Mack Prichard, standing on a bridge above us, shouted out the number of canoes as we paddled by, our group bringing up the rear. He had three cameras hanging around his neck. I paddled with a woman named Cici, who had recently moved to Nashville from California. She was happy to replace the rock I'd planned to stow in my bow and did a great job of propelling the boat forward and reminding me repeatedly without raising her voice which color team we were to follow.

When we reached Bicentennial Park, SOCM volunteers, including Rachael Johns, had unfurled a banner with a bold message to the governor: "Stop Mining Before It Turns Rocky Topless," a reference to Tennessee's theme song, "Rocky Top." As we made the semicircle and headed across the river to the stadium, we whooped and hollered like enlightened Yahoos. Other than those affiliated with SOCM or TSRA, not many stood under the sun to gawk at us or hear our war cries.

The Nashville Tennessean penned Bobby in a small square photo in the local section. Wearing his floppy camo hat, thick black glasses, and a long-sleeved flannel shirt, he's holding up the jar of water with a small grin under his beard. Around his neck hangs a sign that says, "Turkey Knob."

On public radio, Bobby's words were simple and eloquent: "This water was once clear, and now it's dirty. There's something wrong with that."

Dusty, a woman in a brand-new hybrid Toyota took me back to my car at the park. When I returned to the stadium to load my canoe, Vic walked up, soaking wet from a swim in the river. We chatted about how difficult finding time for the river had become. Vic wanted to quit his job at Ford Glass, where he worked a swing shift, often twelve hours at a time. I wanted to stay and talk, but I had a two-hour drive back to Murray, where Julie and I were visiting family.

"You ought to go for a swim before you leave," said Vic. So we walked down the glaring hot concrete steps to the riprap. Across the river a band was setting up for a concert that evening. Beyond was the skyline of Nashville towering in the hazy summer sky. I removed my shoes and stepped carefully down the slimy riprap, backing in Sid style. When I got to my waist I pushed off and dipped my head backward, staying under long enough to shut out the sounds of the city. When I resurfaced, Vic was treading water just a few yards upriver, a big smile on his face.

"That was a great idea," I said.

"Nothing like it," he said, and we tread water in the river that wound through our lives, letting it cool and soothe us as only moving water can.

It's difficult to put into words what place means, how you can grow emotionally attached to a tree, a forest, a pond, a river, or an ocean. Part of it involves what happened there, and it doesn't have to be good; in fact, for a place to really matter in one's life, the good should be mixed with bad, as Randy and I learned when we measured the swings of fortune's pendulum, going from one extreme to the other, in matters great and small. A screaming storm intensified the clarity and warmth of the hard-eyed sunshine afterward. A good meal sharpened the hunger that followed. Exhaustion led to peaceful sleep. Vic talked of the river as if it created possibilities in his life and intensified milestones: his first kiss, his first beer, his first panicked swimming strokes after being tossed into the river. While his parents went through a divorce, he and his brother camped for weeks by the river's side, the moving water helping to calm their emotional turmoil.

Further downstream from Vic, the Cumberland flowed through the formative years of my life. The trip enabled me to feel with more emotional depth the river's history and my connection to it, from the time that the Shawnee paddled dugout canoes to the modern pilgrims whooping it up in rented self-bailing rafts below the falls. As a result of the trip, I grew closer to others who loved the river, not just those I know personally, like Vic and Mack Prichard, but those who killed and died to live near its fertile banks, as well as those who now make a living from it or escape to it on weekends. It is people, after all, who give the river its meaning. Without us it would be just as great, but it would be mute, and the ghost of it would wail into a void without us humans to try to understand how our destinies and well-being are intertwined. The challenge now, for lovers of the river, is to help everyone understand that its worth goes beyond utility and economic value, that keeping it clean and free-flowing will benefit us all in ways that we can't put into numbers or words.

BIBLIOGRAPHY

The research, insight, and analysis of many writers helped me to buttress my personal narrative with historical scope. Foremost in terms of historical and cultural information about frontier life on the Cumberland was Harriet Arnow, whose histories *Seedtime on the Cumberland* and *Flowering of the Cumberland* tell the stories of the first settlers in the area of Middle Tennessee and Kentucky. I am indebted for information from two biographies about Daniel Boone, John Mack Faragher's *Daniel Boone: The Life and Legend of an American Pioneer*, and Lawrence Elliott's *The Long Hunter*. Ted Franklin Belue's *The Long Hunt* and R. E. Banta's *The Ohio* provided fascinating accounts of the lives of the early explorers, long hunters, flatboatmen, and desperadoes. Arnow's *Old Burnside*, Douglas Byrd's *Steamboatin' on the Cumberland*, Warren S. O'Brien's *Adventures Along the Cumberland*, Lynwood Montell's *Don't Go Up Kettle Creek*, and Jack Knox's *Riverman* gave me a sense of what it was like to live and work on the Cumberland before the high dams. Thematic and inspirational touchstones include all of William Least Heat-Moon's work and Joseph Conrad's *Heart of Darkness*.

I also extensively used *The Kentucky Encyclopedia* and the *Tennessee Encyclopedia of History and Culture*.

What follows is a complete list of works I used for background research, with commentary on some works.

PRINT AND VIDEO SOURCES

Albright, Edward. *Early History of Middle Tennessee*. Nashville: Brandon Printing Company, 1909.

Arnow, Harriet Simpson. *Seedtime on the Cumberland*. New York: Macmillan, 1960.

———. *Flowering of the Cumberland*. New York: Macmillan, 1963.

———. *Old Burnside*. Lexington: University Press of Kentucky, 1977. Hardcore historians might accuse Arnow of romanticizing the settlers of Middle Tennessee, led by James Robertson, and there's no doubt where her sympathies lie in the struggle between whites and American Indians. Still, for the detail she provides about the lives of the frontier people and for her storytelling ability, these books are compelling and informative.

Banta, R. E. *The Ohio*. New York: Rinehart, 1949. Like Arnow, Banta is a historian who knows how to tell a good story and to bring to life the frontiersmen, American Indians, and flatboatmen of the Ohio River Valley. Not for the fainthearted, Banta's book accurately reflects the brutality of the period.

Bardach, John E. *Downstream: A Natural History of the River*. New York: Harper and Row, 1964.

Barr, Daniel P. "'A Monster So Brutal': Simon Girty and the Degenerative Myth of the American Frontier, 1783–1900." *Essays in History*. Vol. 40, 1998.

Barret, Elizabeth, dir. *Stranger with a Camera* [videorecording]. Whitesburg, KY: Appalshop, 2000.

Basho, Matsuo. *Narrow Road to the Interior*. Trans. Sam Hamill. Boston: Shambhala Publications, Inc., 1998. Recommended by poet Jeff Hardin for an Eastern perspective on travel and enlightenment.

Belue, Ted Franklin. The *Long Hunt: Death of the Buffalo East of the Mississippi*. Mechanicsburg, PA: Stackpole Books, 1996. Great detail about the buffalo, its place in the ecosystem and in the cultures of whites and American Indians. Belue is clearly an authority on the subject of buffalo and those who hunted them.

Brewer, Alberta and Carson. *Valley So Wild: A Folk History*. Knoxville: East Tennessee Historical Society, 1975.

Buchanan, John. *Jackson's Way: Andrew Jackson and the People of the Western Waters*. New York: John Wiley and Sons, 2001.

Butterfield, Consul Willshire. *History of the Girtys*. Cincinnati: Clark, 1890.

Caruso, John Anthony. *The Appalachian Frontier: America's First Surge Westward*. Indianapolis: Bobbs-Merrill, 1959.

Caudill, Harry M. *Night Comes to the Cumberlands: A Biography of a Depressed Area*. Boston: Little, Brown, 1962.

———. *The Miner, the Mountain, and the Lord, and Other Tales from a Country Law Office*. Lexington: University Press of Kentucky, 1980.

Caudill, Rebecca. *My Appalachia: A Reminiscence*. New York: Henry Holt and Company, 1966.

Clark, Jerry E. *The Shawnee*. Lexington: University Press of Kentucky, 1993.

Conrad, Joseph. *Heart of Darkness*. New York: Pocket Books, Simon and Schuster, 1972. Having taught the novella a couple of times, I'm entranced and troubled by Conrad's vision. Along with Twain and Least Heat-Moon, one of the literary touchstones for my book.

Crabb, Alfred Leland. *Nashville: Personality of a City*. Indianapolis: Bobbs-Merrill, 1960.

Cunningham, Bill. *Castle: The Story of a Kentucky Prison*. Kuttawa, KY: McClanahan Publishing House, 1994.

Dick, David and Lalie. *Rivers of Kentucky*. North Middleton, KY: Plum Lick Publishing, 2001.

Dickey, James. *Deliverance*. New York: Dell Publishing, 1970.

Douglas, Byrd. *Steamboatin' on the Cumberland*. Nashville: Tennessee Book Company, 1961.

Elliott, Lawrence. *The Long Hunter: A New Life of Daniel Boone*. New York: Reader's Digest Books, 1976.

Foote, Shelby. *The Civil War: A Narrative*. New York: Random House, 1958.

Fullerton, Ralph O., et al. *Tennessee Geographical Patterns and Regions*. Dubuque, IA: Kendall/Hunt Publishing Co., 1977.

Howard, James H. *Shawnee! The Ceremonialism of a Native American Tribe and Its Cultural Background*. Athens: Ohio University Press, 1981.

Johnson, Leland R. *Engineers on the Twin Rivers: A History of the Nashville District Corps of Engineers, United States Army*. Nashville: U.S. Army Engineer District, 1968. Hard-to-find book with much historical information about the Tennessee and the Cumberland that cannot be found elsewhere.

Kingsolver, Barbara. "The Memory Place." In *Literature and the Environment: A Reader on Nature and Culture*. Lorraine Anderson, Scott Slovic, John P. O'Grady, eds. New York: Addison, Wesley, Longman, 1999. 199–205.

Kleber, John E., ed. *The Kentucky Encyclopedia*. Lexington: University Press of Kentucky, 1992.

Knox, Jack. *Riverman*. Nashville: Abingdon Press, 1971.

Lane, John. *Chattooga: Descending into the Myth of Deliverance River*. Athens: University of Georgia Press, 2004.

Least Heat-Moon, William. *Blue Highways: A Journey into America*. Boston: Little, Brown, 1982.

Lunch Video Magazine. *The 2004 IR Product Catalog and the LVM Archives DVD*. Penstock Productions, LLC.

McCague, James. *The Cumberland*. New York: Holt, Rinehart and Winston, 1973.

McMurry, Richard M. *John Bell Hood and the War for Southern Independence*. Lincoln: University of Nebraska Press, 1982.

Merrill, Boynton, Jr. *Jefferson's Nephews: A Frontier Tragedy*. Lexington: University Press of Kentucky, 1987. An appalling and fascinating tale of frontier western Kentucky during an extraordinary time.

Montell, William Lynwood. *Ghosts along the Cumberland*. Knoxville: University of Tennessee Press, 1975.

———. *Don't Go Up Kettle Creek*. Knoxville: University of Tennessee Press, 1983.

Moore, Harry L. *A Geologic Trip across Tennessee by Interstate 40*. Knoxville: University of Tennessee Press, 1994.

O'Brien, Warren S. *Adventures along the Cumberland*. New York: Vantage Press, 1963. An eccentric and quaint little book with much firsthand description of the old river before the dams.

Roberts, Diane. "Reynolds Rap." *Oxford American*. Winter 2002. 142–45. One of my teachers at the University of Alabama, she's a Faulkner scholar and a keen observer of contemporary culture.

Roberts, Leonard W. *Up Cutshin' and Down Greasy*. Lexington: University Press of Kentucky, 1959.

Salak, Kira. "Mungo Made Me Do It: Six Hundred Miles on a Surly River to Timbuktu," *National Geographic Adventure*, December 2002/January 2003. 74–84.

Sehlinger, Bob. *A Canoeing and Kayaking Guide to the Streams of Kentucky*. Birmingham, AL: Menasha Ridge Press, 1994.

Sevareid, Eric. *Canoeing with the Cree*. St. Paul: Minnesota Historical Society Press, 1968.

Shaw, Christopher. *Sacred Monkey River: A Canoe Trip with the Gods*. New York: W. W. Norton, 2000.

Sherwin, Holly. *Canoeing in Tennessee*. Franklin, TN: Cool Springs Press, 1996.

Smith, Frank E. *Land between the Lakes*. Lexington: University Press of Kentucky, 1971.

Swift, Jonathan. *Gulliver's Travels*. New York: Oxford University Press, 1977.

Twain, Mark. *Adventures of Huckleberry Finn*. Henry Nash Smith, ed. Cambridge: The Riverside Press, 1958.

United States Corps of Engineers, Nashville District. *Cumberland River Navigational Charts: Smithland, Kentucky, to Celina, Tennessee*. 2000. Every boat, small or large, needs a copy of the charts. Indispensable for us, along with the *Tennessee* and *Kentucky Gazetteers*, which we used above Celina.

Usinger, Robert L. *The Life of Rivers and Streams*. New York: McGraw-Hill, 1967.

West, Carroll Van, ed. *The Tennessee Encyclopedia of History and Culture*. Nashville: Rutledge Hill Press, 1998.

Whicker, Gar. *Fishing the Lower Cumberland River from the Wolf Creek Dam at Lake Cumberland to the Tennessee State Line*. Self-published, 2002.

ONLINE SOURCES

Allen, J. M. Cheatham County Historical and Genealogical Association. <http://www.rootsweb.com/~tncheath/tour.html.> (Information on steamboat, *General Jackson*).

Associated Press. "Suspect in Classic Shooting Incident Arrested." 14 August 2003. <http://espn.go.com/outdoors/bassmaster/s/b_news_030814_classic_shooting_arrest.html>.

Edwards, Holly. "Flooding Puts Dams to the Test." 9 May 2003. *TheTennessean.com*. <http://www.tennessean.com/local/archives/03/05/32542182.shtml>.

Evans, Ed. "A Bad Day at Cheatham." 2 April 2002. U.S. Army Corps of Engineers, Nashville District Web site. <http://www.orn.usace.army.mil/pao/News_Releases/2002Releases/bad%20day%20at%20Cheatham%20Dam.htm>.

Folly, Martin H. "'The News That Stunned the Most Jaded Americans': The North American Press and the Arrest of Two Amish Drug Dealers in 1998." EnterText 1.1. <http://www.brunel.ac.uk/faculty/arts/EnterText/Folly.pdf>.

Garth, Gary. "Mr. Walleye Not Just a Catchy Name." 7 September 2003. *Courier-Journal.com*. <http://www.courier-journal.com/cjsports/news2003/09/07/spt-13-walleye0907-7388.html>.

Goodspeed's History of Tennessee Counties. <http://www.tngenweb.org/goodspeed/>.

"High Lake Waters Are Under Control." 27 March 2003. *Times Journal Online* (Russell County, Kentucky). <http://russellcounty.net/tjarchive_030227_highwater.shtml>.

Kentucky Geological Survey. University of Kentucky Web site. <http://www.uky.edu/KGS/coal/webrokmn/pages/sedrocks.html#sandstone>.

Lewis, Clyde. "Ground Zero Freakuency Modulation." <http://www.clydelewis.com/dis/freak/freak.html>. (Information and theories about strange occurrences in and around Hartsville, TN)

Personal Responsibility in a Desirable Environment (PRIDE). <http://www.kypride.org/>. (Kentucky organization organized after Vic Scoggin's swim to clean up the Cumberland River.)

Scoggin, Vic. <http://www.SavetheCumberland.org>. Vic's Web site is full of information about his swim and about the river.

U.S. Army Corps of Engineers, Nashville District. <http://www.lrn.usace.army.mil>. (For information about camping, history, and statistics regarding the Cumberland River, in particular Lake Cumberland.)

USDA Forest Service. Land Between the Lakes Web site. <http://www.lbl.org/Home.html>.

U.S. Fish and Wildlife Service Fishery Resources, Southwest Region. <http://southwest.fws.gov/fishery/>.

Whicker, Gar and Brenda. Traces on the Cumberland Web site. <http://www.tracesonthecumberland.com/traces.html>.

INDEX